DIVING INTO DREAMS

DIVING INTO DREAMS

Navigating Life's Deepest Waters
to Discover the Secret of Having Enough

by

Szilvia Gogh

First Edition
ISBN: 979-8-9999878-0-8
Printed in the United States of America
Edited by Amy Dorta McIlwaine
Cover design by Lena Semenkova
Interior design by Bostjan Lisec
Published by Limitless Positivity LLC

DISCLAIMER

This memoir is a work of memory and reflection. The events, conversations, and experiences described in this book are recounted to the best of my recollection. However, memory is imperfect, and the passage of time can alter how we remember people, places, and events. Some dialogue has been reconstructed based on my best recollection of the essence and spirit of conversations, rather than verbatim transcription.

To protect the privacy of individuals, some names and identifying details have been changed. In certain instances, composite characters have been created, and timelines may have been compressed for narrative clarity. These changes do not alter the fundamental truth of my experiences or the lessons learned along the way.

The views and opinions expressed in this book are my own and do not necessarily reflect the views of any individuals, organizations, or institutions mentioned within these pages.

While I have made every effort to ensure the accuracy of the information contained in this memoir, I cannot guarantee that all details are completely precise. This book is intended to share my personal journey and the insights gained from it, rather than serve as a factual record of events. Any errors or omissions are unintentional and entirely my own.

Szilvia Gogh

For Mutti and Apu,
who both died too young,
before they could discover
the secret to having enough.

I miss you every day.
I wish you could see me now.
I wish you were here.

CONTENTS

Diving In

Your spark can become a flame and change everything.
– E. D. Nixon

Liquid gold streams through the water, casting an ethereal glow. Imitation coral sways in the artificial currents like a troupe of mesmerized ballerinas. The actors float and move beneath the surface with otherworldly grace.

This is Hollywood magic.

This is my world.

Yet despite the breathtaking visuals, there's nothing glamorous about this moment. One wrong move, one miscalculation, and someone dies.

My heart pounds with the ticking seconds, and not just from physical exertion. We're filming an endless loop of takes for the *Avatar* sequels: four-minute shots, one after the other, with twenty people holding their breath underwater for what feels like an eternity. The burden of responsibility weighs heavy. We've created another world down here—so beautiful, so calm, so inviting in the filtered light!—but my job is more than just making sure the scene looks perfect.

Unless everyone in that tank stays safe, even when pushing their body beyond what seems humanly possible, it's on me.

When the cameras are rolling, the whole crew transforms into a well-oiled machine. At times it's mayhem—like yesterday, when the water in the 650,000-gallon tank erupted into chaos as a massive "whale" thrashed in its death throes. Members of the stunt team hurtled across the tank on personal watercrafts, weaving around the enormous creature at breakneck speed, their engines howling like jet fighters. The entire production crew stared at the churning water, holding their collective breath. Every move was calculated, every person hyper-focused on their part of the puzzle.

It's the same today: a carefully choreographed dance, and we're all in sync. The water, once screaming with action, has become an arena of silent endurance. We're capturing seconds—fractions of seconds, really—that have to be perfect. There's no room for mistakes.

Each take stretches out longer than the last. Every single person, from seasoned stunt performers to Hollywood icons, is holding their breath—muscles straining, lungs burning, waiting for the moment they can break the surface and gulp in air.

I tread water at the edge of the tank, scanning faces, reading the subtle signs that someone is nearing their limit: a twitch, a shift in posture, the smallest signal that it's time to call it.

The pressure is relentless. Hesitation could be deadly.

The air shifts whenever the big names are on set: Kate Winslet, Sigourney Weaver, and of course, James Cameron. When they step into the tank, the water itself becomes a character. Everything gets more intense, more electric. Their presence brings a certain significance—you can feel it in the air, and even in the water sometimes.

I watch them all closely, my eyes constantly moving from face to face, looking for any sign that someone's about to tap out. Every take feels like a lifetime now, stretched thin by the demands of the scene and the pursuit of perfection. Yet amid the tension and the ticking clock, there's a strange beauty in the challenge—an unspoken bond forged in the water's depths, where trust and determination are what keep us going. We're in this together, every single one of us, from the crew working the cameras to the actors fighting to hold their breath just a little bit longer.

Being in the movie business isn't always what people envision. I've been up since five a.m. for my eight-minute daily drive to Manhattan Beach Studios. An ear infection has been bugging me for days—the third one this month—and another day submerged in a huge tank of highly chlorinated water is only going to make it worse. My skin stings from spending twelve or thirteen hours a day in that water, though the burning sensation has become so normal, I hardly notice it anymore. And let's be honest: At a balmy 90°F, the tank is more like a petri dish hosting all of our microscopic secretions.

It's hard. This is where the real work happens—the effort behind the magic. And I love every minute of it.

I've been in constant motion for decades, traveling around the globe and looking inward, always chasing something just beyond the horizon. But how did I end up here? How did I go from a landlocked, communist country in Europe to being submerged in the heart of Hollywood's most ambitious film project?

What is it that draws me to the sea again and again, like a magnet I can't resist?

When did I learn that the biggest dreams require the hardest work—and the deepest faith in yourself?

How did I persevere through illness, heartache, missteps, and the crushing weight of starting over in foreign countries with nothing but determination and a duffel bag?

How did I find my way when every path seemed to lead somewhere I never expected?

When did I finally realize that the journey itself, not the destination, is the point?

And why does this moment—suspended between breaths in a Hollywood tank—feel like both the most unlikely and the most destined outcome of a life lived without limits?

This is a story of going anywhere and everywhere while learning to be present wherever I am—about discovering that integrity, resilience, and sheer, stubborn determination can carry you farther than luck. It's been a wild journey, one I never could have imagined as a kid staring at maps and dreaming of oceans. But I made it here, by diving into my dreams, exploring the depths of my gypsy soul, putting in the hard work, and following my wanderlust, wherever it took me.

And every step of the way has been worth it.

CHAPTER 1

Hungary: Survival in a Shifting World

Life isn't about finding yourself.
Life is about creating yourself.
– Sydney J. Harris

The summer I turn fourteen, my entire life fractures and reshapes itself. It's 1990, and the Berlin Wall has crumbled. Communism ends in Hungary. My period starts. I discover that I love scuba diving. And my dad dies. These seismic shifts happen so close together, they blur into one long, disorienting earthquake that leaves nothing unchanged in my world. But I survive that summer, because I've been preparing for catastrophe my whole life.

Disaster has always felt near, even when I was a baby and had no words for what was happening to me. I wept relentlessly as an infant, or so I've been told. Driven by necessity, my mother returned to work when I was just three months old, and I sobbed myself sick as my tiny body tried to keep her close, to keep her from leaving. She later recalled the desperation of my never-ending cries—my plea for her warmth, her presence.

I was often placed in the bathtub to sleep so my father, exhausted from the weight of our new life, could get some rest. Our family had recently moved from a tiny apartment in a dodgy district of Budapest to a house with a huge garden in the green District XI neighborhood. Too young to understand anything beyond my mother's absence, I spent long days in early childcare yearning for her arms, aching for her voice. Not yet able to express the agony of abandonment, I cried for her until my body surrendered and the pain manifested in other ways. By the time I'd turned two years old, I had undergone nearly twenty ear surgeries, each one a silent testament to trauma I do not remember.

This deep-rooted trauma is woven into the fabric of who I am at age fourteen. It is why I am hardened—why I've learned, far too soon, to rely on no one but myself. This early lesson in self-reliance serves me well when everything falls apart. I already know how to survive when the people who are supposed to protect me can't ... or won't.

As a teenager, already I see that some childhoods are filled with happy moments, with countless memories of a warm, loving family. But my own memories are isolated snapshots—fishing with my dad, hiking through the forest, gatherings with family friends—brief reprieves from an undercurrent of tension that defines our everyday life. Everything was always rushed. My parents—exhausted, impatient, and distracted—only half listened when I spoke. Their minds were preoccupied with dreams of a better future, one they were determined to build, no matter the cost. When their good intentions did not unfold as planned, their frustration seeped into our home, onto my sister and me—a tense, looming storm that we learned to navigate.

Csilla and I might never have picked each other as friends, but we have an unbreakable bond: sisterhood. When we fight, I am usually blamed—the older child who should know better. We are expected to be playmates, and I love my sister deeply, but harmony doesn't come naturally. I take after our father: practical, hands-on, grounded. Csilla is emotional, drawn to excitement and bright lights—our mother's mirror image. Our arguments flare quickly, often escalating beyond words. At a time when the harsh discipline of wooden spoons and leather belts is the norm, my sister and I are just copying what we've seen as the standard way to resolve conflict.

Love existed in our childhood home, but it was complicated, tangled with unspoken expectations and restless ambition. Mutti—my mother—called me her "sunshine" and Csilla her "star," showering us with affection and taking us to art exhibitions and concerts. Apu—my father—taught us to build practical things, like bookshelves, that are both functional and beautiful. His love of animals, nature, and gardening created a closeness with Csilla that I envied. But I've always preferred the solitude of a quiet corner and a good book.

My beloved grandmothers understood me as a child in ways that my parents never could. They had all the time in the world for me and Csilla, and treated us like true young adults. Mutti's parents were eternally cheerful despite facing a lifetime of adversity, and their home in the Pest side of Budapest, only a short bus ride from our house, was like a breath of fresh air—a haven of serenity and generosity. Their patience seemed limitless. Pesti Nagyi (or "Happy Grandma," as I call her) in particular was a beacon of light, radiating warmth, kindness, and an inspirational desire to help others. Around her, I felt unconditionally loved.

Childhood summers with my father's parents in the Komarom countryside were always perfection. We'd help around the farm, feeding ducks, pigs, and chickens, and harvesting fruits and vegetables from her garden. When the chores were done, "Grumpy Grandma," as I call Komaromi Nagyi, taught us to shoot with a shotgun and excel in chess. Most nights, we played gin rummy and other card games for hours—Csilla and I, with Grumpy Grandma, cousin Edit, and Aunt Vera, who usually won. Competitive and sharp, Aunt Vera helped me make sense of the world. In Komarom, I've always felt encouraged and understood.

Back in Budapest, Dad worked three jobs to build our house on the outskirts of the city, close enough to the city center but still quiet and, most important, with space for a garden. He laid the floors, framed the closets, planted vegetables. He was always tired, always working, whether overtime at one of his jobs, in our home, or at his mother's place in Komarom. Even on holiday visits, he was fixing things.

By age eleven, I was on the cusp of adolescence, my world still defined by school and family routines. Then Chernobyl happened.

* * *

The news seeped in slowly, like a dark shadow creeping toward us.

There's no real danger, the media insisted, calm and detached. But my parents exchanged glances that told a different story. My father continued tending his tomato and paprika plants, defying the invisible threat with his calloused hands even as the worry became etched day by day on his face. This was something he could not fix.

The uneasy days dragged on. We followed the advice on the radio and the television, staying indoors and clutching at the normalcy of our routines like a lifeline. The outside world, once so familiar, felt distant and alien, hidden behind closed windows and locked doors.

Hungary is far enough from the disaster to be untouched, the media assured us. Only a few months later, the illusion of safety shattered.

It started with a cough—just my father frequently clearing his throat, a rasp that lingered longer than it should. He waved off Mutti's concerned looks. *It's nothing*, he claimed. *Probably just dust from the electrical factory.*

But the cough didn't go away. Instead, it deepened, becoming wet and violent, shaking his whole body until his face turned red and his eyes watered. Soon, he was struggling to catch his breath after climbing the stairs … then after walking across the room … then simply from sitting up in bed.

The doctor visits became frequent, then urgent. Fragments of hushed conversations between my parents reached my ears, words like *mass* and *spread* and *time* that sent ice through my veins. My mother's face grew hollow, her eyes red-rimmed from crying when she thought we didn't see.

The man who built our house with his bare hands, who could fix anything, carry anything, outlast anyone, began to shrink before our eyes. His clothes hung loose on his frame. His rough and capable hands, once so strong they could split wood with a simple blow, now shake with the effort of holding a coffee cup.

The worst part wasn't watching him waste away—it was watching him try to maintain the illusion that everything would be fine. He still attempted to work on the house, help with homework, make plans for next summer's garden. He tried to hide it from us—stepping outside to cough, muffling the sound with his sleeve, forcing a smile when we caught him doubled over. But you can't hide the sound of a man drowning in his own lungs.

We all knew. The knowledge sat heavy in our home like the toxic air we breathed. Even so, when the final diagnosis came, the words landed like physical blows: *lung cancer, metastasized, liver, lymphatic system.* This man had spent his life working with his body—building, fixing, growing—and now, at thirty-nine years old, his body had betrayed him in the cruelest manner.

The doctors spoke in careful, clinical language about *treatment options* and *managing expectations*, but their eyes told the real story. My mother clung to every word about chemotherapy and radiation, desperate for hope, while my father simply nodded with the resigned acceptance of a man who already knows his fate.

The treatments were brutal. They turned my father's skin gray and made him vomit until there was nothing left but bile. He lost weight so rapidly, his wedding ring slid off his finger—a loss that made my mother sob harder than anything else. When his hair fell out in clumps, she secretly gathered them from his pillow, as though she could somehow put him back together, piece by piece.

When the time comes to let him go, I want to scream. I want to shake my mother until she understands: *This isn't love—it's torture!* But she can't bear to let him go, can't accept that no amount of wanting will bring him back. So he endures weeks of agony on life support, a week past my fourteenth birthday. Machines breathe for him. Tubes feed him. His body is a shell that no longer contains the father I remember.

But I'm fourteen. What do I know about losing the love of your life? What do I know about watching your dreams die in a hospital bed? So I sit beside my father in that sterile room, holding his hand that feels like paper over bone, listening to the mechanical rhythm that keeps him alive when his spirit has already fled. I tell him about school, my friends, anything except the obvious: that we're all just waiting for him to die.

When Mutti finally agrees to turn off life support and Apu's heart stops beating, nine days after my birthday, I feel nothing but relief. The long nightmare is over. No more watching him struggle for breath. No more pretending that everything will be okay. No more hoping for miracles that will never come.

I don't cry at his funeral. Not because I don't love him, because I do—desperately, completely—but because the tears are frozen inside me. Everyone expects grief, but what I feel is more complex and shameful: liberation. I am free from the suffocating weight of watching my father die slowly, free from the false hope that had poisoned our home for months.

But of course, I can't say this out loud. How do you explain to people that your father's death is a mercy? How do you admit that you're relieved when you're supposed to be devastated? So I stand there, dry-eyed and composed, while people whisper about how strong I am, how well I'm handling it, how mature I seem for my age.

I'm not strong, I'm numb! I want to shout. The little girl who once cried herself sick in a bathtub has learned to bury her pain so deep that it can't reach the surface. I've become an expert at surviving, at functioning when the world collapses, at taking care of everyone else when I'm falling apart inside.

The peace that follows my father's death is almost worse than the chaos that preceded it. No more arguments about money, no more fights about the house, no more tension crackling through our dinner conversations—just silence. Just my mother's muffled sobs from behind her bedroom door. Just my sister's confused questions about what's going to happen to us.

Just me, left to pick up the pieces.

* * *

Now that the Iron Curtain has fallen, and our world is opening up, I trace my fingers over the atlas, dreaming of distant shores. For most of my life so far, Hungarians could only travel to Mother Russia, but I've always dreamed of living by the ocean, where the sun shines golden and palm trees frame every view. This deep, out-of-the-blue love for the sea has been a part of me for as long as I can remember.

Magnificent documentaries by David Attenborough and Jacques Cousteau fuel my desire to experience the ocean firsthand. But watching isn't enough—I want to dive in, discover its depths, and live the lifestyle I see on the screen. The mysteries of the deep sea are too compelling to remain just a dream. I long to visit exotic places, taste new foods, and swim in oceans teeming with colorful fish and dazzling coral reef empires.

Unlike my classmates, who can now jet off to foreign destinations for summer vacations, my sister and I spend our summer breaks in Komarom. After my father's passing, when our family's financial situation changes for the worse, we find ourselves with even less disposable income. Summer visits with Grumpy Grandma are a mix of resilience, warmth, and a touch of melancholy.

Her story is one of survival. After World War II, her family was uprooted from their prosperous farm in northern Hungary, now part of the Czech Republic, and relocated to a poor village in southern Hungary. They were forced to leave everything behind—a life of wealth reduced to dismal poverty. My grandfather became ill from the strain, and Grumpy Grandma juggled caring for him with the hard labor needed to survive. She managed the family farm with unwavering dedication and later became a school chef.

Despite hardship—losing her parents, then her husband, and now burying her son—Grumpy Grandma rarely speaks of the pain. Her strength endures, and she fills every corner of her home with the effervescence of life. She is hardened by life, yet filled with courage. She sings and hums folk songs all day long. Her cooking is an especially true reflection of her love and care. When I spend time with her, I feel strong and smart.

To label me as a "tomboy" barely scratches the surface of my true identity, but it's true that I prefer the company of boys over the girls I know.

Once absorbed by dolls, these girls now spend their time on superficial pursuits like makeup, hair, and shopping, all in an effort to capture male attention. Their focus on appearances and validation feels alien to me—a stark contrast to the stimulation and spontaneity I crave.

In my eyes, being one of the boys seems far more appealing. Their easygoing nature and interest in escapades and mischief resonate with me, and we find common ground in our shared enthusiasm for riding bicycles, playing ping-pong in the park, and spending hours swimming and boating. My friends and I seek out heart-pounding, adrenaline-fueled adventures, often skirting the boundaries set by our parents. We are drawn to the thrill of the forbidden, to experiences that defy the constraints of traditional norms. Even more than the exhilaration of dirt-streaked clothes and the exhaustion of physical activity, I revel in the delight of being immersed in the water.

In those brief moments underwater, nobody talks to me or tells me what to do. It's like stepping into a completely different life where I can just … *be.* This is something I can get nowhere in my real life on dry land: absolute freedom.

Hungary, though landlocked, offers plenty of water bodies to explore—lakes, quarries, and rivers that provide infinite opportunities to row, kayak, and swim. I even play ice hockey when they freeze over in the winter. Last year, at age thirteen, I tried orientation diving for the first time and was immediately hooked. I joined the BHG Scuba Diving Club, marking the start of my underwater expeditions.

Orientation diving is a fascinating challenge, like a treasure hunt: finding buoys in near zero-visibility while aiming for the fastest time. We glide through the water with large monofins secured to our feet, keeping our legs together and moving like dolphins. Instead of carrying the air tank on our backs, we push it ahead with our arms to be more streamlined. Attached to the tank's skeg (the fin on its underside, used for steering and stability) are a compass and a distance-measuring device. The air hose dangles from the tank, its loose end a mouthpiece that we grip with our teeth to keep the air flowing into our lungs.

I love everything about diving. Like my younger childhood self, I'm drawn to the thrill of the unknown and forbidden, to experiences that defy the constraints of traditional norms. But at fourteen, I'm no longer a child.

In the wake of my father's passing, the world seems to shift beneath me. Somehow I'm the keeper of our family's fragile stability, the one who has to be strong because everyone else is broken—helping Csilla with homework, managing household finances I'm too young to comprehend, becoming the emotional support system for Mutti, who has collapsed under the weight of her loss. Somewhere in the depths of my frozen heart, I know I'll never fully trust anyone to take care of me again.

As I grapple with this immense loss, another profound shift unfolds—one that reshapes me from top to bottom. Puberty descends upon me with its tumultuous force, ushering in a tempest of changes that leave me disoriented and vulnerable. Overnight, my girlish chest swells to a 34D, a physical transformation that feels alien and uncomfortable. The sudden emergence of breasts is a major inconvenience, a distraction that undermines my adolescent efforts to blend in with the boys. My first period, too, is an unwelcome reminder of my transition from girl to young woman, a painful milestone I feel ill-prepared for. The notion of future childbirth adds to my sense of discomfort and disgust.

At age fifteen, my frustration boils over. One day, in a fit of anger, I take an axe to an old walnut tree in my maternal grandparents' orchard in the hillside of Budapest. My grandfather's usual calm dissolves into genuine anger. It's the first time I see him upset. That moment becomes a pivotal lesson in managing my emotions constructively. From then on, I learn to channel my frustration into gardening and shoveling dirt. Turning over the soil with a shovel each spring to prepare the ground for planting becomes a therapeutic ritual and provides a healthier outlet for my emotions.

I struggle to conceal the changes in my body beneath loose plaid flannel shirts and a hunched posture, hoping the guys will continue to see me as one of them. The thought of being treated differently, of being seen through the lens of womanhood, fills me with dread. I long for the uncomplicated camaraderie of my childhood and the simplicity of that world—a world where I felt at ease and accepted for who I was.

* * *

In high school, the seeds of my ambitions find room to grow.

Academically, I excel in subjects that spark my interest. Math has long been a cherished subject, but now I fall in love with literature and storytelling, imagining myself on quests far beyond the classroom. I develop a love for analytical reasoning and join the debate team, wrestling with thought-provoking ideas and tough topics. My excitement comes not just from winning, but from learning how to present a persuasive argument—a skill that begins to shape how I approach every challenge.

I have started to think for myself.

Emotionally, I'm a storm of highs and lows, a social butterfly who also needs time alone to recharge and often gets lost in a book or a creative project. My teenage years bypass cliques and social division yet are marked by crushes that come and go, each one feeling intense and significant. The drama of young love plays out in stolen glances and whispered conversations, but it's all fleeting—just part of growing up. Each time a whirlwind relationship ends, it feels liberating and bittersweet.

At home, life is still hard without my father. I continue to step into his role, taking on repair duty and learning to drive. This responsibility alters how I see myself. My hair gets shorter, and stress triggers eczema. Compared to my slim, Angelina Jolie–like sister, I struggle with body image and insecurity. While she indulges in Nutella and pizza without consequence, I seem to gain weight just watching her eat.

I try diet after diet, hoping to shed the weight that feels like a drag on my confidence, but end up stuck in a cycle of frustration. Solace arrives in the form of my diving teammate Nóra. Her family becomes a second home to me, offering stability and warmth. Our friendship is special, a lesson in the connections that truly matter.

During physical education class, I show talent in handball and get recruited to the team, but quickly realize that team sports aren't for me. I hunger for more personal pursuits, where success relies entirely on my own efforts. So, I pour all my energy and focus into diving. The underwater world becomes my sanctuary—a place of silence, solitude, and lightness.

Summers are filled with outdoor camping, training in nearby lakes and quarries alongside my teammates and competitors across Hungary. Our schedule is packed with competitions and coaching sessions at the finest diving sites the country has to offer: Ócsa, Ecséd, Budakalász, and my personal favorite, Gyékényes. The team, a mix of older leaders and younger members, becomes like family, creating revered memories. We bond over shared challenges, from navigating murky waters to hitchhiking when our old military truck breaks down. Rarely do we return home except for a quick change of clothes. Even during Hungary's harsh winters, while training in indoor pools or beneath frozen lakes, I embrace the cold with a sense of wonder.

To keep our training affordable, we participate in "Communist Saturdays" at Kopaszi-Gát, our base camp. We maintain the team's equipment, refill scuba tanks, repair neoprene suits, mow the grass, and paint fences—creating a scene that feels a bit like something out of *Tom Sawyer*. These experiences instill in me a sincere sense of responsibility, gratitude, and work ethic.

I realize that to represent my team, my city, and my country effectively, I must train diligently and excel in competitions. Many of my colleagues are superior swimmers, so I work to develop my navigational skills. In clear water, where the buoys are visible from far away, my faster competitors outswim me, but in poor weather and bad visibility, my precision with the compass makes me the winner.

My family's connection to the church further boosts my self-esteem: Sundays bring peaceful services. Wednesday Bible classes deepen my friendships and faith. Saturdays are spent at dance lessons, learning to waltz and tango. The church provides community, love, and acceptance—a place where I feel valued.

Slowly, as I realize my worth isn't tied to a number on a scale, I let go of the pressure to conform. Confidence, I learn, comes not from changing who I am, but from accepting and celebrating it. Embracing my natural shape becomes liberating. I shift focus to what truly matters—living fully, savoring my qualities, and finding contentment in each day.

I dedicate myself fully to the world of competitive scuba diving and get my first glimpse of life beyond Hungary, visiting neighboring countries like Austria and the Czech Republic with my dive team. Their lakes are pristine, bordered by lush plants and wildflowers, not to mention modern amenities like toilets and showers. Their teams are better equipped, too, with new gear and stylish attire, while we make do with hand-me-downs and worn-out scuba gear in constant need of repair.

Being part of the club also comes with other costs that I'm too young to fully understand. Most of our training is funded by military sponsorship, and they don't give money away for free. They depend on us to traverse the pitch-black depths where others can't, using skills that are crucial for search-and-recovery missions and intelligence gathering that no one talks about in daylight.

At age sixteen, I think I'm ready for anything. I've spent years diving in zero visibility, steering by compass and rangefinder alone, pushing my lungs to their limits in freezing water. I've proven myself capable, reliable, unafraid. But nothing prepares you for the moment when your hobby becomes a crime scene.

The call comes on a Tuesday evening. Our coach's voice is different—clipped, official. There's been an incident in Budapest. The police need divers. We're to meet at dawn.

I don't sleep that night. Not because I'm nervous about the dive—I've done hundreds of training dives in worse conditions. But something in the coach's tone, the way he avoided details, sends a chill through me that has nothing to do with the water temperature we'll soon face.

We arrive at a lake in the heart of city just as the sun rises, casting everything in an eerie golden light that feels wrong for what we're about to do. Police cars line the shore, their radios crackling with codes I don't understand. Uniformed officers huddle around maps, pointing at coordinates and speaking in hushed voices.

The briefing is matter-of-fact, almost casual: A high-speed police chase ended here two nights ago. The suspects ditched evidence before they were captured—a duffel bag full of money, thrown from a bridge into the gloomy depths. The water is twenty feet deep, visibility less than a foot. Standard recovery dive.

Except it's not standard at all. This isn't training. This is real crime, real evidence, real consequences if we fail. And I'm sixteen years old, strapping on gear that weighs almost as much as I do, preparing to dive into water as dark as outer space.

The descent is routine … until it isn't. My fins stir up silt with each kick, turning the already poor visibility into complete blindness. I must navigate by touch, my hands extended in front of me, feeling along the lake bottom through thick gloves that make everything alien and distant. After the designated thirty minutes of searching, I surface without the missing bag. Gasping, with the taste of lake water bitter on my tongue, I am both disappointed and relieved.

The atmosphere is tense as my teammates surface, one after another, all empty-handed. Then, an excited scream: "I found something!" our team leader cries. "I think this is it!"

He secures the line thrown to him by the surface support guys, gives the all-clear signal, and watches as they haul up evidence that will put someone in prison for the rest of their life. And somehow, I've become part of that chain of justice, a sixteen-year-old girl who now knows too much about how the adult world really works.

The worst comes three months later—another call, another dawn meeting, another crime scene. This time, the briefing is even more clinical, even more sanitized. A murder case. Missing evidence. Critical to the prosecution. They don't tell us what we're looking for until we're already geared up, already committed: a severed head.

The words leave me nauseous and dizzy on the dive platform.

"We need this evidence to identify the body we found nearby," the detective says, noting my pale face. "Same as any other recovery."

But it's not the same, and we all know it. This is someone's child, someone's parent, reduced to evidence in a waterproof bag. And I'm expected to dive down into that black water and bring it up, as if this is just another training exercise.

The descent feels like falling into hell. Every sound is amplified underwater—my breathing harsh in the regulator, my heartbeat thundering in my ears. The water is even murkier than usual, stirred up by recent storms, and once again I must choose my route by touch alone.

When my hands close around something round and soft, I nearly bolt for the surface. Only years of training and the knowledge that my teammates are counting on me keep me down there, securing the piece with shaking hands, fighting back waves of nausea.

The ascent is the longest of my young life. Each foot upward seems to increase the weight of what I'm carrying, threatening to drag me back down. When I finally break the surface, wheezing and retching, I see my own horror reflected in my teammates' faces.

Then ... relief, like someone has lifted a rock off my shoulders. In my hands is not the disposed head, but an old, torn-up medicine ball—the kind used in PE class or at the gym.

We continue to search for hours without finding the missing piece for this police investigation. Despite returning the next day, luckily—for me—we do not prevail in our search. How would I even have handled it if we did?

This experience follows me. For months, in the dim, cloudy waters of every subsequent dive, I see shadows that might be evidence, shapes that might be secrets, mysteries that might be better left buried. The water, once buoyant and free, now carries the weight of the world's darkness.

* * *

Amidst my teenage struggles, the world around me is undergoing a profound transformation of its own.

In my elementary school, conformity was enforced. We learned Russian as a second language, sang the previous generation's revolutionary songs, and wore red neckerchiefs while participating in propaganda-filled school events. Rebellion seemed impossible. But then the Berlin Wall came down, and communism came to an end in Hungary.

Growing up in a communist country brought a mix of benefits and disadvantages. Education was free and accessible, extending through university. We had free lunches, afterschool programs, and healthcare, along with access to concerts and theater performances. These opportunities enriched our lives and fostered a love for the arts, but the adult world was different. Yes, the government provided a safety net for retirees, offering security in old age after years of hard work. But financial rewards were low regardless of the work, whether you were a doctor or a waiter.

The fall of communism ushers in a new era of empowerment and possibility—an exhilarating contrast to the rigid constraints I've grown up with. Suddenly it feels like stepping into a world without limits, where dreams can finally become reality. The taste of freedom is as sweet as my first Coca-Cola, and it fills me with hope for the future. The world opens up just in time for me, offering opportunities that would have been out of reach just a few years earlier.

Meanwhile, as I dive deeper into the realm of competitive scuba, I discover purpose and connection that transcend the surface world. In the water, I shed the burden of limitations and constraints, and instead find liberation, inner strength, and authenticity. I face each challenge with courage and determination, knowing that every step of my journey holds significance.

I never set my sights on a world championship or envision myself as the best in the field of orienteering diving. The pursuit of such lofty goals, with relentless training six days a week, morning and evening, would strip away the joyful essence of scuba and what it means to me. My devotion to diving isn't driven by rankings; it's derived from fellowship and the sheer pleasure of being immersed in the water.

I already know deep down that my dream will become reality—that my determination to traverse the world and its oceans, from the Arctic to Antarctica, will drive me forward. When I set my sights on something, I pursue it fiercely. The doubts of my friends and family only make me more committed: One day I will live by the ocean, in a place filled with sunshine and life, lined by palm trees, where I will revel in summer all year long.

I just need to find how to get there.

CHAPTER 2

Budapest: Finding My Path

Incredible change happens in your life when you decide to take control of what you have power over instead of craving control over what you don't.
— Steve Maraboli

Growing up with limited means, I learn to be resourceful. My friends get pocket money from their parents. I make mine by turning my hobbies into income—tie-dying shirts, braiding hair, making jewelry, tutoring math. Every little venture fuels my belief that I can create my own opportunities.

By age sixteen, my ambition to roam the world leads me to take on additional weekend gigs in retail, hospitality, and beyond: working at the Benetton store, selling ice cream in a family friend's bakery, waitressing at special events. This not only offers me some financial independence, but also shapes my understanding of how the world works.

Each job brings its own trials and rewards, from managing busy shifts to practicing English to perfecting my communication skills.

Each step means growth and discovery, bringing me closer to the thrill of autonomy.

Each experience further empowers me to pursue my dreams of adventure.

My growing desire for independence clashes with my mother's vision of our family life, creating constant friction at home. Every word, every action is laden with unspoken frustrations. As a single parent, Mutti struggles to raise two kids alone, and her sharp tone often betrays her weariness. We argue constantly.

My deep need for independence clashes with the duty I feel toward our mother. The task of helping my younger sister with her homework after finishing my own becomes a daily aggravation. Reading is the biggest struggle of all. She fights with every word, stumbling through sentences until our study session dissolves into tears—hers, mine, or both. Watching Csilla wrestle with the pages is both heartbreaking and annoying: She resents my bossiness. I am convinced that if only she tried harder, she could overcome the problem.

I love my mother and sister, and no matter how rough the path, we hold on—to each other, to the unbreakable thread of our connection—and always find our way back to one another. Beneath the escalating tension runs a deep, unspoken attachment. Yet at times it feels as though we're living in a reality show like *Big Brother*, a bunch of outlandish characters thrown in the mix together.

The constant competition between sisters engulfs us. I resent Csilla hanging with my friends, looking so effortlessly pretty and natural. When she wants to join me in orienteering diving, I draw the line. Diving is my only escape from reality.

At school we learned about Aboriginal Australians, whose "dream life" occurs alongside their "real life"—a spiritual world outside time and space that is connected to the physical world where they live. I feel the same way with diving. My time under the water feels as important and real as the life I live in the city. The underwater world is where I feel happy and free … where no one else exists … where all obstacles disappear and I am weightless. Csilla's presence would suffocate me.

In defiance, she takes up synchronized swimming instead—and quickly excels, of course, eventually joining the national team.

How is this fair? I wonder. *Why does she become incredibly good, practically overnight, while I struggle to remain mediocre in my own pursuit?* The frustration gnaws at me. I cannot wait to grow up and move out.

Our family life is filled with friction, and our home is a battlefield of daily arguments, public confrontations, and emotional outbursts. Mutti fluctuates between needing my support and asserting her authority, leaving me overwhelmed and longing for escape. I respond by planning trip after trip, venturing farther and farther from Hungary, soaking in European seashores with my friends and my hard-earned money.

The first time I see the ocean—while standing on a rocky Croatian cliff overlooking the Adriatic Sea—something fundamental shifts inside me. The endless blue stretches beyond the horizon. Far below me, waves crash against ancient stones with a rhythm that feels like the heartbeat I've been searching for my entire life. Salt spray hits my face, and I taste possibility. This isn't just water; it's freedom made liquid. My friends are laughing, taking photos, planning which beach to visit next, but I am transfixed.

For seventeen years, I've dreamed of this moment while staring at maps and watching documentaries about coral reefs and underwater worlds. Nothing—no photograph, no film, no flicker of imagination—has prepared me for the ocean's sheer *aliveness*. It breathes, moves, calls to something deep in my soul. Standing there, toes gripping wet rocks, hair whipping in the sea breeze, I know with absolute certainty that this is where I belong. Not in Budapest's cramped scene with its daily battles, not in Hungary's familiar but limiting embrace, but here, where the horizon promises infinite possibilities and every wave whispers of adventures yet to come.

The girl who returns home is different from the one who left—she has tasted salt air and felt the pull of tides, and no amount of family friction can erase that transformation. Yet the arguments with my mother intensify. Her need for control clashes with my growing hunger for independence. In an act of pure rebellion, I forge her signature and sign up for parachute training at a military airfield outside Budapest. The thrill of defying her control is intoxicating.

The training uses old Russian military parachutes—canvas and rope that smell of diesel fuel and history. The Soviet-era facility squats on a windswept plain, its concrete buildings scarred by decades of Hungarian winters. I'm the youngest person and only girl in the class. The instructors are gruff former paratroopers with weathered faces and cigarette-stained fingers. All this only stokes my determination.

The day of my first jump arrives with nervous energy. As the plane climbs, the roar of the engine vibrates through my bones. When the door opens, cold air rushes in, and one by one, the trainees jump. My heart races as I step to the edge and leap into the void.

The freefall is an intense rush—wind roaring, gravity pulling, mind racing between fear and ecstasy. Then, with a jolt, the parachute deploys, and I float in serene silence, awestruck by the vast landscape below. I feel more alive in this moment than ever before in my young life.

During the next day's jump, I studiously aim to avoid the trees below but end up tangled in one, hanging from the branches and laughing at the irony. It's a lesson in focusing on what I want rather than what I fear.

On the final day, tragedy strikes. A fellow trainee's parachute fails, followed by his backup. I watch in helpless horror as he plummets, ending in a sickening impact. The shock leaves me paralyzed. The thrill of the sport is forever tainted. The rush I once craved now feels too dangerous, overshadowed by risk and coarse reality. My daring escapade no longer feels like a grand adventure. After completing the training, I confess to Mutti and promise to parachute no more.

Reaching my final year in high school, I experience a new rush: falling in love. Three years older than me, and a friend from our close-knit group, Balázs becomes a central figure in my life. We spend afternoons playing ping-pong and biking through the neighborhood, our relationship growing with each shared moment. Balázs introduces me to Chinese food and punk culture, shaping my literary and musical tastes and opening my eyes to new ideas and perspectives.

Our connection deepens as we frequent bookstores and theaters together, enjoying long conversations about philosophy and religion, often over almond vanilla tea. Balázs isn't just a romantic partner; he's a mentor and friend, helping me grow. When we watch *Dead Poets Society* together, I am enthralled by its message: *Carpe diem!*

This "seize the day" philosophy speaks to me. I'm eager to expand my horizons and live a life less ordinary. I resolve to embrace every opportunity, to see failure as just a detour on my path to happiness. My optimism helps me view setbacks as chances for growth, and I discover how satisfying it is to help others see things in the same light.

Balázs and I grow closer and closer, our connection solidifying with every shared moment. We talk for hours about everything—his dreams of becoming an established artist, my fantasies of living by the ocean, the books we love, the future we might build together. When the time comes for his mandatory military service, I'm devastated but determined to make our long-distance relationship work.

We write letters back and forth—long, passionate pages where I pour out my heart and he responds with equal intensity. Whenever Balázs gets leave, we spend every possible minute of the weekend together, walking through Budapest's cobblestone streets, stealing kisses in shadowy doorways, planning the life we'll have when his service ends. I have fallen deeply, completely in love with him. The way he looks at me, the tenderness in his voice when he calls me his "little bird"—everything tells me the feeling is mutual.

For months, this becomes my world. I live for his letters, count the days between his visits, dream about our future together. I've never felt anything this intense, this consuming. This must be what the poets write about, what movies try to capture. This is love, real love, and it's mine.

Until one afternoon, walking home from school with a spring in my step after mailing him another letter, I see them: Balázs and his ex-girlfriend, walking hand in hand through the park by our house. He's supposed to be at base—*no leave this weekend*, he'd written just days before. But there he is, laughing at something she's saying, looking at her the way I thought he looked only at me.

The world tilts. My bag slips from my shoulder. The letter I just posted—full of plans for his next visit, declarations of love, dreams of forever—suddenly becomes evidence of my own foolishness.

They don't see me. I stand frozen behind a lamppost, watching the boy I love hold another girl's hand with gentle certainty, just as he'd held mine. It's a brutal education in love and betrayal, delivered in broad daylight. Unable to control myself, I walk up to them and, without saying a word, look into his eyes as I punch his face. Then I walk away, head held high but crying inside.

The realization arrives with devastating clarity: I cannot control what others do, only how I react. The lesson burns, but it also hardens something inside me. If this is what love costs, I'll need to be stronger.

* * *

Law school seems like the obvious path for me after high school, leading to a well-paying career perfectly suited to my debate and logic skills. For months, I've been telling everyone about my plans. My literature teacher, who nurtured my analytical thinking, nods approvingly when I discuss my application strategy. Even my diving teammates joke about having a lawyer in the group

Mutti beams with pride. "My daughter is going to be a lawyer," she tells all the neighbors.

The entrance exam becomes my obsession. I study relentlessly, memorizing history, practicing logic puzzles until my eyes burn, drilling myself on Hungarian and world literature until I can recite authors and their works in my sleep. I'm so confident in my abilities that I put all my eggs in one basket, applying only to Eötvös Loránd University (ELTE), the most prestigious law school in Hungary.

Why waste time on backup options, I rationalize, *when I know I'll get in?*

My confidence isn't unfounded. I've always excelled academically when something interests me. My debate team experience has sharpened my ability to analyze and argue points from various perspectives. My math teacher has praised my analytical mind. Everything points to success. I even start planning my course schedule, imagining myself in lecture halls discussing constitutional theory and criminal procedure.

The night before the exam, I barely sleep—not from nerves, but from excitement: *This is it! The beginning of my prestigious career!* I picture myself in a courtroom, commanding attention, fighting for justice. The image is so clear, so inevitable, that the actual test feels like a formality.

The exam goes well. My preparation pays off, and I breeze through most sections. A few tricky questions surprise me, but nothing shakes my confidence. Walking out of the examination hall, I'm already mentally celebrating. Other students look stressed, and some even cry. Meanwhile, I feel calm and assured. It's done. I'm in.

Weeks pass. I spend them planning my new life—what books I'll need, which professors I want to study under, how I'll balance law school with my diving training. I start introducing myself differently at parties: "I'll be studying law at ELTE in the fall." The words taste sweet and sophisticated.

When the results are finally posted, I rush to the university with my heart pounding—not with fear, but with anticipation. I scan the list once, twice, three times. My name isn't there.

The world stops.

I check again. Surely I've made a mistake! Maybe I'm looking at the wrong list, the wrong faculty? But no—this is definitely the law school admissions list, and my name is definitely not on it.

Around me, other students are celebrating or crying. I just stand there, numb, staring at a piece of paper that has shattered my future.

I find a pay phone and call the admissions office with shaking hands. "I need to check on my application," I say, my voice surprisingly steady. "There must be some mistake."

The secretary's voice is bored, mechanical. "Name and application number?"

I provide the information, gripping the phone so tightly that my knuckles turn white.

"You scored eighty-seven points," she says matter-of-factly. "The cutoff was eighty-eight. You missed admission by one point."

One point. A single point between my dreams and devastation.

"Is there ... is there an appeal process?" I ask. "Any way to—"

"No appeals. The cutoff is final. You can reapply next year."

The phone slips from my hand, clattering against the booth. Students stream past me, some clutching acceptance letters, others comforting friends. I feel invisible, hollow, like someone has reached inside my chest and scooped out everything that made me who I thought I was.

The walk home is a blur. How do I tell Mutti? How do I face everyone who believed in me, who congratulated me prematurely? How do I explain to people who are expecting to celebrate my success tonight? The thought makes me sick.

Mutti is in the kitchen when I arrive home, humming while she prepares my favorite dish for dinner. She turns to me with a radiant smile that immediately falters when she sees my face.

"What's wrong?" she gasps, though I can see she already knows.

"I didn't get in." The words come out as a whisper.

The silence that follows is deafening. My mother's expression cycles through disbelief, disappointment, and something that looks dangerously close to shame. She sinks into a chair, suddenly looking older than her years.

"How is that possible?" she asks at last. "You were so confident. You said it was easy."

"I missed it by one point. One fucking point, Mom."

She flinches at my language but doesn't reprimand me. Instead, she just stares at the half-prepared dinner, as if trying to process this new reality.

"What are you going to do now?" she asks quietly.

And that's when it hits me: *I have no idea.*

I was so arrogantly certain of my success that I never considered failure. No backup option, no alternative applications, no plan B. I've spent months building my identity around being a future lawyer, and now I'm nothing. A high school graduate with big dreams and no direction.

Telling everyone else is even worse than I anticipated.

My literature teacher tries to be encouraging, but I can see the disappointment in her eyes. "These things happen," she says, but we both know she expected better from me.

My diving teammates are sympathetic, but their comforting catchphrases carry an undercurrent of *I told you so.*

The shame is overwhelming. I had been so publicly confident, so vocal about my plans, that my failure feels like a community event. Everyone in my life had opinions about my academic ambitions, and now I have to face them all as a failure. Neighbors who heard about my law school plans now ask awkward questions. Former teachers run into me on the street and inquire about my studies, forcing me to explain my situation over and over again. Each conversation is a fresh humiliation.

Worst of all is the way this disaster unravels my self-image. I've always been the smart one, the achiever, the daughter who would make something of herself. My identity was built on academic success and future potential. Now I'm forced to confront an uncomfortable possibility: Maybe I'm not as special as I thought. Maybe I'm just another small-town girl with big dreams and a limited ability to achieve them.

Sleep becomes elusive. I lie awake, replaying the exam in my head: *Did I misunderstand a question? Did I make an error in calculation? Did I miss some crucial piece of information?*

One point. The margin is so small, it feels like a cosmic joke. If I had double-checked just one more answer … If I had been less confident and more careful … If I had just been slightly better at something I thought I was already good at …

The depression that follows is unlike anything I've experienced since my father's death—not grief over something lost, but the crushing weight of potential squandered, of a future that feels uncertain and suddenly terrifying. I spend days in bed, unable to summon the energy to answer the burning question: *What comes next?*

Weeks pass, and my friends from high school start their university journeys, sharing stories about orientation week and new roommates and exciting courses. I watch from the sidelines, excluded from a future I thought was guaranteed. Some reach out with sympathy, but their pity feels worse than neglect. Others seem almost relieved, as if my failure makes their own success shine brighter by comparison.

My new boyfriend, Mihus, is among those starting at university. We met last spring, at our high school prom, connecting instantly despite barely knowing each other. Our relationship blossomed as we worked side by side at summer jobs, saving up for trips around Europe. Our personalities are complementary: I'm intense and driven. He's quiet, calm, and thoughtful.

Mihus's family welcomes me with open arms—especially his mother, who treats me like the daughter she never had. My mom also grows to trust him, appreciating what a loving partner he is. But the practical questions become urgent as summer fades.

What am I going to do with my life?

How will I support myself?

Should I look for a job, apply to other schools, try again next year?

Every option feels like settling, like accepting a lesser version of the future I had planned.

My mother suggests secretarial school, or maybe something practical like accounting. The idea makes me want to scream. After years of academic excellence, after dreams of courtrooms and legal briefs, she wants me to type letters and file paperwork? But I also can't dismiss her suggestions entirely—at least those paths lead somewhere definite, somewhere stable.

It's a dark period. I'm questioning everything about my intelligence, my judgment, my worth as a person. But sometimes the path forward reveals itself only after everything you thought you wanted has been stripped away.

* * *

That autumn, while encapsulated in the black fog of self-doubt, I wander into a fire enamel class. Arts and crafts have always been my happy place, but I tell myself it's just something to fill the empty days, a way to avoid the pitying looks and awkward conversations about my "plans." Ever since that ELTE admissions list was posted, the only future I've been able to see is one of failure, disappointment, and terrifying uncertainty. But as I discover in the first sessions of the jewelry-making class, this could be a path to something new.

One day, an elderly teacher named Rezső walks into our creative space and takes an interest in my work. He sees potential in my hands and creativity in my approach. For the first time in months, someone is evaluating me based on what I can do, not what I failed to achieve.

When Rezső invites me to join his traditional silver and goldsmithing class, it feels like fate, but it's really desperation—the desperation of someone who has lost her direction. Willing to grab onto anything that might lead somewhere new, I jump at the opportunity. Who knows where it will take me? All I know is, I'm stuck, and staying where I am without moving forward has become unbearable.

The two-year jewelry-making program alternates weekly between art history and classroom theory with hands-on work in the workshop with Rezső. What begins as an escape from my academic failure transforms bit by bit into something much deeper—a genuine passion that surprises everyone, including me.

Soon, people are drawn to my jewelry for its beauty and functionality, and I begin taking custom orders. What started as therapy quickly turns into a business. While my classmates focus on perfecting ancestral techniques, I race through the basics, eager to experiment with new designs. The school workshop becomes my studio, where I lose myself in the thrill of creation.

I befriend Betti, who is loud, rebellious, and free-spirited like me. While most of our classmates are focused on grades, Betti and I think outside of the box and experiment with techniques. Our teacher, as wise and weathered as my maternal grandfather, nurtures our creativity instead of stifling it. He doesn't confine Betti and me to rigid rules, as long as we complete the assigned school projects. Instead, he encourages the two of us to push boundaries, to explore, to trust our instincts.

With his quiet guidance, my confidence grows. For the first time since the law school rejection, I feel the exhilaration of shaping something entirely my own.

There's a freedom in creation, a kind of magic in transforming a shapeless blob of silver into something unique that reflects my personality and passion. I lose myself in the process—the rhythmic hammering, the delicate welding, the slow, careful polishing. Each step brings my vision closer to life, using nothing but raw materials, a few simple tools, and my own hands.

In these moments of genesis, the world fades away, leaving only the rare and beautiful feeling of being completely in the moment. Nothing else exists but me and the art taking shape before my eyes. Some might call it meditation, but it's more than that.

It's escape.

It's presence.

At twenty years old, I am still dating Mihus, and together we plan a road trip to Venice, Italy, with my scuba diving friends, Nóra and her boyfriend. Amidst the annual Carnivale festivities, the four of us dine in the busy, iconic Piazza San Marco. While we converse enthusiastically about the costumes and masks of people walking by, Mihus quietly reaches under the table and slips a ring onto my finger, proposing in the most unexpected and enchanting way.

And just like that … we're engaged, surrounded by charming revelers in a fairy-tale city, marking the start of a new chapter in our lives.

By the time I complete the two-year jewelry-making program, law school feels like a distant and laughable memory. The idea of spending my life arguing for a living holds no appeal. I crave something more dynamic, something that stimulates both mind and body.

Mihus attends Budapest Mechanical Engineering College in a specialized sports program designed for competitive athletes. Striking a balance between academics and training, it's exactly what I need: a place where I can challenge myself intellectually while still nurturing my physical drive. Feeling a flicker of excitement for what may come next, I decide to apply too.

I am drawn to marketing management, a major that fuses creativity and strategy. It will help me understand branding, advertising, and consumer behavior—tools that will help me build something of my own, to shape my growing jewelry business into more than just a passion. And I've decided to minor in paper, press, and packaging, an unconventional choice but one that fascinates me. I want to explore how thoughtful design can elevate my jewelry, transforming each piece into a full sensory experience, from the way it's displayed to the moment it's unwrapped.

When the acceptance letter arrives, it's more than just an invitation to college—it's validation. I'm stepping into a life that truly fits me—not a rigid mold, but an open door to unlimited opportunities for the taking. I'm not just following my boyfriend or choosing a safe career. I'm carving out a future that is uniquely mine, a perfect blend of creativity, business, athletics, and a touch of the unexpected.

I see now that not getting what I wanted was actually a stroke of luck. Missing law school by one point wasn't the end of my story, but a vehement course correction. It pushed me toward something more suitable for me, more important—something I never would have discovered otherwise.

Everything that's happened since high school—both the things I struggled against and the things I stumbled upon—isn't just chance. These events are guiding me toward my true calling. What began as a detour becomes my path.

I'm ready to see where it leads.

CHAPTER 3

The Ionian and Mediterranean Seas: Igniting a Passion for Adventure

Not all those who wander are lost.
– J. R. R. Tolkien

Gliding over the shimmering Ionian Sea in Corfu, I feel an unshakable certainty settle within me. This is it—the moment I've been waiting for my entire life. The boat cruises to a stop, and the engine goes silent. Anticipation builds with every breath as we gear up. My fingers tingle with excitement.

Finally, we take the plunge.

The transformation is instant and otherworldly. This is not the constricting, clouded water of my past dives in Hungary, where diving is more about conquering the challenge than about relishing the experience. Instead, I am enveloped by an underwater world so vivid, so breathtaking, that for a moment I forget to move.

The water is a luminous shade of blue, so crystal-clear that I can see for eternity. Golden sunlight filters through the surface, casting ethereal patterns on the rocky seabed below. Schools of fish flash like liquid silver, darting through vibrant coral gardens. Purple sea fans sway gently with the current. Bright orange starfish cling to the pastel-toned reef like tiny bursts of fire.

My dive buddy Nóra and I look at each other and grin. It is everything we have fantasized about for years, and more.

Every kick propels me into a new dimension of awe. A green sea turtle glides past with effortless grace, its ancient eyes filled with wisdom from a world I am only beginning to understand. The silence is intoxicating, an antidote to the chaos of the world above. I feel completely weightless—not just in body, but in soul. The ocean strips away everything unimportant, leaving only the raw essence of who I am and what I desire.

This is more than a dive. This is a reckoning.

* * *

When I started college two years ago, it marked the end of an era in Hungary: I'm in the last class that doesn't have to pay tuition for college education. Not only do I avoid student loans, but I also receive a monthly payment for my academic achievements through a motivational program: Each year, the government and my school calculate the average GPA, and students who score above that average receive this financial reward. The higher my GPA, the more money I earn monthly. This system motivates me to work harder, knowing that each test and project brings me closer to financial independence.

But college turns out to be far more challenging than I anticipated.

The mechanical engineering curriculum is relentless, packed with demanding courses that teach automation and electrical engineering—subjects that feel worlds away from my creative nature. Instead kindling innovation and imagination, the course load buried me in formulas and memorized information that felt utterly useless.

Amidst all the struggle and boredom, there are moments of clarity. My statistics professor, with her knack for turning numbers into compelling stories, makes the subject unexpectedly fascinating. Under her guidance, data becomes a powerful tool of perception. One day during my first year of college, it hit me: With the same set of numbers, I can paint two entirely different realities. The same figures can prove a company is thriving month after month—or portray it as being on the verge of collapse. It's all in how the numbers are framed.

This realization was both thrilling and unsettling—proof that in business, and ultimately in life, perception often matters just as much as reality.

I quickly lost interest in engineering. My education goals shifted from focusing on the curriculum to seeking the right motivation to finish college. A defining moment occurred when I met a group of mellow seniors at a weekend mixer event, where a casual interaction with leaders of a college cultural alliance evolved into a life-changing connection. Responsible for organizing all the major events on campus, they took me under their wing and invited me into their close-knit circle. Soon I became a well-connected and popular freshman.

Mihus introduced me to his friends too, weaving me into a larger social web that only boosted my rise in the party scene. Before long, I was managing the bar at college parties, making sure the drinks keep flowing and the energy never dips. Organizing parties became my new passion. Nothing compares to the legendary New Year's pool party I orchestrated with Mihus and some of our friends, converting a local pool into a spectacular venue for a night of pure electricity.

The pool was alive—the bass pounded through giant speakers, shaking the water with every beat. Strobe lights sliced through the darkness, painting the crowd in flashes of neon pink, electric blue, and shimmering gold. The scent of chlorine, spilled cocktails, and fresh pizza filled the air as bubbles floated lazily by, catching the lights before bursting into tiny iridescent sparks.

Floaties shaped like flamingos, unicorns, and giant donuts bobbed across the water, bumping into partygoers who splashed and swayed to the music. Girls in bikinis and guys in Speedos danced at the water's edge, their laughter ringing through the humid night. I meandered through the chaos, soaking it all in, as friends raised their drinks, calling my name and clinking cups in celebration. The energy was infectious. This wasn't just a party—it was the party that people would talk about for years. The music pulsed, the lights swirled, and my reputation was sealed as the go-to person for campus parties.

With my new role came financial independence, and I relished the freedom. But as my social circle expanded, my old friendships began to slip away. Deep, cherished connections faded, replaced by fleeting interactions and surface-level camaraderie. Caught up in the thrill of being at the center of it all, I didn't recognize the shift right away. Popularity was intoxicating, and I drank it in without questioning the cost.

The relentless pace of parties and events eventually started to wear me down. Juggling school, work, and an ever-growing social life left little room for relationships that truly mattered. My closest friends quietly drifted away, their absence barely registering in the blur of flashing lights and late nights. Even Mihus and I began to unravel, our bond straining under the encumbrance of my new reality. What once felt exciting now felt exhausting, but I was too deep in our engagement to see a way out.

When my sister enrolled in the same college a year after me, our lives intertwined in ways I never anticipated. I felt unexpectedly comforted to have Csilla by my side. Rather than complicating things, her presence strengthened our bond. We began to lean on each other through academic pressures and social chaos, transforming sibling rivalry into genuine friendship. College life, with all its unpredictability, felt a little less overwhelming with Csilla there—a familiar anchor in turbulent seas.

The other important relationship in my life was provoking an opposite response. By that time I'd been engaged to Mihus for two years, and the brilliant luster of our relationship had dimmed. The distance between us was marked not by fights or betrayal, but by something more insidious: a slow drift. And I was the one pulling away. My love for him hadn't completely vanished, but I wasn't ready for the life we were heading toward. Maybe one day I would be, but not yet.

I was old enough to understand that love and relationships didn't define me, yet still young enough to consider the taboo of going against societal expectations. Mihus loved me in a way most people only dream of, and that made things even harder. How do you walk away from someone who would never walk away from you? Was I making a mistake by choosing the unknown over the comfortable?

People around us had begun settling into their lives: marriage, home, family. Mihus, steady and certain, saw this future for us, too—a settled life, a shared business, maybe even children. But the idea of marriage loomed over me like a door closing on the person I wanted to become: someone who seeks out the thrill of new experiences. I missed having the freedom to roam without considering how my choices affected someone else. Surrounded by people who embraced routine and stability, I wanted to live a bold and unpredictable life, to chase stories that I would tell decades later with a gleam in my eye.

Breaking up with Mihus was one of the hardest things I'd ever done. The moment I said the words, my heart shattered, and the weight of what I was giving up crashed down on me. The thought of him moving on, of loving someone else, left me breathless. Yet beneath the heartbreak, there was something else: relief.

A lightness bubbled up in me, as if I'd peeled off a layer of expectations that weren't actually mine. I had chosen a different path, one I knew was right for me. Suddenly I knew I would get through this experience, just like I'd gotten through everything else. I would be ready to love again someday. For now, I needed to figure out who I was when I wasn't someone's partner, when I was free to chase my own destiny.

I wasn't done growing yet. I wasn't ready to settle in a way that suffocates my dreams. I needed to be selfish for a while, to put my own dreams first, to live a life so full that I would never look back and wonder: *What if?*

Soon enough, fate intervened. The chance came to pursue my long-held dream of those exhilarating dives—to forever leave behind the stagnant, silt-laden waters of quarry lakes. It was a chance that seemed too perfect to be real: The dive club decided to organize a trip to Corfu, Greece, on the Ionian Sea.

Now, finally immersed in this underwater world, every fiber of my being screams that I belong here—not in a classroom, not behind a bar at a campus event, not trapped in a future I never truly envisioned for myself. In my lifetime, I've spent more than five hundred hours underwater, but nothing—certainly not my training in the cold, murky depths of Ócsa—has prepared me for that first voyage beneath the Ionian waves.

This is what I am meant to do.

This is where I come alive.

A rush of clarity floods through me. I cannot—will not—spend my life suffocated by routine, by expectations, by the fear of venturing into the unknown. The sea is vast, infinite in its possibilities, and so is my path. As I ascend to the boat off the coast of Corfu, I know with absolute certainty that I will never be the same.

* * *

The summer after my third year of college brings a twist of serendipity—a golden opportunity just as I'm contemplating the next steps in my journey. My childhood friend Laci, who has made a name for himself as a chef, lands a coveted position on the sun-drenched Mediterranean island of Malta and generously invites all of his close friends to come wait tables at the restaurant. Eager to seize the moment, I sign on for the summer. It seems like a low-risk adventure—an opportunity to see the world, earn some money, and dive into the glassy waters of Malta.

As my plane touches down, I am greeted by the island's striking Mediterranean landscape—an exquisite, colorful interplay of simplicity and complexity. Buildings crafted from sand-colored limestone blend seamlessly with puffs of green cacti dotting the terrain under a blanket of azure sky stretching endlessly over it all. This mesmerizing palette of hues captures my imagination like a painting come to life, a bedazzling backdrop for the adventures ahead.

The romantic vision quickly collides with harsh reality. For the first time in my life, I'm entirely living on my own—no family dinners, no familiar sounds, no safety net. The freedom I craved suddenly feels frightening. And the restaurant work is back-breaking.

The owner, a perpetually sweating Maltese man named Tony, expects us to work twelve-hour shifts in suffocating heat with only one short break. The kitchen pumps out even more heat, and by hour ten, I'm dizzy and nauseous, my feet screaming in cheap shoes. My English, which seemed adequate in Hungary, falls to pieces under pressure.

"Table six wants their steak well done, not medium!" Tony barks at me.

"Yes, I understand," I respond, but I mix up the tables and deliver the wrong order to a table of angry British tourists.

"Are you deaf or just stupid?" one of them snaps. "We ordered fish and chips, not bloody pasta!"

My face burns with embarrassment as I mumble apologies, my carefully practiced English dissolving into a mess of mispronounced words and Hungarian sentence structure. The other waitresses—seasoned locals who speak rapid Maltese to each other—look on with barely concealed amusement.

Each mistake erodes my confidence. By the end of the first week, I cry myself to sleep, questioning everything. The other waitresses don't bother learning my name—they just call me "the Hungarian girl" or point when they need something.

But little by little, something shifts. Loneliness forces me to become resourceful. I start carrying a pocket dictionary and writing down new words every day. I practice conversations with a local who frequents the restaurant. Slowly, painfully, my English improves. And with it comes a fierce independence I've never felt before.

The freedom, when I finally claim it, is invigorating. No curfew. No Mutti questioning my choices. No one monitoring my every move. I can stay out until dawn, eat ice cream for breakfast, or spend my day off reading on the beach, all without explaining myself to anyone. I'm making decisions based purely on what I want, not what's expected of me.

I connect with other young travelers: backpackers from England, working holidaymakers from Israel, fellow students from across continental Europe. We bond over shared struggles: terrible bosses, language mix-ups, homesickness, and the spine-tingling terror of being completely on our own. Our friendships form quickly, forged in the crucible of mutual survival.

But waitressing becomes increasingly unbearable. Tony's demands escalate—he wants us to work split shifts, covering both lunch and dinner with only two hours off in between. The heat is relentless, and some of my coworkers faint in the kitchen. One girl develops heat exhaustion and has to be hospitalized.

Tony's response? "Find someone to cover her shift."

My breaking point comes on a particularly hellish Saturday night. The restaurant is packed, the kitchen is behind on orders, and customers are getting aggressive. I am running on four hours of sleep and haven't eaten anything but stolen bread rolls all day. As I'm rushing from table to table, my hands shaking from fatigue and hunger, I trip and send a tray of drinks crashing into a group of well-dressed couples.

Silence falls like a bomb.

Red wine drips from expensive clothing.

Glasses lie shattered on the floor.

Everyone stares.

Tony appears instantly, his face purple with rage. "You clumsy bitch!" he screams in front of the entire restaurant. "That's coming out of your pay! All of it!"

Something snaps inside me. All the humiliation, the exhaustion, the constant grinding down of my spirit—it crystallizes into pure rage. Instead of exploding, I do something that surprises even me: I untie my apron, drop it on the floor, and walk out.

Not far from the restaurant, there's a dive shop called Diveshack that caught my eye when I arrived in Malta. Every day, I pass by and watch as divers come and go, their excitement palpable. I long to be part of that world, but the cost of diving is out of my reach. Now I have no job—and no excuse.

Determined to make my dream a reality, I muster the courage to walk into the dive shop and speak to the owner. Rita is a woman in her forties with sun-weathered skin and sharp eyes that seem to see right through me.

She has built the shop from nothing, and it shows in every interaction—she's tough, she's meticulous, and doesn't suffer fools.

I approach her with a proposal: I offer to work off the cost of diving and train to become certified at the Professional Association of Diving Instructors (PADI) Divemaster level by taking on various dive-related tasks. I'm prepared to handle any job that will allow me to earn my place in the underwater world.

Rita looks me up and down, taking in my desperation and determination in equal measures. "You ever cleaned gear covered in someone's piss?" she asks bluntly.

"Of course. Everyone pees in their wetsuits," I reply, smiling. "Whether they admit it or not."

Rita smiles back. To my surprise, she sees something in me and says yes. But her approval comes with conditions: Rita expects perfection, and anything less is met with sharp criticism that cuts deeper than Tony's crude yelling.

The work—hauling heavy equipment, picking up and dropping off clients—is more rigorous than I anticipated. My days at Diveshack begin at six a.m. and don't end until after sunset, when the last piece of gear is cleaned and stored. My hands are constantly cut from handling metal tanks and gear. The smell of neoprene and salt water becomes permanently embedded in my clothes, my hair, my skin. And Rita's criticism is endless.

"You're loading that gear wrong. Do you want someone to die?"

"Your English isn't good enough for safety briefings. Practice more."

"You're too slow, too fast, too inexperienced."

Every mistake is a personal failing, every success barely acknowledged.

The worst part is cleaning the diving gear. Wetsuits come back reeking of bodily fluids, vomit, and sometimes worse. Regulators need to be disinfected after being in strangers' mouths all day. Masks fog up with dried snot and spit. I spend hours scrubbing equipment with bleach, trying not to gag, until my hands are raw and cracked.

"This is diving," Rita says flatly. "If you can't handle this, you can't handle being an instructor." Her expectations weigh heavily on my shoulders.

My conversational English steadily improves, but the technical diving terminology creates new frustrations daily. I know all the physics, physiology, and dive equipment we're discussing—but in Hungarian. Although I'm proficient in Russian and German, English is indispensable for the global diving community. I commit to mastering it, but the learning curve is steeper than expected and fraught with challenges.

During safety briefings, I stumble over words like *decompression*, pronouncing it "decomposition," which spooks a group of novice divers who think I'm talking about bodies decomposing underwater. Rita corrects my mistake in front of everyone, casting me a withering look.

Despite her harsh training methods, step by step, my competence and confidence build one day at a time. Then, just when I'm getting the hang of things, everything nearly falls apart, ending my diving career before it really begins.

It's a Tuesday morning, and I'm conducting a try-dive session at the hotel pool, supervising a group of nervous beginners as they get their first taste of breathing underwater. It should be routine, controlled, safe.

Among the group is Margaret, a woman in her sixties from London who's clearly uncomfortable in the water. She's overweight, she's nervous, and she admits she's not a strong swimmer, but she's determined to try diving. "It's been on my bucket list for years," she says.

Everything about Margaret indicates that I should be more cautious than usual, more alert to the warning signs, but I'm still learning to read people underwater. We start in the shallow end—basic breathing exercises, getting comfortable with the regulator. Margaret seems to be doing well. She's breathing steadily, her eyes look calm behind her mask.

When we move to slightly deeper water, something goes wrong.

I'm helping another beginner when I hear the sound every diver dreads: an unmistakable loud gurgling caused by bubbles free-flowing in the water—the signal that a regulator has been ripped from someone's mouth. I turn to see Margaret thrashing at the surface, her eyes wild with panic, water streaming from her mouth and nose. She's trying to scream but only manages choking gasps.

Panic underwater is contagious and deadly. In her terror, Margaret isn't just drowning—she's become a threat to everyone around her. Her arms flail desperately, seeking anything to grab onto, anything to keep her afloat. The other beginners start to panic too, backing away from her in fear.

I swim toward her, knowing I have only seconds to act.

The moment I get close, Margaret's survival instincts kick in. She grabs me with surprising strength, her fingernails digging into my arms as she scrambles on top of me, pushing me underwater in her desperation to keep her head above water. This is what they warn about in rescue training—how a drowning person will use their rescuer as a flotation device, even if it means drowning that person in the process.

Underwater, with Margaret's full weight pressing down on me and her legs kicking frantically, I fight my own rising panic. Her fear transmits through her death grip on my shoulders, and my lungs burn as I struggle to free myself. I can't help her if she drowns me too.

I remember my rescue training: A panicked diver on the surface will not follow you downward. Putting my own regulator back into my mouth, I start going deeper. Breaking free from Margaret's grasp, I swim around and surface behind her, but she spins around, reaching for me again with desperate hands. I have to be quick, decisive, and strong, which feels impossible when adrenaline is flooding my system.

"Margaret, listen to me! You are OK! We are on the surface, and I am here to assist you!" I shout, but she's beyond hearing. Her face is purple, water streaming from her mouth, her movements becoming weaker and more erratic.

I grab her tank valve from behind, and begin towing her toward the pool's edge. She's heavy, waterlogged, and still struggling. My shoulders scream with the effort, but I keep pulling. Other pool guests have noticed the commotion now, and someone shouts for help.

By the time I get her to the pool edge, Margaret has swallowed what feels like half the pool. She's coughing violently, vomiting chlorinated water, and her whole body shakes. Hotel staff rush over with towels and oxygen. Someone mentions calling an ambulance.

As the immediate crisis passes and Margaret begins breathing normally again, the magnitude of what just happened hits me. I almost lost someone—in a pool. If this had happened in open water, she could have died.

Rita arrives within minutes, her face a mask of controlled fury. She doesn't yell—that isn't her way. Instead, she dismisses the other participants, sends Margaret to rest with the hotel staff, and orders me to her office.

"Explain," she says, the single word carrying the weight of my entire future.

I tell her everything—how Margaret seemed comfortable initially, how quickly the panic set in, how I managed the rescue. Rita listens without interruption, her expression unreadable.

"You made three critical errors," she says at last. "You didn't properly assess your participant's comfort level. You didn't maintain close enough supervision. And you let the situation escalate beyond your immediate control."

Each word hits home. I know she's right, but hearing it laid out so clinically makes me feel sick.

"But," she continues, "your rescue technique was solid. You kept your head, you followed protocol, and you saved her life. A less experienced person would have panicked, and we'd have two drowning victims."

The relief I feel is short-lived.

"This can never happen again," Rita insists. "One incident like this can destroy a dive shop's reputation forever. Insurance companies will drop us. Clients will go elsewhere. You understand that, don't you?"

I nod, not trusting my voice.

My confidence, already fragile, is in tatters. For weeks afterward, I second-guess every decision, over-supervise every participant, and wake up in cold sweats replaying those distressing moments in the pool.

But this incident also teaches me something crucial: The ocean doesn't care about my dreams, my determination, my good intentions. It's indifferent to human ambition, and it will kill without hesitation or remorse. If I want to keep my "job" at the dive shop, I need to be better—not just good enough, but flawless.

* * *

One evening, after a punishing day of back-to-back dives with difficult clients, I crumple onto my bed in my tiny shared apartment, so exhausted that I can't even make it to the shower. Lying on my rock-hard mattress, fully clothed, I seriously consider giving up.

Work has taken a crushing physical toll. My days start before dawn and end well after sunset. Between the dive shop work and the evenings out with new friends, I'm getting maybe four hours of sleep a night. My shoulders ache from lifting heavy tanks. My hands are infected from handling rough equipment. My skin is burnt and peeling despite constant sunscreen application. I'm losing weight. My body is breaking down.

Homesickness overwhelms me. I miss my mother's cooking, my sister's laughter, even our family arguments. I miss speaking Hungarian and not having to translate every thought into English. I miss being competent, being understood, being more than just "the Hungarian girl."

From somewhere in the depths of that exhaustion and despair, a stubborn voice reminds me why I'm here. This isn't just about learning to dive as a professional. It's about proving to myself that I can survive anything, that my dream can come true—that I can build the life I want through sheer force of will.

I wake up the next day and start over.

New friendships are my salvation. Patricia, another Hungarian girl working as a tour guide; Lee, a Diveshack diving instructor from England; Sophia, a Czech girl working at a bar—we create our own family of misfits and dreamers. We talk over cheap meals and dance for hours at the summer party scene. We take turns being strong when one of us falls apart.

These relationships teach me that independence doesn't mean isolation. It means choosing your own family, building a support system, and leaning on people who understand your journey.

Gradually, painstakingly, I adapt. My English improves until I can handle complex safety briefings without stumbling. My body toughens to handle the physical demands of working in the dive shop. Most important, my confidence rebounds—not the naïve sureness I arrived with, but something harder, more realistic, earned through failure and recovery.

Surrounded by Malta's beautiful but unforgiving coastline, it's part diving camp, part survival school. My days are still a whirlwind of activity, but it's controlled chaos now. I'm becoming more competent every day. My diving skills sharpen under Rita's exacting tutelage.

The work is hard, harder than anything I've ever done, but it stirs up a boundless sense of accomplishment that no classroom can provide. Every small success—a perfect dive briefing, a satisfied customer, a day without major mistakes—feels like a victory against impossible odds. I'm building something real, something that belongs to me.

My relationship with Rita evolves from pure antagonism to grudging mutual respect. She recognizes my determination and gradual improvement, though she'll never admit it outright. I learn to see her harshness as benevolent fortification—she's preparing me for an industry that doesn't forgive mistakes.

Each dive in the Mediterranean Sea brings me closer to my dream. The thrill of weightlessness and the joy of introducing others to the ocean fill me with contentment. Diveshack feels like the gateway to the life I've always wanted. I'm determined to earn that opportunity through blood, sweat, and more tears than I care to admit.

This summer, far from home, is a turning point—not just a taste of independence, but a no-nonsense education in the cost of independence. I have complete freedom to make my own choices, but I'm learning that freedom isn't free. It comes with responsibility, isolation, failure, and the constant need to prove myself to people who don't believe in my dreams.

Yet through all the struggles, one thing becomes crystal clear: This isn't just what I want to do—it's who I am. Every injury, every mistake, every exhausted night, every language barrier is a gift. By overcoming these hurdles, I'm building the foundation for the life I've always dreamed of. The path is harder than I imagined, but that only makes me more determined to see it through.

* * *

Returning to Hungary after an unforgettable summer in Malta, I reluctantly squeeze myself back into the rigid structure of academia. *Just get through this*, I tell myself, *and put your studying days behind you.*

As my final semester of college approaches, I face a crossroads: Should I follow the well-trodden path and accept a six-month factory internship like most of my classmates? Or should I think outside of the box and create an opportunity that aligns with my true passion?

I decide to return to Malta with a strategic plan. Rather than spending months in a paper mill, I choose to write my thesis on financial planning in seasonal markets, using the scuba diving industry as my case study. This way, I'm not just fulfilling an academic requirement—I'm laying the groundwork for a future that excites me.

My professors don't find my plan amusing. To them, a factory internship represents structure, reliability, the "right" way to complete my degree. My idea—to trade the predictable for the unpredictable, to swap factory floors for sunlit shores—raises more than a few skeptical eyebrows.

But this is my calling—I'm certain of that now. I refuse to settle for conventional or let obstacles stop me. If one path closes, I pivot, adapt, and carve out a new way forward with the same unstoppable determination. If a strategy fails, I tweak it. If a door won't open, I find a window to climb through. Doubt and disapproval from others only strengthen my resolve.

I've learned to see setbacks not as roadblocks, but as stepping stones to something greater. My time in Malta taught me that success isn't just about talent or luck—it's about resilience and courage. I'm not going to wait for opportunities to find me; I'm going to chase them down and make them happen.

My favorite statistics professor sees the potential in my unconventional path. Unlike the others, she doesn't dismiss my plan outright. She recognizes that real-world applications of data and financial planning extend beyond the confines of a traditional internship. Her approval isn't just a bureaucratic green light—it's validation that my approach, though unorthodox, has merit.

Back in Malta, I spend the final semester putting together a comprehensive business plan for Diveshack, drawing from my studies and firsthand experience with the ebb and flow of tourism. I focus on seasonal market trends, strategies to attract more divers, and marketing approaches suited to the industry. It's a rewarding experiment that combines my love for diving with my developing business skills.

With my college degree in hand, the world stretches before me like an open door. I may never use my engineering-focused education in the traditional sense, but my unconventional path reinforces a crucial lesson: Success doesn't have to mean following the expected route. Daring to think differently and pursue what deeply excites me is a far more satisfying accomplishment.

The academic grind is finally behind me, and having met my family's expectations, I am free to embrace the life I've always dreamed of. My wanderlust has been building for years, and now the call of distant horizons feels impossible to resist. My feet are itching to travel, and the oceans of the world are waiting for me to dive in.

But no one else believes in my dream.

Whenever I talk about becoming a scuba instructor and traveling the world, I am met with skepticism, condescending smiles, or outright dismissal. Scuba diving is a pastime, a hobby, a weekend escape at best—not a real career, and certainly not one for a girl from a landlocked country.

Even my maternal grandfather, a man whose wisdom has guided me through life, shakes his head and suggests I stick to watching Jacques Cousteau documentaries instead of chasing a future that seems reckless—it's much safer. My mother, ever practical, urges me to find a stable job—one with security, a paycheck, and a retirement plan.

The only ones who understand are my diving club teammates. They know the intoxicating pull of the water, the way it changes a person—the way it has already changed me. But even their encouragement is tinged with hesitation. They don't outright say it, but I can sense it—the belief that at some point I will have to wake up, come to my senses, and accept reality.

But this *is* my reality.

I refuse to be boxed in by expectations, by the idea that my path should be safe, conventional, and predictable. The thought of staying in one place—waking up every morning to the same beige apartment walls, trudging to the same office job, coming home to cook dinner and watch television until bedtime, repeating this cycle for forty years until retirement—suffocates me far more than the deepest, darkest underwater dive ever could.

I can picture it all too clearly: a life of scheduled meals, weekend grocery shopping, annual two-week vacations to the same lake resort, conversations about weather and television shows, dreams slowly shrinking until they fit inside a china cabinet. That kind of existence, where the biggest adventure is trying a new brand of coffee, where passion gets filed away under "youthful foolishness," where the horizon never changes—terrifies me more than any ocean current, any treacherous depth, any creature lurking in dark water. At least underwater, I'm moving toward something new and unknown. The conventional life my family envisions for me is a different kind of drowning—one where you slowly forget you ever wanted to breathe.

Every doubt, every dismissal, every well-meaning warning only fuels my determination. Because I know, deep in my bones, that this isn't just a dream. It's my destiny. Each time someone tells me it's impossible, I respond with the same unwavering words.

You just watch me.

CHAPTER 4

Malta: Becoming a Pro

The expert in anything was once a beginner.
– Helen Hayes

"Nein!" the course director snaps, returning his masked face to the chlorinated water—a sign for me to drop below the pool's surface and try again.

Klaus is an uninspiring German man in his fifties who treats the entire training process like a tedious chore he'd rather avoid. Lying fully clothed at the pool's edge with a diving mask covering his face, he has asked me to demonstrate the mask clearing skill underwater—a fundamental technique every diver must master.

I try a different approach, thinking maybe I misunderstood.

Klaus simply shakes his head. "Nein. Again."

I make another attempt, this time exaggerating my movements to make them clearer.

"Nein."

"What am I doing wrong?" I finally ask, my voice cracking with frustration.

"You figure it out," he replies.

He's supposed to provide the training I need to pass the PADI instructor exam, but I am starting to think he has no interest in actually teaching.

This becomes our daily routine for a week. I follow the exact protocol that I've been taught, presenting skills from different scuba curriculum, while Klaus offers zero constructive feedback. At first, I'm expecting a positive reaction or guidance on how to improve. But when I mess up somehow, he simply says, "Nein," and moves on. When I do something right, he says nothing at all.

Does he even know what he's looking for? I wonder.

After completing college—largely at my mother's insistence—I have finally seized the opportunity to chase my true dream. No more obligations. No more detours. It's time to do what I've always wanted: earn my certification as a professional scuba diver and travel the world and go where my wanderlust takes me. For me, diving is so much more than just a passing interest. It's my calling, my path to freedom—the key that will unlock the world.

Teaching in the lakes, rivers and quarries of Hungary holds no appeal for me. Determined to explore the world's exuberant oceans and share my love for the underwater realm with others, I've decided to take the course not in Hungary, but in Malta. Saying goodbye to my home indefinitely is a plunge into the unknown. My plan is to pass the instructor exam and then start teaching in the Mediterranean for a while, to gain experience in a familiar environment.

I have intentionally chosen the harder way. Refusing to allow the language barrier to deter me, I focus on passing the exam in English and making my vision a reality. My hopes are high. I am finally doing what I have been waiting for so long. I am ready.

Or at least I thought I was.

Malta in February is at its most unforgiving. The sea, so warm and inviting in summer, now churns gray and hostile under obstinate winter storms. The wind howls across the island, and the rain feels like ice needles against my skin. But Klaus doesn't seem to care about the weather—or about me.

"*Heute*, we practice teaching skills," he announces on the first day of my personal nightmare. His disembodied face appears in the water again and again to observe my performance below, emerging periodically to deliver his dismissive *nein* to my every attempt.

Presentations are a particular treat, when I have to stand in front of Klaus and pretend to teach a diving concept to an imaginary class—with great enthusiasm, so he can evaluate my methods and manner on clarity, accuracy, and engagement. The first one is about buoyancy control, a topic I know inside and out. I explain the physics, display the techniques, try to make the lesson engaging and educational.

When I finish, Klaus writes something in his notebook without looking up.

"How did I do?" I ask, desperate for any feedback.

"Nein gut," he mutters, arms crossed, staring at me with dead eyes through his narrow, dark-framed glasses. "Again tomorrow."

Isolation is the worst part of the ordeal. The dive center in February feels like a ghost town. I'm the only instructor candidate in the class—a detail that transforms what should be a collaborative learning experience into psychological warfare. The few staff members who are present avoid me entirely, as if my clash with Klaus might be contagious. I catch them whispering in corners and imagine they're discussing the Hungarian girl who can't seem to get anything right.

In a normal training course, there would be other candidates practicing the same skills, making the same mistakes, sharing the same frustrations. Instead, I exist in a vacuum where every error feels magnified, every failure feels personal. There's no one to watch and emulate, no fellow student to gauge my performance against, no way to know if Klaus treats everyone this way or just me.

Our breaks are silent and solitary. Klaus reviews his mysterious notes while I sit alone, replaying every moment underwater, wondering what I did wrong this time. There's no one to turn to and ask, *Did you understand what he meant by that?* or *Is it just me, or does he seem impossible to please?*

Evenings are the hardest. Instead of gathering to study with other instructor candidates or blowing off steam about the demanding course director, I have little to do but go over both today's session and tomorrow's, rehearsing presentations in front of the mirror and trying to decode Klaus's cryptic criticisms.

One night, I call my mother from the payphone outside the dive center, my hands shaking from cold and frustration.

"How's the course going?" she asks.

I want to tell her the truth—that Klaus is destroying my confidence, that I'm starting to think this was all a mistake, that I'm drowning in every way but one. But I can't bear to give her the satisfaction of being right about my "unrealistic" dreams.

"It's challenging," I manage. "But I'm learning a lot."

Day by day, my carefully constructed belief in myself crumbles. I begin to question everything I thought I knew about diving. *Maybe I'm not cut out for this,* I think. *Maybe everyone back home was right. Maybe this is just a foolish dream.*

Klaus's attitude toward my training is daunting enough, but the physical demands make everything worse. February in Malta means diving in 59°F water with massive swells that make no-sweat skills feel like life-or-death struggles. My medium-thickness neoprene wetsuit, adequate for spring diving, provides little protection against severe cold. Within minutes underwater, my hands are so numb that I can barely operate my equipment, let alone demonstrate complex skills with the precision Klaus seems to require.

One horrible morning, Klaus makes me repeat the same rescue scenario over and over in rough seas. Each time, I have to swim against the current to retrieve a diver and perform rescue breathing while treading water and towing "the victim" back to shore, taking off both her scuba equipment and mine along the way—all while not missing a breath. By the sixth attempt, I'm so depleted, I can barely keep my own head above water, let alone save anyone else.

"Nein," Klaus says after my eighth attempt. "You are too weak. Real instructors need strength."

His words feel like a dull slap. Weak? I'm in excellent shape—or in way better shape than he is, at least, and he should be my role-model. I've been diving for years, and I've handled far more challenging conditions than this. But his constant criticism is wearing me down, and I'm starting to believe him.

Back in my tiny room that night, I count my remaining Maltese lira and calculate whether I have enough money for a flight home. Am I just fooling myself, thinking I can make a career out of diving? The humiliation of returning to Hungary as a failure seems almost preferable to enduring any more of Klaus's psychological torture.

But then I remember everyone who told me this was impossible—my mother's well-meaning discouragement, my professors' skeptical looks, the neighbors who asked when I'd get a "real job." The unbearable thought of proving them right, of walking back into their pitying smiles and *I told you so* comments, ignites something fierce inside me.

I make a firm decision: Klaus can break my confidence, drain my bank account, and crush my spirit, but I will not let him steal my dream. If he says *nein* a thousand times, I'll try a thousand and one. If he wants to play games, I'll figure out his rules and beat him at them.

The next morning, I approach the course differently. Instead of seeking Klaus's approval, I focus on perfecting my skills regardless of his feedback. In the days to come, I start keeping a diving journal, noting what works and what doesn't, teaching myself through trial and error. If he won't teach me properly, I will figure it out on my own.

I also begin to see Klaus's behavior as preparation for the real world. If I can maintain my composure and competence under his hostile scrutiny, handling difficult clients, less than perfect conditions, and skeptical colleagues will be a breeze. His *nein* becomes my motivation. Each dismissal makes me more determined to prove my worth.

The final exam becomes the ultimate test. Klaus has made it clear all along that he thinks I won't pass. He has planted seeds of doubt about my abilities, my strength, my worthiness to become an instructor. As I prepare for the written and practical assessment by the PADI examiners, my hands shake—not from cold this time, but from the pressure of everything riding on this moment.

The exam takes place on a particularly rough day. The waves are churning, visibility is poor, and the conditions are far from ideal for exhibiting delicate skills. But I've trained in these conditions for weeks now. What once felt impossible now seems manageable.

I demonstrate each skill with methodical precision, drawing on everything I've learned—not *from* Klaus, but *despite* him. When I teach my mock lesson to the examiners about tying a bowline knot, I channel every instructor who ever inspired me, every teacher who believed in my potential. I make the lesson engaging, clear, and supportive—everything Klaus never was.

When I finish, the examiners seem satisfied by my performance. Klaus looks up from his notes with his usual expressionless stare.

"You pass," he says, as if the words pain him.

When other instructors from the previous summer start trickling back to Malta for the new season, they're shocked by my transformation. The Hungarian girl who spent her first season making mistakes and practicing English phrases in her pocket dictionary—eager to please, seeking approval—has been replaced by someone harder, more focused, with steel in her eyes where there used to be nervous energy and quick smiles.

"What happened to you?" asks Lee, the British instructor I worked with last summer.

When I reply, the truth surprises even me: "I learned what I'm made of."

* * *

No congratulations. No recognition of the hell he's put me through. Just a grudging admission that I've met the requirements set by PADI. The Klaus experience scars me, but it also forges a stronger woman. Surviving his course is almost as important as passing it. Now I know that I can endure anything in pursuit of my goals—and that sometimes the biggest obstacles come not from the ocean, but from the people who are supposed to help you navigate it.

Anyway, I don't need his validation anymore. Instructor certificate in hand—paid for with every last cent I had, and earned through more sweat and tears than I care to remember—I make myself a promise: If I ever become a course director, I will remember what it feels like to be dismissed, ignored, undermined. I will be the trainer Klaus never was—supportive, encouraging, and committed to teaching rather than just testing.

I picture myself guiding other divers with empathy, helping them grow in confidence and skill, making a difference in their lives. Klaus may have broken me down, but in doing so, he has inadvertently started me on the path to becoming the instructor—and the person—I am meant to be.

I remain in Malta and get a job working with Aquasphere, a popular dive training center. During my first week, I spend three days with a group of nervous beginners—a family from Finland who've never been underwater before.

I guide the family members through their confined water training in the pool, patiently helping the teenage daughter overcome her fear of putting her face in the water, encouraging the father who struggles with equalizing his ears—the pinch-your-nose-and-blow technique that prevents the painful pressure buildup as you go deeper in the water or fly higher on an airplane—and supporting the mother who panics every time she has to clear water out of her mask. By the time we're ready for their open water certification dives, I've built a real connection with this family. The daughter has gone from terrified to excited, the father has mastered his equalization technique, and the mother trusts me completely. They specifically request me for their final dives.

"You're the reason we've fallen in love with diving," they gush.

But when we reach the dive site, the owner of Aquasphere appears out of nowhere with his wetsuit already on. "I'll take it from here, Szilvia," he says with that practiced smile. "You can help set up the equipment."

Doug is a man in his forties with thinning hair and a permanent tan that speaks of years spent lounging rather than working. He has the kind of easy charm—quick with a joke, generous with compliments, always ready with a beer after a long day—that initially masks his true nature. But underneath the friendly façade lurks someone who sees every situation through the lens of personal gain. Unlike Rita, who inspired me despite her harshness, Doug's leadership feels self-serving and predatory from the very first day.

"But they're my students," I protest. "I've been working with them all week."

"And you've done great work getting them this far," Doug replies smoothly, "but I like to handle the final certification dives personally. Quality control, you understand."

I watch helplessly as Doug charms my students, taking credit for their progress while I'm relegated to carrying tanks and assisting them in setting up gear. When the family completes their certification, they thank Doug profusely, not realizing that he just swooped in for the moment of glory. In the logbooks, Doug records himself as their certifying instructor, which means his name will be on their dive cards—adding four more certifications to his tally while mine remains at zero.

The pattern soon becomes clear: I do all the hard work—the classroom sessions where students grapple with dive tables and safety procedures, the pool sessions where they fumble with equipment and fight their natural fear of breathing underwater, the shore dives where they practice unfamiliar skills in gloomy water and limited visibility. Then Doug appears for the final, fun dives in crystal-clear water where students feel confident and grateful, taking them on his flashy boat to the best dive sites.

Doug's system ensures that while I work full-time, my official statistics tallied by PADI show almost no productivity. "You're still learning, Szilvia," he says after poaching another group of my students. "I'm protecting your reputation by making sure these certifications go smoothly. Once you have more experience, you'll understand why this is best for everyone."

When I confront him directly, he turns it into a lesson about patience and humility.

"Success in this business isn't about ego," he lectures, leaning back in his leather chair with his hands behind his head, feet up on the top of his desk. "It's about teamwork. You do your part, I do mine. The students have a great dive experience and get certified. Everyone's happy. Why are you making this complicated?"

"Because I'm doing most of the work and getting none of the credit," I snap back, well aware that in the diving industry, reputation and certification numbers mean everything.

"Credit?" He laughs as if the concept is foreign to him. "Szilvia, you're getting paid the same whether your name is on their certification cards or mine. What matters is that you're learning. Think of me as your mentor."

But this isn't mentorship—it's exploitation. A real mentor would gradually hand over more responsibility, not systematically steal recognition for work already completed. In Doug's version of teaching, I do all the work, and he reaps the rewards.

One evening, after Doug has stolen my students yet again—this time a couple celebrating their anniversary, who specifically requested the young Hungarian instructor who made them feel so safe—I reach my breaking point.

"This has to stop," I tell him after the other staff have left.

"What has to stop?" he asks innocently.

"You know exactly what. Taking my students, stealing my certifications. Treating me like paid labor while you collect all the student count and the credit."

Doug's friendly mask slips for just a moment, revealing something cold and calculating underneath. "Let me explain something to you, Szilvia," he growls. "This is *my* dive center. These are *my* clients. You work for *me*, which means your students are actually *my* students. If you don't like how I run my business, you're welcome to find another job."

But how can I find a proper job when my student count—idling near zero—doesn't reflect my true level of experience? Trapped in a cycle of stolen dive certifications and gaslighted frustration, I realize I have two choices: continue to accept this exploitation, or find a way to break free from Doug's parasitic scheme.

In the meantime, I have fantastic teammates to commiserate with. Living above the dive shop with fellow instructors from an eclectic mix of nations offers some relief. We share laughs, bond over World Cup soccer games, and unwind after long days in the local pubs or in the living room of our shared apartment with feet up on the coffee table and cold drinks in hand. Weekly bonfires on the beach bring the dive community together, creating cherished moments of camaraderie. Night dives with the dive staff—without clients—provide rare moments of peace amidst the havoc.

For long months now, I've juggled a packed schedule, managing multiple groups of divers with a limited inventory of gear. Long days of diving, tank-swapping, and driving clients around the island stretch me thin, but the experience strengthens my resilience and adaptability.

While the workload is hard, the diving is simply incredible. Malta is famous for its shipwrecks-turned-reefs—sunken treasures like the *Um El Faroud* oil tanker, now home to a diverse array of marine life. Exploring rusted hulls covered in coral and sponges while surrounded by glittering schools of fish, you magically become part of the big blue. The underwater landscape is dotted with fascinating caves and tunnels carved into the limestone over centuries. Swimming through these natural mazes, with sunlight filtering through cracks in the rock, is like discovering a secret world hidden beneath the waves.

This summer turns out to be one of the most fulfilling of my life. Nights are filled with dinner parties and outings with friends, marking milestones and creating memories together. Driving around Malta in the company car, basking in the sun or reveling under the stars, I often pinch myself, amazed that this dream has become my reality. All the hard work and challenges are worth it.

But living away from Hungary and my mother fills me with mixed emotions—it's a balancing act between the cheer of independence and the weight of responsibility. Beneath the gratification of free will, a lingering ache reminds me how far away I am from home and my loved ones. I did not think I would miss them so soon.

Hoping to bridge that distance, I invite my sister to join me in Malta. Csilla embraces the bustling island life but quickly grows restless working at a slow-paced water sports rental shop. She yearns for the water—kayaking, snorkeling, surfing—rather than the monotony of retail work, and I certainly don't blame her.

Living with all of us in the *Big Brother*–like apartment, Csilla gets a taste of life abroad and soon realizes it's not for her. She misses her friends and just doesn't find the lifestyle appealing. Why leave behind all the wonderful things about home, the safety net of the people and places where we grew up? I am sorry to see her go, but nothing could make me return to Hungary right now. My gypsy heart thrives on the thrill of new pursuits.

For me, the choice to explore the world, forge my own path, and go with the wind is electrifying.

* * *

As time passes, it becomes more and more evident to me that being a scuba instructor is more than a job—it's a commitment to safety and survival. Each dive is a test of my skills and judgment, and the stakes are always high. The tranquil beauty of Malta's waters belies the danger that awaits.

One Thursday morning, I'm guiding six divers to one of Malta's deep wreck sites—a challenging dive, even for experienced divers, that requires both skill and respect for the ocean's power. The group is mixed: Two experienced divers are celebrating their wedding anniversary. A father-son duo has arrived from Italy. And Emma, a woman in her thirties from Holland, has booked the trip with her boyfriend, Trevor.

From the moment I meet Emma, warning bells start ringing in my head. She's clearly uncomfortable during the dive briefing, fidgeting with her gear and sweating profusely. She admits she's not a strong swimmer and reveals that she barely passed her open water course two years ago in a quarry in the Netherlands. More concerning, she's a large woman wearing a thick, winter-appropriate wetsuit she brought from home—a size 4XL that barely fits her frame, the neoprene straining at the seams. It's overkill for the hot summer, but our rentals only go up to 2XL. While the rest of our group is sporting light "shorties" for the summer weather, she is already overheating.

"Are you sure about this dive, Emma?" I confirm during our equipment check. "It's quite deep. We have to swim a fair amount, and the currents can be demanding."

"Oh, I'll be fine," Emma insists, though her voice wavers. "Trevor's been diving here before. He says it's spectacular. I can't miss it."

Trevor waves off my concerns with casual arrogance, saying, "She'll be fine. I'll keep an eye on her. We've done plenty of dives together." His response betrays him as one of those overconfident divers who mistakes bravado for competence, because I know from experience that panic underwater doesn't discriminate based on who's watching you.

Still, Emma has her certification. She has passed the medical clearance. And they paid for the day. Technically, she meets the requirements for diving. Against my better judgment, I agree to take her.

We enter the water by making a giant stride off a cliff twenty feet above—a leap that would intimidate many people even without forty pounds of gear attached to them. The exit promises to be even more challenging: a rusty ladder that we must climb back up after an exhausting dive, hauling ourselves twenty vertical feet while wearing all of our equipment and weight belts.

The cliff jump before our actual dive goes relatively smoothly. One by one, we launch ourselves from the rocky edge with a rush of air and adrenaline before hitting the surface with a solid impact and a satisfying splash that sends spray in all directions. Each entry is a controlled plunge that leaves us gasping and grinning as we surface.

The water is angrier and more uneven than I'd like, with a noticeable swell that makes maintaining our position difficult, even at the surface. As we prepare to descend, I'm already on high alert, keeping Emma in my peripheral vision while managing the rest of the group.

The descent begins normally. We follow the cliff wall downward, using the hunk of rock as a visual reference while I monitor everyone's depth and air consumption. Emma is working harder than the others; her movements are less fluid, her positioning less controlled. But she seems to be managing well—her breathing appears steady, and she's staying close to the group.

About five minutes into the dive, at forty feet in depth, we leave the comfort of the wall and head into the deep blue, navigating toward the *Rozi*, one of Malta's famed wrecks. This is always the moment that separates confident divers from nervous ones—when the bottom drops away, and suddenly we're swimming in underwater space 100 feet off the ocean floor, relying entirely on my compass and experience.

When you're conducting an underwater orchestra, a single missed note could spell disaster. My focus becomes laser-sharp. I'm simultaneously checking my depth gauge, consulting my compass, scanning for the wreck (which many instructors miss due to its unusual location far offshore), and monitoring six divers' positions and air levels. When I glance back to ensure everyone is following, my heart stops.

Emma is sinking.

Her regulator has popped out of her mouth and is trailing beside her, bubbling precious air into the sea. Behind her mask, her eyes are wide with terror, but she's not reaching for her regulator—she's just sinking, paralyzed by panic. Her heavy weight belt is pulling her down fast.

I react instinctively, abandoning my position at the front of the group and swimming hard toward her. In the few seconds it takes me to reach her, she's dropped another ten feet, putting her at a dangerous depth with no air source. I grab her regulator with my right hand and shove it back into her mouth while purging the water out of it. Simultaneously, my left hand secures her gear and begins inflating her buoyancy control device, or BCD, to stop her descent.

When I check her face next, she does not seem to be conscious. Her eyes are glazing in the distance, without focusing on anything.

I must make a split-second decision. Emma needs to get to the surface immediately, but bringing her up too fast could give her (and me) decompression sickness or an arterial gas embolism. Neither is good.

I start a controlled ascent, trying to maintain a safe ascent rate. Every fiber of my being wants to rocket to the surface, but I know that could kill her just as surely as drowning. Once we are on the move, I signal for everyone in our group to follow me.

The ascent takes forever. Emma is a rag doll, and I am doing all the work, kicking fiercely to propel us toward the surface. I keep one hand on her regulator, ensuring it stays in her mouth, while using my other hand to control our buoyancy and ascent rate. All the while, I'm talking to her through my regulator, projecting calm even though my own heart is racing.

When we finally break the surface, Emma is still unconscious. Her face is pale, but she is breathing on her own—weakly.

During the brief period we were underwater, the surface conditions have worsened. The swell is significant, and we're being pushed around by waves that seem much larger amid an emergency. I inflate Emma's BCD to establish her buoyancy and remove her mask to give her easier access to air, but she's still laboring to breathe properly.

I begin the exhausting swim back to the cliff face, towing Emma while fighting against the current. I keep talking to her, checking that her chest is rising and falling.

The other divers have surfaced by now, and I can see Trevor frantically swimming toward us. But he's not helping—he's panicking, asking questions I don't have time to answer and getting in the way of the rescue.

"Stay back!" I bark. "Give me room to work."

The swim to the ladder seems like it will never end. My shoulders and legs are screaming with the effort of dragging Emma's full weight while fighting the current and swell. My own breathing is becoming labored, and I have to consciously fight my own rising panic. If I lose control now, we could both be in serious trouble.

When we reach the rickety ladder at last, the real challenge begins. Emma is still unconscious and limp, and that twenty-foot vertical climb up a cliff face while wearing full scuba gear is looking more daunting than ever. I unclip my heavy equipment and hers as well, letting it float with the rest of the group, but it still takes the combined strength and balancing act of three people to physically haul Emma to the top.

When we lay her down on solid ground at last, her skin is pale, and her lips are turning blue. She finally opens her eyes and looks around as if seeing the world for the first time. "Well, that was exciting," she says weakly, as if she'd just finished an amusement park ride instead of nearly drowning.

I stare at her in disbelief. "Emma, you almost died down there. You lost your regulator and were sinking with no air source."

"Oh, I'm sure it wasn't that serious," she replies, already beginning to rewrite the narrative in her head. "I just got a bit tired. These things happen, don't they?"

Trevor nods eagerly, supporting her denial. "See? She's fine. Emma's tougher than she looks."

But I'm not fine. Their casual attitude is both astonishing and infuriating. My hands are shaking with residual adrenaline as my mind replays every moment of the rescue. The knowledge of what almost happened is crushing—I came so close of losing someone on my watch.

The rest of the group still expects the full expedition they paid for, so we prepare for the second dive of the day. And I make the decision that defines me as an instructor, pulling Emma aside and insist she sit this one out. "After what happened down there," I insist, "it's not safe for you to dive again today."

Emma's casual demeanor evaporates. "Absolutely not!" she blusters. "We paid for two dives, and I'm getting two dives. There's nothing wrong with me."

Trevor steps in aggressively. "You can't discriminate against her because she had a minor issue! Her doctor cleared her for diving. It's your duty as an instructor to take paying customers."

"My duty," I reply, my voice steady despite my racing heart, "is to ensure the safety of all my divers. What happened down there wasn't minor—it was a near-drowning incident that could have killed her."

"You're being overcautious," Trevor threatens. "This is Malta, not some dangerous location. The conditions are perfect."

The confrontation escalates quickly. They demand to speak to my supervisor, threaten legal action, accuse me of being inexperienced, swear they'll report me to PADI. Other divers start to gather, watching the argument unfold. I can feel my professional reputation hanging in the balance.

As a new instructor facing this kind of aggressive pushback, part of me wants to give in. Why not avoid confrontation and potential complaints? The industry pressure to keep customers happy, regardless of safety concerns, is enormous. Dive shops depend on positive reviews and repeat business.

But I think about Emma's face underwater—the terror, the helplessness—and the very real possibility that she could have died. How would I live with myself if I took her on another dive and something worse happened? I have to listen to my gut feeling.

"I'm sorry," I say, "but my decision is final. Emma will not be diving again today—at least, not with me."

The argument continues for another twenty minutes, with threats of complaints and legal action flying back and forth while the remaining four divers and I are gearing up for our second dive.

Back at the dive center, Emma and Trevor make good on their threat, lodging a formal complaint with the dive shop management. They paint me as an overcautious rookie instructor who ruined their vacation over a "minor incident." They demand a refund and grumble about posting negative reviews online.

I wait anxiously as the shop manager reviews their complaint and my incident report, my entire career hanging by a thread. If the shop sides with the customers, word could spread that I'm difficult to work with ... overly cautious ... bad for business.

But after hearing all the details, the manager supports my decision completely. "Safety is paramount," she tells Emma and Trevor firmly. "Our instructor made the right call. Your near-drowning incident was serious, and attempting another dive could have been fatal."

The validation is an incredible relief. It fundamentally changes how I approach instruction. I become more assertive during dive briefings, more willing to refuse divers who don't meet safety standards, more insistent on proper equipment fits.

For weeks afterward, the rescue haunts my dreams. I wake up in cold sweats, reliving those terrifying moments when Emma was sinking, with no air source. *Am I cut out for this level of responsibility?* I ask myself. *Are the stress and pressure worth it?*

But gradually, my first serious test as a professional instructor becomes a source of strength rather than trauma—not just because of the technical skills I demonstrated under pressure, but because of the character it revealed. I handled a life-threatening emergency and saved someone's life. I stood up to aggressive customers and prioritized safety over profit. In that moment of crisis, I discovered what kind of instructor I wanted to be: one who trusts her instincts and accepts the full weight of responsibility that comes with taking people into an environment where mistakes can be fatal.

Every time I take someone underwater, their life is literally in my hands. One moment of inattention, one poor decision, one failure to recognize danger signs could result in tragedy. Being liked is less important than keeping people alive.

The ocean taught me that day that it doesn't care about customer satisfaction, positive reviews, or business considerations. It cares only about respect, preparation, and the skill required to handle whatever tests it presents. And sometimes, the biggest challenge isn't the dive itself. It's having the courage to make the right decision when everyone is pressuring you to make the wrong one.

CHAPTER 5

Manchester: Plunging into the Unknown

If you don't like where you are, change it.
You're not a tree.
– Jim Rohn

Diving in Malta is like lunging into a splendid painting, where glimmering sapphire waters offer a mesmerizing contrast to the island's white limestone backdrop. Each dive brings a new exposure, whether I'm exploring hidden shipwrecks or gliding through crystalline cavern waters.

One of my favorite dives is on Gozo Island: the Blue Hole, a natural rock formation with a deep, circular pool that connects to the open sea through an ancient underwater arch. Surrounded by an astounding dance of colorful fish, I feel like I'm swimming in a clear aquarium.

I love teaching scuba diving and embrace the island lifestyle. Every dive, every celebration feels like a scene from a perfect summer. After dropping off the last clients each day, I cruise back to the apartment, sipping ice-cold Coca-Cola and blasting music. I am living my dream, and it's more extraordinary than I ever imagined.

But as a young female instructor, I face entrenched stereotypes that turn every day into a battle for basic respect. The persistent discrimination isn't always overt—it can be subtle and insidious.

It starts the moment clients first see me. When they realize they've been assigned to a twenty-three-year-old female instructor who looks even younger, their faces fall. Their eyes immediately start scanning for a man—any man—who might be the "real" instructor.

"How long have you been doing this?" they ask, in a tone that suggests no answer will be long enough. When I explain my background, training, and experience, I can see them mentally calculating whether to trust me or ask for someone else.

Despite my low official PADI student count—which now shows only about twenty certified divers under my belt—I have ten years of scuba experience, and my competence is obvious. Yet clients consistently seek validation from male staff members—even when those men know less than I do. During dive briefings, I explain the depth, currents, and potential hazards in detail. When I finish, someone in the group invariably turns to one of our male instructors with half my experience.

"So what do you think?" they'll ask. "Is she right about the conditions?"

The male instructors, to their credit, typically gesture back to me. "She's the expert on this site. I'd trust her judgment over mine any day."

My age compounds the problem. Not only am I female in a male-dominated industry, but I look young enough that clients assume I'm inexperienced regardless of my actual qualifications and the 700-plus dives under my belt. The combination of youth and femininity creates a perfect storm of doubt about my competence.

What's most puzzling and discouraging is how other women sometimes contribute to the problem. Some female clients, perhaps influenced by societal biases, show more confidence in male instructors than in me. It's heartbreaking to realize that the very people I'm hoping to inspire are sometimes the most skeptical of my abilities.

Some days, I consider giving up. Between the constant battle for respect, the financial disadvantages, and the institutional barriers, I question whether this career is worth the struggle. Having to prove myself every single day, with every single client, in every single situation, takes a toll that my male colleagues can't understand. They get to focus on diving, teaching, and having fun, while I get to deal with the extra physical, emotional, and psychological exhaustion from needing to perpetually assert my right to even be here.

But then I remember why I started—to share my love of the underwater world—and I resolve to prove that women belong in every aspect of this industry. Every *nein* Klaus threw at me, every student Doug has stolen, every client who doubts my abilities—it all feeds my determination to succeed not despite being a woman, but as a proud example of what women can achieve in this incredible field.

I refuse to let stereotypes and biases define my career and my life, but standing up against discrimination isn't just about me. It's about supporting every woman who might consider a career in diving but assumes she doesn't belong. It's about changing an industry culture that still treats female professionals as exceptions rather than equals. And it's about proving, one dive at a time, that the ocean doesn't care about your gender—only about your skill, your knowledge, and your respect for its power.

For a female dive instructor, the path may be tougher, the obstacles more numerous, and the victories harder-won. But every small victory feels monumental. When a family specifically requests me for their advanced training because their daughter found me inspiring, it validates everything I've endured. When a nervous male diver thanks me for making him feel safe during his first deep dive—for literally holding his hand—it reminds me that competence transcends gender stereotypes. When I guide someone through their first underwater experience or handle an emergency with composure, I'm not just building my own career—I'm opening doors for the women who will follow.

On the dive boat after one particularly frustrating day, I hear a group of male instructors loudly dismissing Sarah, a newly certified divemaster from Australia, because she's blonde and "looks too pretty to know anything about diving." She's actually one of the most skilled divers I've worked with this season, but today they've relegated her to equipment washing and deckhand duty while giving the prime dive jobs to guys with half her experience.

"It's always like this," Sarah says quietly, toweling off her gear beside me. "At home, in Indonesia, here in Malta—doesn't matter where I go. They see the ponytail and assume I'm just here to meet guys or work on my tan."

I watch her carefully coiling her dive line with the precision that comes from hundreds of dives, her movements efficient and practiced, and I know she's right. I've seen it too—talented women relegated to shallow dives or "easy" groups while men with the same certification level but questionable skills get the technical assignments.

"What if we had our own space?" I say suddenly. "Not competing against each other, but supporting each other."

Sarah looks up, interested. "What do you mean?"

That evening, back in my tiny room in our cramped apartment, I pull out my laptop and start typing. The name comes to me immediately: Miss-Scuba.com. But this isn't about crowning the prettiest diver or competing for some meaningless title. It's the exact opposite: a platform designed to unite women, to elevate skill over appearance, to focus on experience rather than stereotypes.

As the words pour out of me, I hold tight to this stubborn intention to dismantle stereotypes and rebel against mediocrity, to be grateful for being healthy and capable, to celebrate free will and wanderlust. This rising awareness of how fortunate I am, and how much I have to share with other dive enthusiasts, spurs me to create something revolutionary: a space where a marine biologist from Kenya can connect with a commercial diver from Norway, where Sarah's and my expertise would be valued, not questioned.

I type late into the night, until the mission becomes clear: Miss-Scuba.com will offer advice to new divers from a female perspective. It will serve as a place for offering tips and personal travel experiences with others who share my passion for adventure, diving, and exploration. It will be a community where women can embrace their adventurous spirit and redefine what's possible in a world that still clings to old biases—a community where we prove that our strength lies not in competing against each other, but in lifting each other up.

With women increasingly present in high-paying jobs and owning their love for travel and discovery, scuba brands have an opportunity to rethink their strategies and offerings. Miss Scuba represents a call to action: for the dive industry to recognize and cater to a burgeoning market of women who are ready to explore the depths of the ocean with the same intensity and enthusiasm they bring to every other aspect of their lives. By acknowledging and addressing this untapped market, the industry could foster a more inclusive and dynamic community, celebrating the contributions and experiences of female divers and paving the way for a more equitable and adventurous future.

My ultimate goal, with Miss Scuba and with my career as a dive instructor, is to inspire others—not just women—to look beyond their immediate surroundings and recognize that the world is much larger and more vibrant than it may appear. It's easy to get caught up in our daily routines and remain confined to our comfort zone. But life is rich with diverse cultures, extraordinary individuals, and countless opportunities waiting to be explored. When you have good health, you possess everything you need to chase your dreams, unlock incredible possibilities, and pursue your goals.

The real challenge lies in taking that leap into the unknown—a leap that many fear, despite its potential to unlock incredible possibilities. Of course, if it were easy, everyone would do it. But my belief that the hardest paths are often the most rewarding pushes me to stay focused and on course. The difficulties along the way are proof that I'm on a journey few are willing to take.

* * *

As the summer heat rises and the dive season gets busier, a new instructor joins the team, and suddenly the universe seems perfectly aligned.

Harry is from England—strong and stocky, with sun-bleached hair, tattoos snaking up his arms, and piercing blue eyes that seem to see right through me. He has an easy confidence that borders on arrogance—a magnetic spark that captivates everyone around him. Watching him teach diving is like witnessing an artist at work. His instruction makes people fall in love with the underwater world.

Harry's dangerous appeal draws me in despite every rational warning. When he talks about diving, his passion is infectious. When he looks at me, I feel like I'm the only person in the world. He is everything I never realized I was missing.

It's intoxicating and terrifying all at once.

Within a week, we're swept up in a romance that feels like something out of a movie. Our connection is immediate and intense, as though we've known each other forever. We spend every free moment together—diving during the day, exploring Malta's hidden coves at sunset, talking until dawn about our dreams of globe-trotting together. Then, in a spontaneous moment that takes my breath away, Harry drops to one knee on a secluded beach and proposes under a canopy of stars.

Without hesitation, I say yes, imagining a future full of love and adventure. We envision ourselves as a diving power couple, traveling from one exotic location to another, building a life around our shared passion for the ocean.

Eager to start this new chapter, I ask my mother to send my birth certificate so Harry and I can get married right away. But in her wise way, Mutti gently suggests we take time to live together before making such a big commitment. Though it stings at the time, I realize she's right—love needs time to grow in everyday moments, not just romantic ones. So, I follow her advice, and we decide to live together first, discovering more about each other with every passing day.

When Harry suggests we relocate to the UK together, it feels like destiny. Doug's constant theft of my students has reached a breaking point, and the idea of starting fresh somewhere new with the man I love seems perfect. Harry paints a dazzling picture: running a successful dive operation near his hometown of Manchester, building our reputation in the clear waters of English quarries, and eventually expanding internationally.

"We'll be partners in everything," he promises, his eyes bright with possibility. "Business partners, life partners, dive partners. We'll build something amazing together."

The decision feels right, especially after Doug steals yet another group of my students, I know it's time to finally break free. Harry and I pack our bags and make the life-changing decision to relocate to Cheshire, near Manchester.

Having grown accustomed to the clear, warm Mediterranean Sea, I am struck by the bleakness of Astbury Lake—the main dive location used by the dive shop, Limitless Diver Training. This small quarry is freezing cold and darker than any water from my orienteering days in Hungary. The visibility is so poor it feels like a nasty joke—often less than three feet on a good day. Maneuvering in these murky waters becomes a constant hurdle, requiring me to tether students together with guide ropes to avoid losing them in the gloom.

Teaching in these conditions is like conducting a symphony while blindfolded—everything is twice as hard and half as rewarding. Despite the sunken wrecks and guide ropes strategically placed throughout the quarry, my students often surface in complete confusion, unsure of what they've seen or whether they've completed their training requirements properly.

Occasionally, we escape to Capernwray, a quarry lake with water as clear as glass and filled with whimsical underwater attractions, from submerged aircraft to a rocking horse to a gnome "garden." These trips become a rare treat, brief stand-ins for the kind of diving that made me fall in love with the underwater world.

The relentless gloom of the UK becomes a suffocating weight on my soul. Days blend into weeks of gray skies and persistent drizzle. The seasonal depression hits harder than I expected, sapping my enthusiasm for everything I once loved. I desperately miss the energizing Mediterranean sunshine.

Living arrangements add another layer of misery to the situation. We're staying with the dive center owner, Connie, and her three children in Alderley Edge, a posh but super eerie neighborhood of Cheshire, near Manchester. Ancient trees loom over narrow lanes that twist and disappear into shadows, their gnarled branches forming canopies so thick, they block out daylight even at noon.

The house itself is a Victorian relic with creaking floorboards that announce every footstep, windows that rattle in their frames when the wind picks up, and a persistent dampness that seeps into your bones no matter how high you turn up the heating. At night, fog rolls in from the moors, muffling all sound except for the occasional cry of some unseen creature in the darkness. Even the locals speak in hushed tones about the woods behind the house, warning against walking there after sunset. Between the suffocating dive conditions and this gothic nightmare of a living situation, I feel like I'm trapped in some twisted fairy tale where the princess never gets rescued.

Connie works as a nurse, pulling long shifts at the local hospital, which means that in addition to managing the dive business, I often end up babysitting her kids. The children are sweet, but they're not my responsibility, and I resent being treated like live-in help when I'm supposed to be building a career as a dive instructor.

Worse, I suspect Connie has romantic feelings for Harry, which creates an uncomfortable tension in an already stressful cohabitation. I catch her watching him with longing when she thinks no one is looking. She laughs a little too loudly at his jokes, finds excuses to touch his arm during conversations, and always asks for his help with things she could easily handle herself. Whether Harry encourages this attention or simply doesn't notice it, the situation makes me feel like a third wheel.

As the weeks pass, Harry's behavior becomes increasingly erratic. He has a talent for appearing just long enough to charm new students during their initial consultation, promising them expert instruction and personalized attention. Then, once they've paid and committed to the course, he vanishes, leaving me to handle everything from classroom theory to pool sessions to open water certification dives. More and more, I am forced to make excuses for him, cover for his absences, and work twice as hard to maintain the quality of instruction our students deserve and expect. The stress is overwhelming.

I keep hoping that this is just a rough patch, that the man I met in Malta will resurface and we can get back on track. But Harry's carefully constructed façade begins to crumble, shaking the foundation of everything I believed about our relationship.

The first shock wave comes when I answer the dive shop phone one evening, and a woman's voice, sharp with anger, demands to speak to Harry. "Tell him Ingrid called about the child support," she snaps. "He's three months behind again, and if he doesn't pay up, I'm calling my solicitor."

When I confront Harry, he laughs it off with casual indifference. "Oh, that. Yeah, I have a kid with Ingrid. Didn't I mention it?"

The revelation hits me like a physical blow. Not only does Harry have a child he never mentioned, but he's been avoiding his financial responsibilities. As the weeks pass, more calls come in about four more children—with three different women. And he's behind on support payments for all of them.

"It's not a big deal," he says when I express the shock and pain of learning about these children he'd kept secret from me. "They're all in the past. You're my future."

But how can he dismiss his own children as just part of his past? What are we supposed to live on when he starts sending our limited income in sporadic payments to appease the angriest mothers? And why does he disappear for hours without explanation, returning with the smell of perfume that isn't mine?

What happened to the charming, passionate man I fell in love with?

Despite our supposed partnership, Harry squirrels away all of our business earnings, leaving me to survive on occasional tips from students. When I confront him about our agreement to share everything, he becomes defensive.

"I'm handling the business side," he explains in a manner usually reserved for children. "You just focus on the teaching. Trust me, I know what I'm doing."

But I can see exactly what he's doing. While I work double shifts teaching nervous students in freezing quarries, Harry pockets the money and spends it on things that have nothing to do with our business or our future together: new clothes, nights out with friends I never meet, expensive dinners at restaurants he never invites me to. And what started as casual drinking after work escalates into daily consumption that is beginning to affect his ability to function.

When I discover Harry has been stealing money directly from our joint account—money I've earned through my own teaching—I confront him with bank statements showing unexplained withdrawals.

He doesn't even try to deny it. "I needed cash for business expenses," he says with a shrug, as if taking money without permission is perfectly normal.

"What business expenses?" I ask. "I handle all of our business accounting. Nothing justifies these withdrawals."

"You wouldn't understand," he replies dismissively. "There are things you don't need to worry about."

But I do understand. I understand that he's been funding his drug habit and irresponsible lifestyle with money I've earned through hard work and dedication. I understand that our "partnership" has been a one-way street from the beginning, with me providing the labor and him reaping the benefits.

As winter deepens, Harry increasingly abandons his responsibilities, and the drug and alcohol problem becomes impossible to ignore. He begins showing up to work high or hungover, his pupils dilated and his speech slurred. Sometimes he doesn't show up at all.

"Where were you?" I demand after he misses an entire day of classes, leaving me to handle twice the workload. "We had eight students scheduled, and I had to manage them all alone."

"Relax," he mumbles, reeking of alcohol and something else I can't identify. "They got their training, didn't they? What's the problem?"

The problem is that I'm running a dive operation single-handedly in harsh conditions while he disappears on drug-fueled binges. The problem is that students are starting to ask where their "lead instructor" is. The problem is that I'm working myself to exhaustion while he's destroying everything we're supposed to be building together.

The breaking point comes during one of the worst weeks of my life. It's been raining for six straight days, and Harry has been missing for three of those days without any explanation. I'm teaching back-to-back classes in the freezing quarry—in conditions that would demoralize far more experienced instructors—trying to maintain professional standards and an upbeat atmosphere while privately falling apart. I'm dealing with personal betrayal that cuts deeper than anything I've ever experienced. And my love for diving—the one constant in my life—has begun to feel tainted by the trauma of this relationship.

I feel like I'm drowning on dry land.

When Harry finally returns, he's high and unapologetic, strolling into the dive shop as if he's been gone for an hour. He doesn't ask how I managed without him, doesn't apologize for leaving me to handle everything alone, doesn't even seem to realize that his absence has put enormous strain on our business and my sanity.

"Where have you been?" I question him, my voice trembling with fatigue and rage.

"Out," he replies casually, already looking around for something else to occupy his attention.

"Out where? I've been covering for you, making excuses to students, working double shifts because you disappeared without a word."

"Relax, Szilvia. Everything's fine. You worry too much."

That's when I realize that nothing is fine, and it never will be as long as I stay in this toxic situation. Harry isn't going to change. He's not going to suddenly become responsible, honest, or capable of the partnership I thought we were building. He has shown me exactly who he is, and believing his promises of change would be foolish beyond measure.

Our relationship isn't just troubled—it's dangerous.

After eight months of relentless rain, only three hours of sunshine, and a never-ending string of betrayals, I pack my dive gear and book the first available flight back to Hungary. I don't leave a note or try to explain my departure to Harry. By the time he sobers up enough from his latest night out to notice I'm gone, I'm already in the air, seeking refuge from the soul-crushing environment that nearly destroyed me.

The flight feels like escape. As the plane climbs away from Manchester's gray landscape, the burden of Harry's duplicity and England's gloom begins to lift. I may be broke, humiliated, and heartbroken, but I'm alive and free from a situation that was slowly killing my spirit.

The gray skies fade below me as the plane heads above the clouds, into the eternal blue, and east toward home, toward family, toward the possibility of healing and starting over. The experience has taught me something I'll never forget: Sometimes the bravest thing you can do is walk away from everything you thought you wanted, because it's the only way to preserve what you know you need.

* * *

Back in Budapest, the heavy clouds and autumn chill mirror the gloom I've left behind. Desperate for an escape, I spin the globe on my desk, letting fate decide my next move.

I stayed in England longer than I should have, driven by the stubbornness of not wanting to admit failure and the hope that love could overcome any obstacle. I finally left carrying the painful knowledge that love alone isn't enough. Trust, respect, shared values, and mutual support are equally essential to sustain a relationship. Harry taught me what I don't want in a partner, which turns out to be almost as valuable as knowing what I do want.

It's a harsh but necessary lesson about the difference between persistence and self-destruction, between fighting for love and enabling someone else's destructive behavior. When the circumstances threatened to consume me, admitting defeat was the only way to claim victory.

Leaving Harry behind is one of the hardest things I've ever done, not because I still love him, but because it means admitting our relationship was a lie. The future I'd imagined, the partnership I'd invested in, the love I thought we shared—all of it was built on deception and false promises.

But staying would have been worse. Staying would have meant accepting a life of financial exploitation, emotional manipulation, and watching someone I cared about destroy himself with drugs and irresponsibility. It would have meant sacrificing my own dreams and well-being for someone who had already proven he wasn't worth it.

England tested my soul. It also built my character. I lost almost everything, but I gained something more valuable: the knowledge that I'm strong enough to leave a toxic situation, even when it means admitting I was wrong about everything I believed. Now I'm determined to get my life back on track.

I reach out to poke at the globe and stop it from spinning. My finger lands on Thailand, a tropical haven bathed in sunlight. Stormy skies and betrayals fade, replaced by the promise of Thailand's vibrant culture and sunlit shores. There is something special and exciting about plunging into the unknown, with no plans—but a future full of opportunities.

Without hesitation, I book my ticket.

I'm ready for a new beginning.

CHAPTER 6

Koh Phi Phi: Wild and Free

To live is the rarest thing in the world.
Most people exist, that is all.
– Oscar Wilde

I arrive in Bangkok with zero job prospects but heaps of optimism. I saved up just enough money in the UK to live in Asia for about a month. Even as I prepared for the journey, the weight of my past began to lift. Now, equipped with a rekindled sense of determination and an overstuffed duffel bag, I'm stepping into the next chapter of my life, hopeful that it will be filled with light, revelation, and healing.

My ultimate goal is not to travel as a tourist, but to find a scuba diving job on a beautiful Thai island. A friend from my time in Manchester, now teaching English in the city, offers me a place to stay for now and shows me around Bangkok. The traffic is wild—that's the first thing I notice. Motorcycles zip through congested streets, often carrying entire families, babies included. It makes me wonder: Do Westerners overdo safety? Or does life here simply follow different rules?

Bangkok's contrasts fascinate me. From the chaotic rush of traffic, crowded street markets, and noisy tuk-tuks to the serene corners, hidden courtyards, and quiet alleys, the city is a whirlwind of sensory experiences. It's frantic, dirty, and bustling, yet I feel an unexpected sense of harmony and belonging.

The city's energy, combined with my growing connection to Buddhism, creates a harmony that resonates deeply with me. It starts with a book I find in a dusty Bangkok bookshop: Thich Nhat Hanh's *The Miracle of Mindfulness*. As I read his words about finding peace in simple moments, about breathing as meditation, about washing dishes not to get them clean but simply to wash dishes—to be fully present in that moment—something clicks. I think of all the times I've rushed through life, always reaching for the next destination, the next certification, the next adventure.

At Wat Pho temple, I sit cross-legged on cool marble floors, watching monks in saffron robes move with deliberate slowness. Their chanting isn't just sound—it's vibration that seems to settle something restless inside me. I try to follow their rhythm with my breathing, the way Thich Nhat Hanh describes. In, pause, out, pause. For the first time in years, I'm not planning my next move.

Later, in a small temple near the backpacker's haven of Khao San Road, I light incense and read posted quotes from the revered Dalai Lama: "Sometimes not getting what you want is a wonderful stroke of luck." The words stop me cold. I think about missing law school by a single point, and about all the other things that didn't work out in my life—jobs I didn't get, relationships that ended, plans that fell through. Yet each disappointment somehow led me here, to this moment of understanding.

Surrounded by the sweet, earthy scent of nag champa and the soft murmur of prayers, I realize I've been chasing happiness in destinations instead of finding it in moments.

Every intricately designed temple in Bangkok becomes a peaceful escape, filled with soft chants, fragrant incense, and a sense of tranquility. Amidst the urban frenzy, I find plenty of spots where life slows down—

where the Buddhist teaching of mindfulness starts to make sense not as philosophy, but as practice.

Thai street food captivates me, especially the fresh-made pad thai. I fall in love with the aromatic, spicy flavors and the casual, friendly atmosphere among the street vendors. King Bhumibol Adulyadej's image is everywhere, reflecting the nation's deep respect and affection for their beloved monarch. Thailand truly lives up to its reputation as the "Land of Smiles."

Every day in Bangkok brings new encounters: travelers with intriguing stories, locals eager to share their culture, expats who've made the city their home. The mix of tradition and modernity, commotion and calm, leaves a lasting impression on me.

From rooftop bars where the city sprawls endlessly below in a carpet of neon and twinkling lights leading to Khao San Road, every evening feels like a leap of faith. One day, my friend and I find ourselves in a hidden speakeasy behind a tailor shop, sipping cocktails in an intimate, vintage setting. Another night takes a darker turn when we stumble upon a strip club ping-pong show whose bizarre and unsettling acts leave me feeling uneasy.

Despite the sensory overload, I feel drawn to the richness of Thai culture and determined to explore it further, seeking experiences that celebrate the country's beauty rather than exploit it. After a few days of the city's overwhelming pace, I am ready to head south to the coast.

I travel via a night bus to Phuket, a lively tourist hub, especially around Patong Beach, which never sleeps. This is a popular spot featuring an abundance of dive shops, but I long for a quieter place. At the ferry station, I buy a ticket to Koh Phi Phi. Boarding that ferry becomes one of the best decisions of my life.

When I arrive one afternoon in 2000, Koh Phi Phi still feels like a hidden gem, untouched by mass tourism. The island, made famous by the film *The Beach*, starring Leonardo DiCaprio, is a breathtaking paradise—sparkling, warm water full of hidden coves, towering cliffs, and coral reefs teeming with life. The turquoise waters and pristine white sandy beaches create a picture-perfect paradise—no cars, no stress, just dive shops, bars, and barefoot, sun-tanned globe-trotters.

The small village is charming, dotted with bamboo huts and open-air cafes where backpackers share stories over fresh coconuts or Chang beers. The camaraderie is evident, and the locals are welcoming, living life at a relaxed pace. The simplicity and contentment here are striking compared with the frenzy I left behind.

I visit the local dive shops that first afternoon, lined along the one paved street stretching from the pier, each offering its own charm. I'm soon hired by Hippo Divers, one of the island's largest dive centers. Known for its prime location and exceptional boats, it's the perfect place to start my new undertaking. All in all, Koh Phi Phi seems like a dream come true, blending work and thrill-seeking in a picture-perfect setting.

It's pure bliss, and I know I want to stay.

* * *

Life feels like a dream. In Koh Phi Phi, I find solace and inspiration, a fresh canvas for my next work of living art.

I rent a room from a kind local man who invites me to his table each evening. Over shared meals, we talk about our home countries, local politics, and religion. More than 90 percent of Thailand is Buddhist, while about 5 percent are Muslim and the remaining communities Christian and Hindu—all of whom pretty much live in harmony here on the island. My landlord explains why I rarely see locals swimming: They believe the water harbors bad spirits. It's the only thing about this fascinating place that I disagree on. The only spirit I feel here is one of adventure.

I'm not surprised to learn that most Thai families live modest, happy lives, untouched by the desire for material wealth. Indeed, every day on this island feels like a gift—an escape from the complexities of my past and the outside world, allowing me to embrace the island's tranquility. Shoes are a rarity, worn only at night to avoid stepping on broken glass. With no TV, no newspapers, WiFi access available only in internet cafés, and almost no running hot water, life on Koh Phi Phi is beautifully simple.

My routine at the dive center is wonderfully uncomplicated, with little to worry about: After three dives a day to incandescent coral reefs, I spend afternoons lounging on the beach with friends, soaking up the sun and the joy of the moment. Highlights include naps, beach volleyball, and delicious, affordable Thai food. Watermelon, pineapple, and baby bananas are plentiful, picked fresh each morning by the guy who works at our dive shop. The intense flavors remind me of homegrown produce from my grandparents' garden.

I quickly become friends with Jarod from Australia, the other newly hired instructor, and we share laughs and explore the island together. Our go-to spot becomes Carlito's Bar, where we wind down after long days with clients, sharing stories over gin and tonics and Koh Phi Phi's dreamy sunsets. The bars and cafes hold impromptu gatherings, where people take pleasure in the view with a drink and live music. As the sun dips below the horizon, the sky bursts into deep purples, fiery oranges, and soft pinks, casting a golden glow over the island.

After a quick nap, I'm back out, hopping between local restaurants with pirated movies playing in the background, and beach bars with fire dancing shows and Buddha Bar music filling the air. The nightlife is energetic but chill, and we dance well past midnight, surrounded by laughter and clinking glasses. On the way home, we grab a late-night snack and treat ourselves to a soothing three-dollar massage, a wonderful way to unwind before I head back to my bungalow, completely content.

It's the life I've always envisioned—freedom, fun, and amazing diving, all wrapped up in one perfect package. It's a place for easy friendships, where every night feels like a celebration.

I learn fire dancing from Solej, a Thai performer, and immerse myself in Muay Thai, the martial art and combat sport. Rosie from London becomes my best girlfriend; we form a tight-knit bond, laughing all day with the other instructors on the boat between dives, and we always watch out for each other. Geri, my childhood friend from orienteering diving, follows me to Koh Phi Phi in pursuit of his own dreams, and it's good to have another Hungarian on the island.

Diving in the Andaman Sea is nothing short of magical. At first, I don't understand why they call it "work": I swim daily with leopard sharks, turtles, manta rays, and lionfish, eating fresh pineapple between dives, and get paid for it. My favorite spots are a three-hour boat ride from our island: Hin Daeng (Red Rock) and Hin Muang (Purple Rock), whose names come from their blankets of soft red and purple corals. Barely visible from the surface, both attract fish like magnets, which also draws sharks to the area. The water is so clear, you can see as far as you would on land, and the temperature is perfect, close to 90°F. The dives on these pinnacle islands feel like walking in a colorful flower garden.

I persuade my mother to visit—a life-changing experience for both of us. She's enchanted by the underwater world, spending hours snorkeling and sharing in the island's simple pleasures. This island, so far removed from everyday reality, offers her a glimpse into the life I always wanted. Watching Mutti soak up this new lifestyle deepens our bond, making her stay one of the most gratifying and heartfelt times we've ever shared. I feel that she finally gets me.

My passion, my drive, and my love for the ocean are paying off. I've proven to my family—and myself—that a career does not need to be a nine-to-five job. I can make money doing what I love every day. And that's what I plan on doing.

* * *

Working in Thailand has its own rhythm, and it's not always smooth sailing. As dive instructors, we're on the job seven days a week, diving through Christmas and New Year's, with only a few parties to break up the underwater routine. In my first eight months on Koh Phi Phi, I have just two days off, and that's only after I get an ear infection.

Throughout 238 days of nonstop diving, I work hard and party hard. That strenuous combination often lands instructors in the decompression chamber after developing "the bends"—decompression sickness because of the nature of our work.

Decompression sickness happens when you either stay underwater too long or ascend faster than the nitrogen bubbles can safely escape from your bloodstream. But prolonged exposure to high-pressure environments can also cause the bends. Even when scuba professionals follow proper dive protocols, the effects from daily dives over extended periods can be cumulative—it's called a "silent bubble build-up." Dehydration from long hours in the sun, post-dive alcoholic drinks, and physical exhaustion only amplify the risk.

The hyperbaric chamber—a cylindrical metal tank that looks like it's straight out of a sci-fi movie—is a lifesaver for those suffering from the bends. Medics adjust the air pressure inside to help the body safely release nitrogen bubbles built up from frequent dives. Even with all precautions, nitrogen can still build up after months of constant diving, making decompression sickness a regular hazard in our profession.

But hey, that's the life we signed up for—the thrill of exploring Thailand's underwater wonders, mixed with a dash of adventure and a pinch of risk. It's not just a job; it's a way of life. Every dive could end up being a story. Every visit to the decompression chamber is a cautionary tale with a touch of island flavor.

Each dive center on Koh Phi Phi adds its own unique flair to the diving experience, thanks to its English, Swedish, Israeli, French, or Korean influence. A welcoming vibe unites them, with rustic signs and colorful murals reflecting the vibrant marine life just offshore.

Dealing with language barriers is a common experience in many diving shops—and our charismatic shop owner, Mr. Ha, attracts a lot of business from his homeland, Korea. Communication can be tricky: I don't speak Korean, and most of our Korean divers don't speak English. But all of our staff members are driven and eager to share our love for the underwater world with everyone from beginners to seasoned divers.

We all dread Wednesdays, however, as they bring a peculiar experience none of my fellow instructors look forward to. That's when we get a fresh batch of Korean honeymooners flooding the island for a day of excitement—happy newlyweds who've all gotten married at the same time and are now traveling together and doing every activity together, including scuba diving. To anyone outside the Korean culture, it's the strangest thing.

Our Korean clientele also presents some other notable challenges, such as unfamiliarity with swimming. I encounter many Korean divers who adopt a bicycling-like motion in the water, inadvertently disturbing coral with their kicks. People who can't swim well tend to hold my forearms in death grip, and women with long nails leave long-lasting marks that make me look like a rival in a catfight. I take extra precaution when we host the wedding travel groups, on a boat packed with thirty honeymooning couples, all dressed to the nines, the women in fresh nails and full makeup that dissolves underwater like a clown's face paint.

Mr. Ha delivers elaborate diving briefings with dramatic hand gestures and sound effects, attempting to bridge the language gap between divers and instructors. Uncertain about communicating effectively, I feel uneasy taking some groups on deep dives. So, I devise a clever workaround to ensure both enjoyment and safety.

I inflate my BCD and use my snorkel while swimming on the surface toward shallow waters, where the bottom is crowded with colorful coral and fish. Then I deflate the diving couple' BCDs so they dip underwater and, holding on to their tank valves, take them on a picturesque tour. I kick for the three of us while they watch the corals sway lazily and the brightly colored fish dart by, and squeal with excitement as an occasional turtle swims past. When we reach our time limit, I steer them back toward deeper water and the boat, giving them the gratifying illusion of coming up from a deep dive.

Throughout the experience, Korean divers often hold hands under-water, a heartwarming sight. Upon resurfacing they eagerly ask how deep we ventured, I reply with a grin, "Really deep!"

Their faces light up with joy, and Mr. Ha beams with satisfaction. It's a creative solution that fulfills the clients' expectations while also ensuring their safety.

Threading the nuances of scuba instruction on Koh Phi Phi, I observe how communication and cultural differences shape each diving experience. A local saying, translated into a memorable English expression, captures this fascinating insight: *Same same but different.* While the fundamentals of diving and the locations we visit are largely consistent, each diver brings their own style and mindset underwater. Mr. Ha's inventive briefings and my adaptive techniques underscore the need to acknowledge these differences to enrich the diving experience for everyone involved.

Same same but different also reflects the distinct approaches I start to notice in scuba diving among women versus men, where the biggest difference is in their receptiveness to instruction. Women students, I observe, tend to think everything through and hang on every word the instructor says. Men, on the other hand, often try to figure things out on their own, assuming they know more than the instructor—especially when she's a younger female like me, regardless of my hundreds of logged dives.

Women even have different reasons for signing up for a diving class—all too often, it's not because they want to scuba dive, but merely because their boyfriend does. Men are more likely to dive for the thrill and adventure of the sport. But women who dive for the same reason—to try something out of the ordinary—get more excited about taking the big step, and they are some of my favorite students.

The more I dive, the more it seems to me that female divers are apt to know their limits and make wiser choices. Women are generally more conservative and careful when planning a dive, while most guys follow the *Let's figure it out as we go* route. And women seem to make better diving buddies than men: When they agree to dive together, they frequently check on each other and are willing to cut the dive short if their buddy encounters a problem. When men agree to be dive buddies, it often just means diving in the same ocean.

The ratio of men to women is about eight to one, and I see more out-of-shape men than women in my classes. Women tend to be more body-conscious, which results in better physique and smoother underwater moves, leading to more efficient air consumption. Meanwhile, guys tend to be more gear-oriented. If they like diving, they purchase all sorts of scuba gear.

The first piece of equipment my male students want to acquire is a knife, and not just any knife—a big knife. This is followed by the latest scuba gadgets, a sling for spear fishing, or a fancy underwater camera. In contrast, only avid dive girls own more than a basic warm-water wetsuit. Women may be less interested in owning equipment, but they are keen on seeing pretty, colorful fish in tropical waters. Of course, through Miss-Scuba. com, I hear more and more from hardcore girls who scuba dive under ice, through shipwrecks, or in raging rivers—and I hope and expect that trend will continue.

Upon completing their training, newly certified female divers seem more excited and proud of their accomplishments than men. A scuba certificate may be just another hobby for men, alongside skydiving, snowboarding, surfing, what have you, but for many women, it's a huge, bold achievement. Perhaps that's why, women instructors typically are more patient and attentive with students than their male counterparts: Instructors who once feared the water and are not daredevils by nature become more empathetic than those who can't relate to the apprehension of new divers.

Of course, diving depends on the individual, not the gender. There's no way—and no reason—to deem men or women the better divers, better students, or better instructors. Regardless of who is adventuring underwater with me, I am loving every minute of it, and I feel the same way about this island lifestyle. Everyone feels the same when they first arrive in Phi Phi, thinking they've found paradise on Earth.

* * *

One morning, when another instructor has overindulged the night before and is far too hungover to take out a brand-new diver, I step in to cover for him. As soon as we anchor, all the experienced divers eagerly jump into the water, disappearing beneath the waves. By the time my beginner student and I are ready to enter the ocean, something extraordinary happens: Out of nowhere, a majestic whale shark appears, slicing gracefully through the water.

In this bewitching moment, all thoughts of practicing new skills vanish. We are completely spellbound by this gentle giant. Whale sharks are elusive creatures, and spotting one is a rare and precious event; we are incredibly fortunate to be in the right place at the right time. Some of my fellow instructors have spent five years in Phi Phi without ever encountering one. Yet here is my student, on his very first ocean dive, experiencing the awe-inspiring presence of a whale shark.

None of the seasoned divers from our boat see the whale shark—only the two of us. We swim alongside the colossal beauty, mesmerized by its sheer size and grace. As the sunlight dances on its spotted skin as it moves effortlessly through the water, I record every second in my memory, amazed at the infinite power of my ardent connection to the ocean and its wonders.

At the end of my first season, Mr. Ha invites me back for the next year and offers me the position of manager. It's a boost to my ego, a clear sign of his trust in me, and it feels like validation for all my hard work. But as much as I appreciate the opportunity, I'm conflicted. The simplicity of my current life—the freedom, the diving, the easy friendships—is something I'm not ready to complicate. It's a tough decision. I am torn between the allure of professional growth and the laid-back life I've grown to love.

After a few months of backpacking in Australia and a brief visit to Hungary, I return to Koh Phi Phi and accept the manager position, filled with anticipation and a sense of renewal. Living in a rustic bungalow by the beach, waking up to fresh pineapple, and spending evenings with gin and tonics under a star-filled sky, transporting me to moments of pure bliss. But as my second year in Thailand unfolds, I begin to feel a creeping discontent that grows with every passing day: an internal retreat from the vagabond lifestyle.

No one stays on the island for long, and I get a kick out of that—at first. Through work, I'm always meeting new people, especially when the bustling high season arrives. The island pulsates as before, with tourists flocking to and from its shores like the ebb and flow of the tides. But something inside me has changed. My passion for diving remains, but after months of teaching without pause, burnout starts to set in. I'm growing tired of the constant stream of new faces. As soon as I get to know and like someone, they leave.

After two years, I feel like paradise is closing in. Koh Phi Phi is becoming a prison.

I still love Thailand—the beaches, the diving, the Muay Thai, the nightlife—but I'm yearning for something more, something different. Amidst the tropical beauty, I start to crave intellectual stimulation, something beyond the rhythm of the waves and the daily routine. And the intimacy of island life, where everyone knows everyone else's business, is starting to feel suffocating. The island's timeless charm and predictable pace are stifling my growing need for the energy of cities, the culture of museums, and the excitement of new ideas.

Saying yes to becoming the manager was a mistake I didn't realize until too late. Despite my best efforts to fix the flaws in the operation and boost morale with incentives, Mr. Ha repeatedly undermines my decisions. His behavior speaks volumes about the culture he grew up in: even modern Korean men, it seems, aren't accustomed to taking orders from a woman. I should have anticipated this, but I didn't.

Reality settles heavily on my shoulders.

Standing at the crossroads of my future, I feel torn. The tranquility of the island, this place I've come to love, is at odds with the pull of new possibilities, new horizons—a call to something more. One night, as I share drinks with friends at Carlito's Bar, the conversation turns to what comes next. We all agree it's time for a change.

I'm not yet sure what that change will look like, but once I make the decision to move on, excitement floods through me. The anticipation of new adventures and opportunities feels like a cold, refreshing shower, waking me up to a renewed sense of purpose.

* * *

My cousin Andrea, who lives in Florida, has extended an invite for me to come visit her and think about what to do next. I've never been to the United States, so I can only hope that not all Americans are like those on *The Jerry Springer Show*.

Where should I go? What part of the world is calling to me? I look forward to brainstorming with Andi. We're so alike in so many ways that our thoughts and ideas flow seamlessly, as if we were sisters. The thought of reuniting with her feels like the perfect next step, a chance to explore fresh opportunities and reconnect with someone who knows and understands me like only family does.

I stop working on January 1, 2002, and spend my final week on the island—the first week of a new year—doing my favorite things and those I never had time for: leisurely reading on the beach with my morning coffee, rock climbing with Solej, snorkeling with blacktip sharks at sunrise, lounging in a hammock with a gin and tonic at Carlito's Bar at sunset. I hardly say goodbye to anyone: I value the friendships made here, but goodbyes have always felt like something I'm not quite ready for.

Soon it's time to take the ferry back to the mainland. From Phuket, I make my way to Bangkok to catch a flight out of Asia. Sorting out my visa is surprisingly easy, and with the paperwork in hand, I start looking for a ticket to Fort Myers, where Andi lives. But the travel industry is reeling in the aftermath of 9/11, and flights to Florida are few and far between.

Three weeks pass, and still no seats to Florida are available. I start to wonder if the universe is nudging me toward something different. In an impulsive moment, I switch gears and book a flight to the West Coast instead. It's an unexpected about-face, but I figure that once I'm in the US, moving from one coast to the other will be easy.

I call a former student who once offered me a place to stay if I ever go to California. "Felix? This is Szilvia, your instructor from Phi Phi. Remember me?"

"Of course!" Felix replies. "How are you? I miss the island, and you guys, and everything …"

"Great!" I reply eagerly. "So, remember that offer to stay with you? I am landing tomorrow at seven p.m. Can you pick me up?"

"Uh, which airport?"

"San Francisco!"

Felix pauses, then laughs. "Do you know how far that is? It's a six-hour drive!"

This was a hiccup I had not expected. On the map, San Francisco seems barely an inch away from Los Angeles! But when Felix urges me to fly to LAX instead and says he'll meet me there, one American city sounds as good as the next. And they're both on the ocean.

Los Angeles, I think. *Why not?*

My next call to spontaneity has arrived.

CHAPTER 7

Los Angeles: Questioning the Gypsy Lifestyle

Wild woman are an unexplainable spark of life.
They ooze freedom and seek awareness,
they belong to nobody but themselves yet give
a piece of who they are to everyone they meet.
– Nikki Rowe

Towering kelp fronds rise from the ocean floor like underwater redwoods, reaching through the chill of the Pacific toward sunlight that filters down in ghostly green and golden beams. These giant seaweed forests sway with the currents—dense, shifting walls that provide shelter and food for a vast array of marine life. Swimming through the kelp canopy is like moving through an ancient, enchanted forest. At times, you lose sight of open water as the kelp enfolds you in its unearthly lullaby.

From curious sea lions darting through water to bat rays gliding silently over the sandy bottoms to the occasional leopard shark weaving between kelp stalks, diving in California is unlike anywhere else. Every dive holds the thrill of discovery, the perfect blend of adventure and mystery.

But the next episode in my personal quest begins many weeks before my first dive off the California coast. The moment I step off the plane surrounded by fellow travelers, it hits me: *I've left Asia.*

Despite bizarre questioning by US customs officers—*Are you part of a terrorist organization? Were you working as a prostitute in Thailand?*—it's exciting to be in a new country, on a continent I've never visited before. And seeing Felix's familiar face at the airport is comforting.

We head to his place in Tarzana so I can drop off my belongings—a dive bag and a small duffle bag. Stopping for lunch in Santa Monica, I'm overwhelmed by the endless options: bread! cheese! sides! But my turkey and cranberry sauce sandwich is perfect, something I've missed while living off fried rice in Thailand.

Life in America feels different right away: Portion sizes are massive. The tipping culture is strange to me. Smoking, so common among my friends in Thailand, is almost taboo here. And the driving rules! Felix lets me borrow his Porsche, and in less than a week, I rack up three fines—one for not yielding to a pedestrian, another for parking during street cleaning, and a third for a no-parking sign I never saw.

I arrived in my Thai flip-flops, so adjusting to American life includes buying shoes—and of course, a pair of Rollerblades for twenty bucks at Venice Beach. Skating along the promenade, watching all the performers, quickly becomes my favorite pastime.

California is beautiful, but the social scene is unlike the easygoing vibes I'm used to. People look cool but often seem like they're trying too hard. Parties are full of snobs who measure your worth by your zip code and brand of sunglasses.

Exploring Hollywood alone while Felix works is eye-opening. I meet people who seem completely disconnected from reality—like the aspiring actress at a coffee shop who won't give me her real name because she's "protecting her brand," or the guy at a Venice Beach party who introduces himself as a "pre-successful screenwriter" and spends twenty minutes explaining why his script about talking dolphins will revolutionize cinema. At another gathering, a woman refuses to sit on the couch because the lighting "isn't flattering for photos" and proceeds to spend the entire evening positioning herself near windows.

Everyone seems to be an actor waiting to be discovered, treating every conversation like an audition and every interaction like a networking opportunity. Even ordering coffee becomes a performance: People speak loudly enough for surrounding tables to hear about their "meeting with producers" and their "callback for a major studio film." It's exhausting being around people who are always trying to be something, and never just themselves.

Two weeks fly by. Intrigued by California, I decide to linger a little longer. Flights to Florida are still scarce after 9/11, and though I'm eager to reunite with my cousin Andi, there's no real rush.

My visit to San Diego, where Felix's family lives, instantly captures my heart. With its sun-soaked vibe, miles of postcard-worthy coastline, and inviting beaches, the city feels like paradise. A boat trip to see migrating whales—massive, graceful creatures gliding through deep blue waters—leaves me in awe. The warmth and charm of San Diego, from the energetic waterfront to the historic, colorful streets of Old Town, makes me feel completely at peace.

Felix even offers me a room in his place indefinitely, which tempts me to stay in Los Angeles. But my savings are dwindling fast, and California's cost of living is astronomical—especially after Thailand, where daily expenses are minimal. If I were still traveling through Asia, I could stretch my savings for half a year. Here, I may only have enough for one more month.

Should I stay or should I go? California has grown on me, pulling me into a life I never imagined. Living in America was never part of my dreams, but now that I'm here, I can't help but fall in love with the lifestyle. It's a place like no other, and I see why they call it the land of opportunity.

Once again, I decide to leave the decision in the hands of destiny: If I get a job at the first dive center, I'll stay. If not, it's off to Florida.

The first listing in the Yellow Pages is Aqua Adventures, but I prefer eye-to-eye conversations, so rather than call, I decide to show up and check out the place in person. Pulling up to the dive center in Burbank, I'm not impressed. The shop looks old-school, with pegboards instead of computers—like a dusty garage sale rather than a professional dive center. The owner, Greg Tash, is old-school too—bearded and macho, the stereotype of a grizzled boat captain.

"Girls," he declares, "cannot dive."

My extensive experience in ice, cave, and wreck diving, including two thousand dives in Hungary, Malta, England, Thailand, and Australia, says differently. Greg starts to show interest in hiring me. "But since September 11," he confesses, "everything has slowed down. Nobody's spending money. Nobody's diving."

It sounds like a dead end.

A few days later, just as I'm about to book my flight to Florida, the phone rings. "When can you start?" Greg asks.

In that moment, everything changes.

But even as I accept the job, a nagging voice in my head whispers: *Is this just another stop on an endless journey? Am I incapable of being satisfied anywhere? What if the problem isn't* where *I am, but* who *I am?*

The thought claws at me, threatening to drag me under, like being caught in a rip current with no way to swim free.

* * *

After nearly two years of diving daily in Thailand with a constantly rotating crowd of clients, the slower pace of California diving feels refreshing. Most dives here are reserved for weekends, so I spend weekdays at the shop, renting out gear, doing repairs, selling equipment, and planning classes and upcoming trips. It's a mellow rhythm that balances the marvels of diving with the routine of preparation and planning.

Aqua Adventures feels like a clubhouse, where locals hang out and talk for hours. People come and go all day, and I persuade them to join my classes, sign up for upcoming trips, and browse through all the new gear they should buy. Greg starts introducing me as his "expert instructor."

Expert?

I want to correct him. I'm not even twenty-six years old and still adjusting to California's diving conditions. The old-timers hanging around the shop have forgotten more about these waters than I'll ever learn. Yet it's flattering that he thinks so highly of me and my abilities.

My one-month anniversary in the US has me reflecting on my life. I'm still uncertain about the direction I'm going—I tend to make decisions quickly and think about consequences later. A few weeks ago, I arrived in LA for an overnight stay. Now, unexpectedly, I'm building a life here.

My days have fallen into a routine: Have morning coffee on the patio with Felix, discussing interesting topics. Drive to work in his car, which he generously lets me use. Then spend my day at the dive shop teaching basic, advanced, and rescue scuba skills to locals—office workers looking for weekend adventures, college students earning their certifications, retirees finally pursuing dreams they'd put off for decades. I check equipment, organize gear, and guide people through their first underwater experiences.

After work, I change into running shoes and pound the pavement through our neighborhood, trying to shake off the restlessness that follows me everywhere these days. The evening runs become my salvation, a way to clear my head.

Thursday evenings bring a different kind of adventure: cooking classes with Laurah, an eclectic artist who came to me as a dive student and is becoming one of my closest friends. She's a Hollywood special effects genius with paint-stained fingers and an infectious laugh, who insists that cooking is both an art form and a weapon of seduction.

"The way to most guys' hearts is through their stomach," Laurah declares, teaching me to sauté garlic until it sings and explaining why presentation matters as much as flavor. We drink Chianti while chopping vegetables, and she regales me with stories from movie sets while showing me how to make bruschetta and ceviche from scratch. These Thursday sessions feel like the highlight of my week. I learn something new, laugh until my sides hurt, and temporarily forget that I'm still searching for my real path.

One evening, a strange thought pops into my head: *I'm too old to keep living this gypsy lifestyle but too young to settle down.* I feel stuck between two paths, like in the lyric from a sad song, something about *I'm too old to cry after breaking up but too young to worry about being alone.* I'm caught between the wisdom of my experiences and the naiveté of my longing for more.

Emotionally, it's a confusing place to be.

Meanwhile, Felix has fallen for me. He acts like my boyfriend, and the irony is, he could be—at least on paper. He's a talented composer with an incredible smile, charming in conversation, a gentleman who always plans thoughtful activities. We cook together, indulge in candlelit dinners, dance at LA nightclubs, and in-line skate along the beach in Venice. He's one of the nicest, funniest, and most caring people I've ever met, and he always wants to make me happy. We spend hours talking and laughing about everything under the sun. But there's no chemistry between us.

I don't want to hurt him—Felix is genuinely one of the kindest person on Earth. But I also can't force myself to feel something that isn't there.

I would love to be in love with him. It would make everything perfect, solve all my problems. But that's not how attraction works with me. He's neither athletic nor conventionally good-looking—despite that amazing smile—and I'm just not physically attracted to him. I knew Felix fancied me, yet I've always seen him as a friend. He's simply not my type.

Here's the uncomfortable truth: I haven't put a stop to his romantic gestures because it feels nice. When Felix buys me gifts, I accept them. When he invites me to elegant dinner parties, I enjoy them. When he lets me use his car and offers me a place to stay, I accept his generosity. I tell myself that I'm not leading him on—that we're just friends who enjoy each other's company. But deep down, I know better.

Am I using him? I don't want to admit it. The thought makes me sick with guilt ... but not sick enough to change my behavior. I need the housing. I need the car. I need the stability he provides while I figure out my life in California.

Yet I'm terrified by how easily I could slip into Felix's comfortable routine permanently: coffee on the patio, work, dinner, television, bed. Rinse and repeat. It's stable, predictable, safe—and soul-crushingly ordinary. That small, nagging voice in my head is whispering again: *What if I get too comfortable? What if I start to crave this normalcy? What if I become one of those people who talks about travel but never goes anywhere?*

* * *

Things start to crack open when I meet Carlos, a Colombian guy who walks into the dive shop one day. Nothing serious develops between us, but I'm drawn to his energy and his feisty group of friends. We start spending time together at barbecues that stretch late into the night, filled with laughter, music, and passionate salsa dancing that makes me feel alive.

Felix notices the change immediately. At first, he tries to be understanding, even supportive, but I can see the hurt creeping into his eyes every time I mention Carlos or come home late from another gathering. The tension in our shared space becomes palpable.

One evening, as I'm getting ready to leave for yet another barbecue, Felix confronts me. "I don't understand what's happening," he says, his voice strained. "I thought we had something special. I've given you everything—a place to live, my car, my time, my heart. And now you're running off with some guy you barely know."

His pain cuts through me like a knife. I want to explain that Carlos isn't the issue—that this isn't about choosing someone else over him. It's about the suffocating feeling that I'm living a life that isn't mine, playing a role I never auditioned for.

But how do you tell someone who's been nothing but generous and kind that their love feels like a cage? How do you explain that their devotion makes you feel guilty rather than grateful?

"Felix, you're an amazing person," I start, but the words sound hollow even to me. "You deserve someone who can love you the way you deserve to be loved."

"I don't want someone else," he replies, desperation creeping into his voice. "I thought we had a magical bond building. What's wrong with wanting to build a life together?"

Everything and nothing, I think.

But I can't say that, so instead I just stand there feeling like the worst person in the world and hug him tightly. The guilt and self-loathing are eating me alive. While trying to figure out who I am and what I want, I've hurt someone who is genuinely good. I pride myself on being honest, on living authentically, but I've been dishonest in the worst possible way: letting Felix hope when I knew there was no future for us. I'm in danger of becoming the kind of person I never wanted to be.

I keep telling myself that it wasn't intentional—that I never meant to take advantage of his feelings. But intentions don't matter when you've broken someone's heart. I've been living in his space, driving his Porsche, accepting his generosity, all while knowing I could never give him what he really wanted. Felix deserves better than someone who sees his love as a burden rather than a gift.

It's time to find my own place. I'm going to stay in California for a while, and moving out feels like the only way to curtail the damage.

The following week, I start paying rent to Felix, pass my driving test, and buy a car for five hundred dollars at an auction. It's not much, but it's mine.

I tell myself the car is essential—after all, I need it to get to work. Without a car in LA, where public transportation isn't all that reliable, you're constantly limited, and I don't want to feel stuck. But soon, the reality sets in: I'm not just buying a car—I'm tying myself down, both emotionally and financially.

The payments, the maintenance, the continual thought of what might go wrong—all of this is starting to feel like deadweight rather than the freedom I imagined. This new life, while full of exciting potential, is also wrapped in commitments that tether me to a reality I didn't expect. That small voice inside me is saying even more terrifying things now: *What if I keep running from stability and nothing amazing happens? What if I only discover that adventure gets lonelier with each passing year?*

My little red sports car is just the first sign: I'm starting to sacrifice flexibility for stability.

* * *

As I continue to explore all California has to offer, Muay Thai is a mainstay—a tie to the vagabond life I was living in Phi Phi, and a source of strength and empowerment amid a confusion of possibilities. Training with Paulo Tocha, a world-renowned master, actor and stunt double—best known for his performance in *Bloodsport*, *In Hell* and *Strange Days*—whose presence in the ring commands respect, is an intense journey—a fusion of discipline, technique, and mental fortitude. Each session challenges my body and mind, pushing me beyond any needless limits I may set. Through Muay Thai, I forge bonds with fellow enthusiasts—individuals driven by a shared pursuit of physical and mental discipline.

At the same time, I'm surprised to find myself embracing my inner Californian—and my more feminine side. I'm driving around in a cute little red sports car and filling my closet with a growing collection of stylish clothes and shoes. Then I decide to do something I never imagined I'd enjoy: go for a manicure and pedicure. What could be more *California girl* than that? It's funny, but I'm starting to appreciate these girly touches.

But sitting in the nail salon, watching the technician paint my fingernails orange, doubt surges through me. I'm the girl who lived in flip-flops for two years, who owned three shirts total, who could pack her entire life into two duffel bags! Now I have a closet full of clothes, a drawer full of face creams and hair goo, and perfectly polished nails.

This isn't me! I panic. *When did I become the kind of person who spends time in a nail salon? When did I start caring about matching my shoes to my outfit?*

The women to either side of me hold out their hands lazily for shades of beige and pearlescent lacquer, chirping about their husbands, their kids, their weekend plans at Costco. They seem happy, content. But listening to their chatter feels like glimpsing my future, and terrifying thoughts pester me.

What if this is what growing up means?

What if all my talk about adventure and freedom is just delayed adolescence?

What if the thing I've been running from—ordinary life—is actually what I want?

Perhaps this is an awakening—a realization that I'm ready to stop running. Perhaps it's time to fully accept and celebrate this new side of myself and open up to deeper connections with others.

I delve further into Buddhism, my practice evolving since those temple visits in Thailand. California doesn't have all those ornate temples filled with chanting monks, but I've discovered something equally powerful here: books. I spend evenings on the patio with Thich Nhat Hanh's teachings spread across my lap, his words about mindfulness hitting differently in this new context.

"The present moment is the only moment available to us, and it is the door to all moments," he writes, and I finally understand what he means. Instead of constantly planning my next escape, my next adventure, I'm learning to be where I am—to be present in the moment, not just physically but mentally.

The Dalai Lama's writings are equally transformative for me. I read one touching quote over and over: "If you do not love yourself, you can not love others." I think about all the ways I've sought validation through achievements, certifications, and constant motion toward the next big thing. Sitting in the California sunshine, surrounded by books rather than incense, I'm discovering that spiritual practice doesn't require a specific location or ritual—it requires honest reflection and the courage to sit with uncomfortable truths.

With time, experience, and the wisdom of masters, I'm learning that vulnerability is not only natural but an essential part of the human experience. I understand more about the need for inner bliss and peace. True fulfillment, I'm discovering, can't be found at any specific point on the globe. Joy, growth, awareness, satisfaction—these things start from within.

I eagerly absorb this new knowledge and perspective, sensing an alternative path from the wanderlust of my past.

But am I evolving? I ask. *Or am I losing myself?*

* * *

In spite of inner turbulence and introspection, my dating life settles into a casual rhythm, a pattern of carefree encounters that rarely build into anything serious. There's a certain freedom to drifting without clear direction, but also a lingering feeling that maybe, just maybe, something more meaningful could be out there waiting for me.

In the meantime, I find real comfort and joy in evenings spent at close friends' homes. We gather in cozy spaces, where familiar laughter echoes through the room and shared stories layer over each other, weaving a tapestry of connection and belonging. Many of my friends are part of the AA community, embracing lives free from drugs and alcohol. California seems to attract folks who have chosen the path of sober living after a troubled childhood—people who stopped taking drugs and drinking at age fourteen or fifteen, an unusual scenario compared with my experience. But their self-awareness is powerful, and these gatherings feel like a grounding force, a reminder of the beauty in friendships that are steady and true, even when other parts of life remain in flux.

Working at Aqua Adventures turns out to be a great fit, and I've been lucky to secure authorization to work in the US. I love my job, especially after Greg lets me redesign the shop. After getting rid of the dusty pegboards cluttered with faded equipment catalogs and doing some serious cleaning—scrubbing salt residue from display cases, organizing rows of colorful fins by size, arranging masks and regulators so they catch the light—it feels like a cool hangout for local divers. I add comfortable seating where people can gear up without crouching on the floor, install better lighting that makes the wetsuits look sleek instead of dingy, and create a bulletin board for dive trip photos and local underwater sightings. The back corner becomes a proper coffee station where divers can hang out and swap stories. I arrange the certification materials into an actual learning area instead of a chaotic pile. Now people linger after buying gear and finishing their class, sharing stories about weekend dives and planning their next underwater adventures.

Burbank is filled with lighting technicians, grips, and other people working in the movie business. Located near NBC, Disney, Nickelodeon, and other major studios, we're always busy with stunt coordinators, directors, and actors coming in for gear or scuba training. Greg's stories about the business are intriguing, and each time he mentions working with director James Cameron on *Titanic* and *The Abyss*, or filming *Pirates of the Caribbean* in Mexico with actor Johnny Depp, it feeds my dreams about living that kind of life.

Several months have passed, and I relish the camaraderie with regulars who frequent the shop and sign up to join our boat charters. There's something special about diving with the same group, trip after trip—a shared understanding that deepens with every dive. We get our gear ready together, carpool to the boat, swap stories, and build the types of bonds that I've been missing ever since leaving island life behind. Anecdotes, banter, and revelations slowly morph into friendships.

Eileen, with her unshakable positivity, becomes one of my closest girlfriends in California. She's a self-made woman of fierce strength and determination, who put herself through nursing school while raising her son alone. I admire her deeply, and we bond over shared experiences and an understanding of hard work and dedication.

Eileen introduces me to her friend Susy, a veterinarian and passionate dive enthusiast who spends all her free time underwater, even volunteering at the Long Beach Aquarium. Susy is someone who says yes to every dive trip, and I can always persuade her to take another specialty class with me. She is super easygoing and loves diving as much as I do.

Uncle Pete and Steve Sr., the biggest troublemakers around, quickly become like family to me, the older male role models I never had while growing up—always pushing me to be my best while keeping things fun and lighthearted. Most afternoons find them at the shop, turning work into celebration thanks to their mischievous nature and that timeless spark in their eyes. Then there's Earl, a former bodyguard and man of few words but a comforting presence, and Franky Five-Knives, an avid collector who dives with the eponymous knives strapped to his body. These guys always have my back, no questions asked, guiding me through the challenges of managing daily life with a foundation of respect and care that I didn't realize I needed.

Two couples—Eo and her husband, Paul, along with Lisa and her partner, James—become regulars on our dive trips and are always the life of the party, always up for adventure. Lisa and Eo share my devotion to living boldly and freely. Soon we are planning a girls-only Miss Scuba trip to San Diego, where we mix surfing and scuba diving with visits to art galleries and evenings spent around a campfire, drinks in hand, These new experiences deepen my connection with women who inspire me to live fully and unapologetically.

When Josh walks into Aqua Adventures for an open water class, we click instantly, and soon we become inseparable friends. He gets hooked on diving, enrolling in every course I teach and eventually earning his Divemaster rating. Josh is a walking storybook, from his tattooed skin to his charismatic tales and eternal sense of adventure, who introduces me to more incredible, hilarious friends than I can count.

After hearing so many of my stories from living in Thailand, one day Josh offers a pact that I cannot refuse: *You get me a job in Thailand, and while I'm gone, you can sublease my house in Hollywood.* A few weeks later, Josh is heading to Koh Phi Phi while I am packing my bags and saying farewell to Felix. I thank him profusely for everything he has done for me, but we both know it's time for me to get my own place.

Everything feels different in California, including the ocean itself. In the luxurious, tropical waters off Thailand, a thin shorty wetsuit was more than enough, but these coastal waters are a different story. To stay warm here, even in August with the warmest water temperature at 70°F, we need a super-thick, cumbersome wetsuit. This adds both weight and bulk, making each dive feel more physically exhausting. But all that is forgotten as we embark on an exhilarating mini-expedition to the Channel Islands—a group of eight charming islands and diverse underwater seascapes off Southern California's coast.

Each of these islands is a paradise in its own right, from the rugged, untouched wilderness of San Miguel through the iconic Arch Rock of Anacapa to the bustling, sunlit shores of Santa Catalina. For this voyage, we've planned a three-day trip to the Northern Channel Islands with Truth

Aquatics, a liveaboard dive fleet. The incredible crew and our great group of divers meet on a Friday night in Santa Barbara, where our boat awaits us. Onboard, we claim our bunks, set up our gear, and settle in for the night, lulled to sleep by the gentle rocking of the harbor and the welcome drinks mixed by Uncle Steve and Pete.

At four a.m., while we're still in deep sleep, the boat quietly heads out into the open ocean. We wake up two hours later to the warm, welcoming smells of coffee and bacon wafting from the galley—a perfect start to the adventure ahead.

We anchor at a remote spot near San Miguel Island where no other boats are in sight. I've brought my handmade dolphin monofin, and during one dive, a curious seal swims over to me, mimicking my movements as we play among the rocks. It feels like something straight out of a Discovery Channel special. Our comical Simon Says interaction—I spin, the seal spins, then I flip, the seal flips—would have made for incredible footage, but of course no one is there to film it.

Even so, in that moment everything is perfect. The encounter is etched in my mind, creating that same notion I've had many times before: *I belong here.* I secretly wish the boat would break down so we could stay at this remote island and dive forever, living off the ocean.

The three days fly by, yet the experience feels like a full week of vacation abroad. The escape from Los Angeles to the quiet, vast beauty just offshore offers such a contrast to the sensory overload of city life. Trips like these remind me why I started traveling in the first place: because being near the ocean is all the serenity I need.

* * *

Several months later, an unexpected opportunity comes up: Greg asks me to attend a scuba equipment seminar in Las Vegas while he stays behind to run the shop. I'm finally on the move again, and it seems like the perfect chance to mix business with pleasure. The city's energy hits me like a rush. Everyone's here for the same reason: to play.

Gambling pulls me in immediately. It's all too easy to lose track of time when the thrill of blackjack and roulette consumes my day. After hours in the casinos, I hit my limit and decide to stroll along the iconic Strip before heading back to my hotel.

After a few minutes in the sticky Vegas heat, I bump into a guy with a Harley Davidson. He offers me a ride—no flirting, no weird vibes, just a friendly gesture. I've hitchhiked my entire life—across Europe, through Thailand and Australia, all over the world. Without thinking too much, I hop onto the bike.

We head out toward the desert, wind whipping my face as the city disappears. The desert is incredible, vast stretches of sand as far as the eye can see, and for a while, I'm too caught up in the moment to care that the city is receding behind us.

Suddenly, the reality of my situation hits me like a sledgehammer: I'm completely alone. Nobody knows where I am. I didn't tell anyone about taking a ride with a stranger. Greg thinks I'm at the seminar, and I won't be missed at Aqua Adventures for days. If something happens to me out here, I could vanish without a trace.

We drive deeper and deeper into the desert, miles from any civilization—nothing but endless sand and rock. This isn't a scenic detour—we've been driving for over half an hour in the wrong direction.

"Hey, where are we going?" I ask, fighting the urge to panic. "My hotel's in the other direction."

"We're making a quick detour to pick up my Corvette," he says, his tone different now. "It's way more comfortable."

Every alarm bell in my head is screaming now, but I force a smile. "I'm actually really enjoying the bike. No need to switch."

He doesn't reply, just keeps driving deeper into the vast nothing. My heart starts racing as I calculate how far we are from anything—at least thirty miles from Vegas, probably more. Even if I could somehow get away from him, how would I survive walking back through the desert at night?

We finally arrive at a rundown trailer in the middle of absolutely nowhere, and he casually invites me in for a drink. The predatory confidence in his voice makes my skin crawl.

"No, thanks, I really need to get back," I say, keeping my voice steady. "My friends saw me leave with you, and they'll be waiting. We have dinner plans." It's a lie, but it's all I have.

He parks the bike anyway and gets off, expecting me to follow. When I don't move, his demeanor shifts completely. The friendly stranger is gone, replaced by someone much more menacing.

"Come on," he says, his voice hardening. "I brought you all the way out here. The least you can do is have a drink."

I slide off the bike but stay near it, my mind racing through escape scenarios. There are no neighbors, no other houses, no passing traffic. Just empty desert stretching in every direction.

"I'm not going inside," I say firmly, sitting down on the dusty ground beside the bike. "If you want to talk, we can talk out here."

The tension is thick enough to cut. He's clearly angry that I'm not playing along with whatever he had planned. We're locked in a risky standoff: He's trying to convince me to go inside. I'm refusing, making up increasingly elaborate lies about people who are expecting me back.

Finally, I stand up and start walking—just start walking into the desert, toward what I hope is the direction of the highway, even though I know it's probably a death sentence. The sun is starting to set, and soon it will be pitch black. But staying feels even more dangerous.

"Where the hell are you going?" he calls after me.

"I'm walking back to Vegas," I say without turning around. "Thanks for the ride."

I keep walking, my heart pounding so hard, I can hear it in my ears. The desert stretches endlessly ahead. I have no water, no food, no idea how far I am from civilization. Every step takes me further from any shelter, but also further from him.

After I've walked maybe half a mile, I hear the sound of an engine behind me. He's following me in his flashy sports car—apparently he did have the Corvette at the house after all.

"Get in," he says, pulling up beside me. "This is stupid. You'll die out here."

He's right, and we both know it. Getting in that car might be an even worse mistake, but I don't see much of a choice.

"Take me back to Vegas," I say. "Right now. No stops, no detours."

The ride back is the longest thirty minutes of my life. He's clearly furious, angry that I didn't go along with his plan, whatever it was. The uncomfortable silence is thick and heavy, and I keep my hand on the door handle the entire time, ready to jump out if he tries to take another detour.

When we reach the Strip at last, I practically leap from the car before he's fully stopped. I don't say thank you, don't look back, just walk quickly toward the bright lights and crowds of people.

Back in my hotel room, I'm shaking so hard, I can barely hold my phone. In third-world countries where everyone warned me to be careful, I never once felt truly afraid, even as a solo female traveler. Strange how it's here, in America, where I felt threatened.

I was lucky to escape unharmed. How easily it could have gone differently! If I hadn't trusted my instincts, if I'd gone inside that trailer, if I hadn't been willing to walk into the desert …

That experience changes something fundamental in me. I know I'll never hitchhike again or even pick up hitchhikers. The carefree trust I once had in strangers is gone, replaced by wariness that I hate but can't shake. The adventurous spirit that made life worth living feels damaged.

I wonder if some experiences change you so completely, you can never go back to who you were before.

CHAPTER 8

Coast to Coast: Looking for Enough

Watch your thoughts, they become words.
Watch your words, they become actions.
Watch your actions, they become habits.
Watch your habits, they become character.
Watch your character, for it becomes your destiny.
– Frank Outlaw

My journey to the United States started with a simple plan to visit my cousin in Florida, but nearly a year has flown by before I finally book a flight to the East Coast. I've come to love California and the life I'm building here. Returning from my trip to Las Vegas in one piece felt like returning home.

Before I travel to Florida, however, Aqua Adventures has planned another multi-day diving trip to the Channel Islands. I'm more than ready for a relaxing getaway with people I know and trust. Everything is aligning perfectly—the weather, the company, the dives. Things couldn't be better.

We kick off the voyage at San Miguel Island, Greg's favorite place to dive. In the northern islands, the fish are bigger and the water is colder—especially in November. But it's not as icy as I expected, or have I just toughened up? We dive for scallops, hauling in enough for the whole boat to devour. One guest whips up his infamous wasabi sauce, which is an unbeatable partner with fresh seafood as we cruise around the islands. The dives at our next stop at Santa Cruz Island are spectacular too, as are Uncle Pete's infamous coladas.

Evenings are spent playing dominoes and backgammon, swapping dive tales with Greg and the seasoned crew. Two music industry executives have joined us on this trip, one of whom—Hilaire Brosio—is luxuriating in a two-year paid sabbatical after a savvy contract in a record company buyout. Hilaire's vivacious personality—along with his lively stories about touring with AC/DC, Metallica, and Sarah McLachlan—immediately draws me in, and we become fast friends. We end the night with Cuban cigars on deck, gazing at stars and sharing stories, like a scene from a mafia movie.

On our final day, we approach the back side of Santa Catalina Island and anchor at my favorite dive site: Farnsworth Bank. My excitement builds as we gear up. This is an advanced dive, not for the faint of heart. For those ready to embrace the ocean's depths, it offers unparalleled beauty and serenity. The ocean is a stunning shade of blue, and I can't wait to plunge into its depths.

As we drop into the water, I feel the familiar rush of exhilaration. We swim down, and the surface world fades, replaced by the mesmerizing underwater realm.

At sixty feet, we reach the top of Farnsworth Bank, and the view through crystal-clear water is breathtaking. The pinnacle rises from the ocean floor, a towering monument of marine life. Delicate hydrocorals in hues of purple and pink stand out against the rocky backdrop, swaying with the currents, adding to the meditative rhythm of the dive. Each coral structure is unique, a testament to the ocean's artistry.

Descending further, I spot a playful seal darting through a school of fish, its sleek body cutting through the water, weaving in and out of the shimmering mass with grace and agility. The fish scatter and regroup, a synchronized dance of survival.

Below me, bat rays glide through the water like giant butterflies, their wings flapping gently, a picture of tranquility and elegance. Time has slowed down. I am at peace.

The deeper I go, the more I feel like I'm in a Jacques Cousteau documentary. As I reach one hundred feet, the dive becomes surreal. The colors are more muted, but the life is no less vibrant. Schools of fish move in unison, creating patterns that shift and change with each passing moment.

I pause for a second, taking it all in: the silence of the deep, broken only by the sound of my own breathing ... the marvelous weightlessness of being underwater ... the meditative beauty of the marine life surrounding me.

After a while, we begin our ascent. The light above grows brighter as we move toward the surface. Back on the boat, I breathe in the salty air, already anticipating my next dive at this incredible paradise.

Everyone needs a sanctuary, and the underwater realm is mine—my escape from the world above.

* * *

I arrive in Fort Myers just in time for Christmas, excited to reunite with Andi and her twin brother, Csaba, who is visiting from New Jersey—my only family in America. Stepping off the plane, I'm welcomed by the sultry Florida air. Andi's lively home, surrounded by mango trees, animals, and constant laughter, is a welcome respite and a reflection of her effervescent spirit.

Over the next few days together, we explore Florida's coastal beauty, such a sharp contrast to California's cool, kelp-filled waters. It's fascinating to see my cousin Andi in her element—as a natural healer, with her salt cave for treating skin and lung ailments—and to learn about Csaba's life as a successful pulmonologist. Both help people in their own intriguing ways, and this personal and professional ambition only adds to the comfort and harmony I feel in their presence.

Thanks to our free-spirited nature and a shared acceptance of life's imperfections, Andi and I share an unbreakable bond. Visiting her feels like a reunion— a reminder that family is always an anchor, no matter the distance, fastening me to a steady life. But it also highlights everything I've given up to live the vagabond life. Watching Andi and her husband with their established lives, their routines, their deep connections to their community, I realize what I've traded for my freedom.

They ask about my plans, my relationships, my future. I have no solid answers. I'm living as though I'm still twenty-two years old, as though commitment and stability are diseases to be avoided at all costs. But I'm almost twenty-seven and still asking: *When does the adventure have to end? When do I have to grow up? When do I have to go home and get a "real" job?*

It's easy to see that my older cousins are worried about me. They're too polite to say it directly, but I can see it in their eyes: concern that I'm running from something, that all this traveling is just avoidance disguised as adventure.

Maybe they're right. Maybe I've been running so long, I've forgotten what I'm running from. Or maybe I'm running from the very thing I want and need: a real life, with real connections and real roots.

I've always had "itchy feet syndrome"—settling into a new spot, making friends, even finding love, only to feel restless once everything is in place. I never seem to stay anywhere longer than six months at a time. Even in Thailand, after teaching diving through the high season, I took off to Australia for a backpacking trip for the low season, staying on the move for months until the next high season arrived.

Will I ever settle for good?

My time in Florida nears its end. Under the fireworks of a new year, my cousins and I toast to new beginnings and enduring connections alike. Soon, I'll return to the kelp forests, chilled waters, and rugged coastlines of California, but I'll carry with me a renewed sense of connection—along with treasured memories, fresh perspectives, and a heart full of gratitude.

* * *

As I learned in Koh Phi Phi, returning to an old haunt never quite recaptures the magic. It's been just over a year in California now, the longest stretch I have spent anywhere since I started globe-trotting. Restlessness will surely catch up with me soon.

Greg sees my dilemma and comes up with a solution, surprising me with a thoughtful proposal: He offers to financially support my dream of becoming a PADI Course Director, a goal I've discussed with him many times—and a commitment of about ten thousand dollars. It's a gesture of faith that means the world to me.

In the PADI system, a Course Director holds the most prestigious and elite position, representing the pinnacle of scuba instruction. As the highest-ranking professionals, Course Directors are entrusted with the crucial responsibility of shaping the next generation of diving instructors by holding Instructor Development Courses and certifying Divemasters and Assistant Instructors as Open Water Scuba Instructors. Their job is to uphold the highest standards of education, safety, and professionalism in the diving industry.

More than prestige, though, the Course Director level opens doors that remain closed to other instructors. Course Directors can work anywhere in the world, commanding premium rates for their expertise. They're invited to lead exclusive dive expeditions to remote locations—places like the Red Sea, the Maldives, and Indonesia's Raja Ampat—where wealthy clients pay top dollar for expert guidance. The certification also grants access to the lucrative world of instructor training programs, where a single weeklong course can generate more income than months of regular teaching.

Beyond the financial rewards, Course Directors become part of an elite network, connecting with dive operators, marine biologists, and un-derwater photographers who can smooth the way to opportunities I can't even imagine yet. This isn't just another certification—it's a passport to the kind of diving career I've dreamed about since I first saw Jacques Cousteau's documentaries as a kid in Hungary.

Becoming a Course Director is a remarkable achievement that requires exceptional skill and dedication, not to mention experience. Achieving this goal elevates divers to the top tier of the global diving community. Their influence and expertise set the tone for the entire PADI ecosystem, ensuring the quality of diving instruction worldwide.

Much time has passed since I'd bothered with incremental steps in this system, due to the cost associated with each ranking. Now the opportunity to go all the way had presented itself, thanks to Greg and Aqua Adventures. Why not just take the leap?

I spend the winter and spring ranking up the certifications—when I am not working in the shop—that are prerequisites to achieve my grandiose goal. When the water temperatures drop, our winter wetsuit just doesn't cut it anymore, so we switch to dry suits. The thicker gear takes some getting used to, but it's essential for diving comfortably in the cold Pacific currents coming from Alaska.

Summer arrives, and I am still consumed with diving and completing the various prerequisite Specialty Instructor courses, Master Instructor certification, and other certifications I need in order to be eligible for the CD program. For part of the application, I spend months developing business plans based on market research data I'm collecting. My constantly wandering spirit feels anchored—for now.

By the following September, I am ready to apply for the Course Director training course, but it's not just a matter of meeting a deadline and paying the course fee—I also need to be selected by PADI. The opportunity comes only once a year, and thousands of instructors apply from around the globe. Approximately 130 are accepted.

If chosen for the upcoming session, I would become the youngest female course director in the world and the first female CD from Hungary to enter the course. Mutti would be so proud! She already tells everyone about my achievements, ever since her visit to Thailand—sharing pictures and stories at every chance. After anxiously waiting for three months, the news finally arrives: I've been accepted.

I feel like I'm on top of the world.

But even in this moment of triumph, a cold, empty feeling creeps into my bones. When I call my mother to share my achievement, it's hard not to imagine her sitting alone in our big, empty house in Budapest. While I'm celebrating my success in California, she's taking the same bus to the same job she's had for twenty-odd years. She sacrificed everything for me and supported my diving dreams even when she thought they were impractical. Now that I finally have the success she wanted for me, I'm too far away for her to enjoy it.

What Mutti really wants is her family. What would really make her happy is her daughters, grandchildren, family dinners, someone to grow old with. Instead, she has postcards from exotic locations and second-hand stories she tells her friends about her daughter, the world traveler.

Some nights, I lie awake calculating: *If I stay in California for ten more years, will Mutti still be alive when I'm ready to come home?* The thought makes me sick with guilt—but not sick enough to book a one-way flight back to Hungary.

* * *

On the first day of the training course, we visit the headquarters and meet John Cronin, the co-founder of PADI. It's a great chance to network. My team includes people from New Zealand, Florida, Guadeloupe, St. Martin, and St. Thomas. Mary from Indonesia keeps everyone laughing with her youthful spirit, despite being my mom's age. I'm already planning to visit the Brazilian girls for Carnival season next February. Then there's CJ from San Diego and Ian from Phuket, both full of humor and easy laughter.

The two weeks of training—presentations, friendly competitions, homework, study groups, evening parties by the pool—feel like the most intense summer camp imaginable. Most of my fellow candidates are older, and some are surprisingly out of shape. Many are scuba shop owners, which likely helped them reach this level. Sitting among these seasoned professionals, I feel like an imposter—a child playing dress-up. These folks have been running successful dive operations for decades. They have gray hair, crow's feet from years of squinting into the sun, hands scarred from countless gear repairs.

Training feels like a Jacques Cousteau expedition with a corporate twist. In the pool, we perform rescue scenarios like underwater ballet—precise and graceful yet life-saving. In the classroom, we present topics ranging from dive theory to business management, each testing our knowledge and dedication. Evening study groups turn into brainstorming sessions where decades of collective diving wisdom gets shared freely.

The coursework is demanding—we're cramming years of business education into two weeks while maintaining the physical and technical standards expected of Course Directors. Some nights we're up until two a.m. helping each other prepare presentations, only to be in the pool by seven a.m. for rescue scenario practice.

But something magical happens as the days pass: Rather than competing against each other, we become a tribe. When I struggle with the business management presentations, CJ shares his spreadsheets and walks me through profit margins. When Mary fumbles with the technical rescue scenarios, Ian and I spend hours practicing in the pool with her until she nails every skill.

The practical exams are grueling, but we approach them as a team. During the underwater rescue scenarios, we push each other to be better and support our classmates when they falter. In the classroom presentations, we offer genuine feedback and encouragement, even shifting our schedules to accommodate those that go overtime.

The standards are high—higher than anything I've experienced in diving: Every skill must be demonstrated to perfection. Every presentation must meet professional standards. Every written exam requires a thorough understanding of dive theory and business practices. I doubt myself sometimes, wondering if I really belong here.

My fellow candidates refuse to let me sink into self-doubt. "You're here for a reason," CJ encourages me after a particularly challenging day. "PADI doesn't make mistakes with Course Director selections."

The Brazilian girls share their business experiences from running operations in remote locations. Mary teaches us about cultural differences in diving instruction across Southeast Asia. The Caribbean contingent shows us how to manage dive operations during hurricane season. Despite our different backgrounds, we're all dealing with the same challenge: proving we can uphold the highest standards of diving instruction.

The friendships formed over two intense weeks feel lifelong. As graduation day approaches, we plan a pool party to celebrate not just our individual achievements but the bonds we've forged. We promise to visit each other's operations, to refer students back and forth, to maintain this network of excellence we've built together. As the youngest candidate, I feel especially lucky. Some trainees have waited decades for this chance. I'm grateful to be part of this group. What's more, I'm inspired by their generosity in sharing their knowledge and experience.

By the final day—July 25, 2003—exhaustion has set in, but it's the good kind, the satisfaction that comes from being pushed to your limits and discovering you're stronger than you thought. I stand there on the sun-bleached deck of the dive boat, salt spray still clinging to my wetsuit, the Pacific Ocean stretching endlessly behind me. The smell of neoprene and diesel fuel mixes in my nostrils as the California sunshine warms my face. Around me, fellow candidates are laughing and embracing, their voices carrying across the water as they celebrate this achievement.

The sound of waves slapping against the hull provides a steady rhythm beneath the celebration, and I taste the lingering salt on my lips from our final underwater evaluation just minutes before. I am officially the youngest female PADI Course Director in the world and the first Hungarian woman to earn this title. It's a prestigious moment, the result of years of dedication—and two weeks of the most challenging, supportive, and transformative training of my life.

My hands are still jittery—from adrenaline, not nerves—as I hold my Course Director certificate, the paper surprisingly crisp and substantial in my hands. Its weight somehow represents all those early mornings, the countless hours underwater, the moments of doubt I pushed through. I should feel triumphant.

Yet instead of elation, cold dread settles in my stomach.

This was supposed to be the high point of my career, the moment that would prove I'd made it, that all the sacrifices were worth it. But now that I'm here, the achievement feels hollow, like someone scooped out all the meaning. Suddenly I realize there's a void somewhere inside me—and I'm not sure what will fill it.

Why isn't this enough? I wonder.

All around me, my fellow graduates celebrate with wide grins on their faces. They have lives to return to, people who care about their success. I have … what? A tiny, rented one-bedroom house—until Josh decides to come back from Thailand? A boss who invested in me for business reasons?

The terror hits me like a wave: *What if there is no "enough"?*

What if I keep chasing the next certification, the next adventure, the next achievement, only to discover that the restlessness inside me can never be satisfied?

What if I'm doomed to search perpetually for something that doesn't exist?

Everything in California is going perfectly—too perfectly. I have a job I love, friends who care about me, opportunities opening up everywhere. So why do I feel this gnawing anxiety in my chest? It's like I'm waiting for the other shoe to drop, expecting something to go wrong—maybe even hoping something will go wrong. Because if life can be this good and I still feel empty inside, what does that say about me?

Maybe I'm one of those people who is only happy when struggling—when there's a mountain to climb or an obstacle to overcome. Maybe I'm addicted to chaos. Maybe I don't know how to handle contentment.

These thoughts make my stomach drop, like I'm falling from a cliff with no parachute. But in that sickening moment when I realize there's nothing to catch me, one thought rises above them all.

I'm about to start living the dream I've envisioned ever since I was a child.

CHAPTER 9

Wanderlust: Achieving Elite Status

Life is a journey, not a destination.
– Anonymous

From diving with hundreds of hammerhead sharks at Cocos Island to watching the sunrise at Cambodia's famed Angkor Wat temple, my bucket list is coming to life. I've always been a natural salesperson, able to sell salt water to mermaids. Now, as a PADI Course Director, I host trips through Aqua Adventures, which brings in extra money for Greg and fun adventures for me. But soon I'm pitching wild ideas for incredible Miss Scuba dive tours as well, catering to wealthy female clients who are ready for anything.

My exotic destination picks resonate with would-be travelers, inspiring them to follow my lead to faraway places where these women would hesitate to venture on their own. When I host the Miss Scuba expeditions, I take time off from the dive shop—doing the extra work on my own and also keeping the profits.

Greg is surprisingly supportive of me doing a few trips each year on my own, as long as I keep his trips full too. Any client who isn't ready for an extreme adventure can be funneled into Aqua Adventures' more traditional offerings. Plus, I'm helping the shop make money, by bringing in new divers to take our certification courses and buy specialized equipment before they join my expeditions.

Is this the solution to my dilemma? Can I satisfy my wanderlust while also creating a solid foundation, a true home?

I have the privilege of working in a financially thriving niche that has opened doors to remote, fascinating parts of the world that I could never have afforded visiting on my own. Since I'm bringing a group with me, I get to go for free. Whether it's wreck diving, night diving, or deep diving, I teach classes during these trips and end up coming home with more money in my pocket than I left with.

Once I realize that diving is just one thing I have in common with all the people signing up for my trips, I expand the itineraries. Building Miss Scuba into a legitimate business is a gradual process that starts with late nights at my laptop after long days at Aqua Adventures. I begin by reaching out to women I've met through my website or traveling, creating email lists of divers from different regions, and researching destinations that offer more than just underwater experiences.

The real breakthrough comes when I start treating each trip like a curated experience rather than just a dive vacation. I spend hours researching local culture, connecting with guides who can show us hidden temples or local markets, finding photographers who can capture both underwater and cultural moments. I incorporate activities that the whole group will enjoy: yoga, cooking classes, wine tastings. Word of mouth becomes my best marketing tool: Women return from a Miss Scuba trip and immediately start recruiting friends for the next one.

Managing the logistics means early mornings spent answering emails before heading to the dive shop, coordinating with international operators over my lunch breaks, and planning itineraries in the evenings. The effort is exhausting, but exhilaration and satisfaction are my reward. I'm transforming something I dreamed up back in that cramped Malta apartment into a business that is changing women's lives—including my own.

Soon, I'm leading female-only and female-friendly (where husbands, boyfriends, and guy friends can join us too) Miss Scuba trips for groups of twenty to thirty clients, traveling to extraordinary spots like the Wakatobi archipelago in Indonesia and the jungles of Fiji. Our far-flung expeditions are packed with zip-lining, bicycle riding, spa treatments, white water rafting, you name it. And they sell out *fast*.

I travel to destinations that test both my skills as a guide and my forbearance as a human being. Tobago and Trinidad is one that breaks my heart in a million ways. What should have been resplendent underwater gardens are bone-white graveyards—coral reefs devastated by high water temperatures and bleaching. Fish populations have dwindled to a few hardy survivors darting among the skeletal coral remains. I have to explain to disappointed clients why we're swimming through a subaquatic cemetery instead of the tropical paradise they paid to see.

Environmental destruction breaks my heart, but managing spoiled, rude clients threatens to break my spirit.

"This isn't what I expected when I booked with Miss Scuba," one guest announces during our wine tasting in Tuscany, her voice carrying across the vineyard terrace. "I mean, for this price, I could have gone to the Maldives."

The sommelier pauses mid-pour. The other guests' faces fall. We're sitting in the middle of a pastel Tuscan masterpiece, surrounded by rolling hills covered in ancient vines, sipping wines crafted here for centuries, and Linda can only compare it to a beach resort.

Every morning becomes an exercise in group patience as we wait for the same guest to finish her extensive preparation ritual. Arriving for lunch one day at a charming coastal restaurant I've been excited to share with the guests, she asks loudly, "Are we really eating here? I saw much better places on TripAdvisor."

When we finally get underwater, the Mediterranean Sea itself becomes her next target. "This is nothing like the Red Sea," she complains during our surface interval, loud enough for the entire boat to hear. "And why are there so few fish?"

I want to explain about overfishing, about decades of environmental pressure on the Mediterranean, but I know it won't matter. Some people are just determined to be disappointed.

One toxic personality can poison even the most beautiful destination. Entitled complaints and negativity can infect an entire group: People stop sharing their excitement about the day's discoveries. Easy laughter becomes forced. That sense of community is broken, as guests roll their eyes or whisper among themselves. At times, I spend more time managing one guest's dogged dissatisfaction than actually guiding the trip.

Not every trip is a disaster, of course. The majority of them are transformative experiences that leave clients planning their next adventure before they've even returned home. And they're proving that I've finally cracked the code: I can be a perpetual wanderer and a successful entrepreneur at the same time. My restless spirit isn't a liability anymore. It's my greatest business asset.

On a muck diving expedition to the Philippines and Sulawesi, we spend hours rummaging through what most people would consider underwater garbage dumps—black sandy sea bottoms littered with human debris. It's a completely different kind of diving that requires patience and a trained eye, and my clients initially wrinkle their noses at diving in aquatic junkyards. But this ecosystem harbors a multitude of tiny, bizarre creatures—the ocean's most extraordinary macro life. Their skepticism turns to wonder when we discover the payoff hiding among the muck: frogfish, electric clam, ornate ghost pipefish, and a host of other creatures so alien, they seem straight out of a science fiction movie.

Our Hawaii trip delivers equal parts enchantment and challenge as we take clients night diving with manta rays off the Kona coast of the Big Island. The darkness can be disorienting, and coordinating the dive with nervous, first-time clients requires constant vigilance. The mantas feed with their mouths wide open, coming so close that you can see their individual gill slits, and in the excitement of seeing these magnificent creatures, people sometimes forget basic safety protocols. But there's something mystical about floating in the dark Pacific, surrounded by lights to attract plankton, watching these graceful giants with twenty-foot wingspans glide through the water like undersea ballet dancers.

In Croatia, I sail with a group of ten fun-loving guys who treat the entire Adriatic like their personal playground. Investment bankers and tech executives by trade, they become overgrown fraternity brothers once they step onto a sailboat with unlimited Croatian wine. We dive ancient Roman ruins, explore hidden coves accessible only by boat, and spend evenings in waterfront tavernas, arguing about everything from soccer to internet security. Their boundless energy and competitive banter keep everyone laughing, though managing ten alpha personalities contained on a floating vessel—especially when it comes to who gets which cabin, and whose turn it is to help with sailing duties—requires the diplomatic skills of a UN negotiator.

Every trip, every dive, introduces new knowledge, new ideas, new lessons that can only be found when you treat life as a journey. I'm a wandering soul, living exactly how I pictured it. But saving a whale in Costa Rica is the coolest thing I've ever seen.

From the boat's deck, we hear it: a gut-wrenching cry that pierces the calm of the ocean and fills the air with desperation. My pulse quickens as I scan the water, searching for the source: a distressed whale calf. When I catch sight of it, my stomach drops—a young humpback, thrashing helplessly, tangled in a web of ropes and fishing lines.

The mother circles nearby, her massive body moving with anxious energy, unable to help her baby. My mind races, quivering between the thrill of this close encounter and the urgency of the lives at stake. This is no longer a dive holiday; it's a rescue mission.

Knowing mother whales can be protective, our captain positions the boat very carefully. I jump in with the divemaster to help cut the net, but all I see are a bunch of divers floating around with cameras. The whales are gone.

Disappointed, we climb back onto the boat. "Nobody else goes in the water but my two guys," the captain demands, circling back to relocate the whales.

This time, one of the Costa Rican crew jumps off the boat, dive knife clenched between his teeth, and straddles the baby whale. Holding its dorsal fin, he begins cutting through the enormous nylon fishing net, inch by inch. The other diver catches its tail and works his way up toward the head, cutting the remaining mesh.

Sensing freedom near, the calf takes off like a rodeo bronco. As more of the buoyant net is cut away, the young whale can finally dive under, dragging the divers down too.

The mother whale moves closer, her body tensing. She could crush the divers in an instant by simply rolling on the calf. But after a long, investigating look, she seems to realize they're helping her baby. She stays right alongside them until the net is fully cut away.

With a final breath and a huge theatrical splash with their flukes—what I'll always remember as a thank-you—the whale family descends into the deep.

Passing boats greet our crew with applause, celebrating their bravery. Everyone aboard our boat feels the significance of what just occurred. Swimming with whales is dangerous and illegal, but the rescue was necessary.

I'm thirty years old now, and after traveling the world and diving in countless locations, ticking off one sensational destination after another, I start to think I've seen it all—until I swim with great white sharks.

* * *

Greg has led the Aqua Adventures trip to Guadalupe Island, off the western coast of Mexico, for six years in a row. Although he loves the opportunity to dive among these sharks, he reluctantly hands the reins to me for a new experience this time around.

The journey to the boat is an endeavor in itself. We meet at the dive shop at three a.m., take the train to San Diego, and embark on a bus that drives us further south to cross the border into Mexico, where we board our vessel for the next week, in the Ensenada harbor. The voyage to Guadalupe takes twenty hours, and by the time we arrive the next morning, we are eager to get into the water.

As we suit up, the anticipation is electric. The crew erects the shark cages on the stern of the vessel while we're briefed on safety procedures and the hookah breathing apparatus—a surface-supplied system that delivers air through long hoses from compressors on the boat, eliminating the need for scuba tanks. The cages—two just below the surface and one submersible—will offer front-row seats to the underwater world.

Everything is blue as far as the eye can see. We are in the middle of the open ocean, with deep water columns below us. Distant shadows are all that alerts us to the presence of these large creatures at first, but as the day progresses, the sharks grow bolder, circling closer, drawn by the scent of chum in the water.

The submersible cage takes us deeper into their realm. As soon as AC/DC blasts through the submerged sound system, the sharks are drawn to the vibrations. The divemaster opens the submersible cage door, allowing the most daring of us to step onto the top. Adrenaline pumping, I am standing just feet away from great white sharks—a feeling both surreal and pure.

Sharks love rock music, I think. It's wild, unbelievable.

The second day brings the unexpected appearance of a scalloped hammerhead shark, a rare and thrilling find in these waters. The weather turns rough on the final day, so instead of diving, we tour the island, spotting sea lions, elephant seals, and tons of birds. Leaving Guadalupe, we all vow to return. Now I get why Greg can never seem to get enough of this rush.

This experience redefines my understanding of sharks. Far from the fearsome reputation they carry, these creatures are mind-blowing and powerful yet uninterested in harming us. Feeling inspired, I organize a Miss Scuba trip to Grand Bahama with twelve women of all ages—some I've spent time diving with before, others I'm meeting for the first time—to dive with "shark mom" Cristina Zenato.

After packing my bag at the last minute as always, I arrive at the airport only to have my flip-flop break. Luckily, a TSA agent helps me patch it up with duct tape, and we all giggle at the absurdity. Traveling with my friends from LA—Eo and Lisa, as well as Maryann and Julia—feels like a carefree school trip.

Over the past few years, the ratio of men to women in my classes has shrunk to about three to one—an increase that shows up at every level, which is gratifying. Some of those women become not just clients but close friends: Maryann, a Filipino friend of Eo's, juggles two jobs yet still finds time to seek exhilarating experiences and live to the fullest. Having raised her daughter as a single young mom, she's now diving headfirst into the adventures she had put on hold, making up for lost time and savoring every moment. Julia, an unexpected addition to our adventurous girls' gang, is an adult film star who brings out our wild side, encouraging us to let go, be bold, and revel in the joy of gallivanting without a care in the world. Her energy is infectious—with her, there's never a dull moment—yet she has a big heart and a surprising soft side, especially as someone who rescues dogs with the same care and devotion she shows in everything she does.

After a layover in Miami, and a taxi driver who welcomes us to Grand Bahama with stories about the island, our group of twelve women finally unite over mojitos in Freeport, setting the stage for what should be a memorable trip—a perfect blend of diving, yoga, and camaraderie.

Sunrise rooftop yoga, facing the ocean and surrounded by flickering candles, is a peaceful way to greet each day. Once we've nourished our bodies with a fresh breakfast and coffee, we head to the dock, and the relaxed atmosphere shifts to a buzz of excitement.

Meeting Cristina Zenato, I am starstruck. The other women and I giggle while donning our heavy stainless steel chainmail suits in preparation for Cristina's shark feeder course. She has spent decades building trust with Caribbean reef sharks, removing fishing hooks from their mouths and even inducing tonic immobility: calming the sharks into a trancelike state, a technique she uses to educate people about their misunderstood nature. Cristina is truly a legend, and now we are diving alongside her.

The sharks glide gracefully around us, their primal energy palpable and invigorating. I feel a healthy, intense mix of fear and love for these majestic predators. Surrounded by sharks, the adrenaline I felt in Guadalupe returns, every bit as surreal—especially when I take my turn holding the feeding tube.

All shark eyes focus on me. I pull out the small fish from my tube, positioning it where Cristina directs me, and suddenly I am hand-feeding an apex predator. My mind is blank. I am in the flow.

Later, we explore the underwater caverns of Ben's Cavern and Mermaid's Layers, descending into a labyrinth of stalactites and ancient fossils. Cristina's passion for cave diving adds to the rush we feel as she shares stories of rare creatures and hidden chambers.

The next day brings another spellbinding encounter as we scuba dive with dolphins. These intelligent creatures seem to sense our excitement, responding with graceful movements and playful antics. Swimming with a dolphin alongside me is a singular experience—an incredible connection with nature.

After washing off the salt and sand, we gather each evening at the Dive Bar, refreshed, dressed up, and ready to unwind. Stories and laughter flow as freely as the drinks. One memorable night, we cross paths with Miss Grand Bahama herself, bonding over shared tales of adventure and discovery. These nights aren't just about having fun—they solidify our relationships, building lasting memories that keep our team strong both above and below the waves.

On the flight home, it's impossible not to reflect on the incredible experiences and friendships formed on this trip and all the others stretching back through the months and years. Hosting these trips isn't just about diving; it's about creating moments that resonate with others, deepening our connection to the sea and to each other.

Over ten years as a scuba instructor—ever since my first dives as an instructor in Malta—I've witnessed firsthand how diving transforms lives. More than just mastering a skill, diving is about experiencing a profound shift in perspective. Nothing is more magical than that moment when someone takes their first breath underwater—when they discover a new world where weightlessness and tranquility reign. That moment changes everything.

It changes lives.

I change lives.

People are never the same after that very first dive, and yet every dive reveals wonders both large and small. Throughout years of diving, I have explored countless inner depths, illuminated layer upon layer of awareness, and developed essential ties to the world around me. Where does it all lead? I don't know yet.

But I intend to find out.

* * *

Back home in Los Angeles, I've just finished unpacking my bags when my sister arrives from Hungary. She plans to stay for a month, eager to shake off the weight of a recent breakup and escape the harsh Hungarian winter. Over coffee, she excitedly pulls out a travel magazine featuring a thrill-seeking day in California: sunrise surfing at Redondo Beach, scuba diving, skiing at Big Bear, and biking scenic trails.

"Let's do it all—in one day!" Csilla exclaims, her eyes lighting up.

It's an ambitious goal, but we make it happen. And we don't stop after that adventure-packed day. By the time we reach San Francisco on an impromptu Pacific Coast road trip, driving north through ancient redwoods to our right and dramatic coastal cliffs to our left, we are rediscovering that unbreakable bond of sisterhood. This incredible scenery seems to trigger epic conversations. Time and distance mean nothing. Both the years apart and the activities we're tackling together now bring us ever closer.

But sisters also have a knack for getting under each other's skin. As our trip draws to a close, Csilla nonchalantly says, "You've become dumb in America."

I am proud of the life I've built, yet her words sting.

For Csilla, who has earned multiple degrees and successfully climbed the career ladder right in her own backyard, it must be hard to understand why I chose such a different path—one filled with worldwide wandering guided by risk-taking and self-discovery. Her accomplishments are even more impressive given the truth we learned many years after childhood: Csilla has dyslexia.

The diagnosis arrived like a key, unlocking the mystery of her frustration and my misplaced impatience. If we had known sooner, I would have been more understanding. But in those days, we did not have special education teachers; no one understood that some kids learned differently and needed to be taught differently.

Csilla overcame that disadvantage and achieved something extraordinary, but I've created something extraordinary too—on my own terms. I know this to be true. But her comment plants a seed of doubt nonetheless.

Determined to prove her wrong, as is customary for sisters, I set myself a challenge: to enhance my academic credentials in a way that will further my ambitions. I don't need another diploma collecting dust. I want practical skills that will enrich my life and career.

Already deep in the process of organizing travel groups, I begin by becoming a certified Travel Agent. I also enroll in a nearby community college, taking classes on my days off. I start with English as a Second Language to refine my language skills. But that's just the beginning.

My desire to continue learning persists, even gathering steam, and I sign up for courses in basic coding, web design, creative writing, and Photoshop—all skills I can use to elevate the Miss-Scuba.com website. Soon, I've added an online shop for apparel and jewelry.

Returning to the practice of jewelry-making feeds my creative soul just as it did back in Budapest years earlier. Crafting jewelry that portrays the essence of exploration and nature's beauty, shaped in silver and adorned with healing gemstones, releases an entrenched sense of purpose in me. Inspired by my love for the ocean, travel, and the spirit of adventure, each piece carries a story of adventure, resilience, and wanderlust. In many ways, designing jewelry feels like teaching diving: Just as I guide divers deliberately to discover the wonders beneath the ocean, I infuse each piece of jewelry I create with intention, hoping to inspire and empower the wearer.

My journey takes an unexpected turn a year or so later, when I discover a passion for telling stories through captured images. What begins as a series of classes in black-and-white photography culminates in a degree in photojournalism from Pasadena City College. This path is no longer about proving Csilla wrong. As I showcase articles written in class on my website and start submitting them to travel and dive magazines, I uncover a newfound devotion and sense of fulfillment.

Drawn toward a fresh challenge as ever, I decide to fuse this creative pursuit with my love of diving, reaching for the next step in this natural progression: underwater photography.

* * *

I have long been captivated by the radiance of life seething and swarming beneath the surface. Now I'm eager to document the ocean's beauty and diversity through the lens of a camera.

Photography, like diving, requires equal parts passion, patience, and presence. Each painstaking photo is a small piece of the day's experience preserved forever. That's what stirs my motivation—not posed or staged shots, but those that tell a story through each frame, depicting the essence of a moment, an emotion, a place. I'll wait as long as it takes to portray these candid moments of the raw, unfiltered beauty of everyday creatures in their element.

Guided by this passion, I plan a group trip to Papua New Guinea, a region famous for its rugged, breathtaking, sometimes hazardous terrain. Amid the country's untamed beauty, the resort we stay in is a beacon of serene safety, overlooking the tranquil ocean and dense jungle alike. The luxury hotel is secured by an electric fence— a stark reminder that beyond our manicured grounds, Papua New Guinea remains gloriously wild.

Saltwater crocodiles patrol the rivers, some growing over twenty feet long. Six-foot-tall cassowaries stalk through the jungle like feathered dinosaurs, their bone-crushing kicks capable of splitting a tree trunk. At night, we hear the haunting calls of wild boars and the splash of unknown creatures in the darkness beyond our safe haven. The fence also deters the local tribes who, while generally peaceful, sometimes venture close to the resort boundaries in search of food or supplies.

Waking up on our first morning there, surrounded by the alluring calls of unfamiliar birds and the soft rustle of jungle leaves, I reflect and recharge before heading out on the day's diving adventures. Everyone who signed up for the trip to PNG is drawn here by a shared passion for exploration. As the boat meanders through sheltered waters near the mainland and enters the open channel, and the calm, mirrored surface gives way to a playful dance of wind and waves, we find common ground in our love of the sea—a sense of unity that breaks down the usual barriers separating people.

We laugh as the boat bounces along, with the wind tugging at our clothes and the water occasionally spraying up to greet us. The group is in high spirits, almost childlike, as though stretching out before us is one big amusement park filled with unpredictable thrills. In many ways, that is true. And the capricious beauty of these diving expeditions unfurls not just in the underwater landscapes but in the diverse group of people who come together—often strangers who impulsively become friends.

But as we approach our first dive site, my dreams of photographing an array of remarkable marine life begin to dissolve. My new digital underwater camera, which took an entire year to save up for, sits useless in my hands.

Hundreds of dollars in underwater housing and months of anticipation seem suddenly pointless. I'm in one of the world's most pristine diving locations, thousands of miles from the nearest camera shop, and ready to witness and record the most astonishing assortment of marine life I've ever seen, but my camera's screen remains stubbornly black. I fiddle desperately with settings and batteries, trying not to think about every shockingly colorful nudibranch, every perfectly positioned reef fish, every instant of underwater magic that is passing by undocumented.

Why now? I agonize, as if the camera has deliberately chosen this moment to fail. But equipment failure soon becomes the least of my problems.

While the shared love of diving usually cultivates camaraderie, I sometimes notice subtle competition among a group's divers. This time, the culprits are a longtime regular at Aqua Adventures—reliable, enthusiastic, and genuinely passionate about underwater photography—and a seasoned travel writer who carries himself with the confidence of someone who has seen it all and isn't easily impressed. When the photography enthusiast mentions a rare fish he spotted, the travel writer one-ups him with a story from Raja Ampat, a haven of biodiversity. When I'm explaining the dive plan, the two men strive to position themselves closest to me, each trying to engage me in private conversation.

"That's not exactly how the current works here," the travel writer interrupts. "The real action is on the north side of that reef."

The photo enthusiast's jaw tightens. "Well, Szilvia and I were just discussing the photo opportunities on the south wall, weren't we?"

By day's end, my camera is working again, and despite a few technical setbacks, I manage to snap five or six solid shots—not as many as I'd hoped, but it feels like a victory. I'm experimenting with wide-angle photography, depicting divers framed against the coral with the thick jungle above casting shadows through the water. Simultaneously photographing above and below water with the surface creating a split in the middle of the frame is challenging work, and I am here to revel in and learn this new craft. But realizing my underwater photography dreams soon becomes secondary to managing the testosterone-fueled soap opera above the surface.

By day two, the alpha males are openly bickering over everything: who gets which spot on the boat, whose underwater photos are superior, who knows more about PNG marine life. The rest of the group walks on eggshells, afraid any comment will detonate another argument. Dive briefings become minefields, where I have to carefully balance attention between the two men. The breaking point comes when they demand to be on separate boats.

"I didn't pay this much money to listen to his amateur observations," the travel writer announces at dinner, his voice carrying across the restaurant.

The photo enthusiast's face flushes red, and I can see him calculating his response.

I'm in one of the world's most beautiful diving destinations, but instead of marveling at the marine life, I'm jury-rigging photo equipment and strategizing how to keep two clients from ruining everyone else's trip—like a camp counselor managing two children who refuse to share their toys. I strive to remain calm and empathetic on the outside while I quell the screams within.

Even in paradise, there are predicaments and impediments.

But the moment we jump in the water, everybody forgets the tension. Today's dive spot, an underwater cliff, reminds me of Malta's dramatic drop-offs, where soft blazes of orange coral cascade down the rockface like underwater waterfalls. Wall diving has so much to offer—a combination of beautiful coral gardens and the vast watery expanse that feels like you're standing on the edge of the planet. The abyss beckons, a deep blue mystery that stirs both fear and fascination.

Gazing into that endless blue, I am humbled. How small and insignificant we are in the grand scale of the ocean!

In my bungalow later that afternoon, while downloading and sorting the day's diving photos, I take a moment to simply exist in the present, letting the serenity of my surroundings seep into my bones. The ocean always has this effect on me—its vastness slows my thoughts, stilling the chaos of daily life.

It's something Thich Nhat Hanh writes about in his teachings on mindfulness: how nature can become our teacher, showing us how to simply *be* rather than constantly *do*. The rhythmic sound of waves mirrors the breathing meditation I've been practicing, each surge and retreat a reminder that life, like the tides, has its own natural rhythm, one that we can either fight against or flow with. Sitting here, watching the water catch the afternoon light, I understand what the Buddhist masters mean when they speak of finding peace in the present moment. The ocean doesn't worry about yesterday's storms or tomorrow's tides—it simply exists, fully and completely, in each wave.

For the first time in years, I feel myself doing the same. I am not thinking about the next dive, the next destination, or the next achievement, but simply allowing myself to enjoy being here, breathing slowly and deeply.

Outside my window, a single leaf falls from a tree toward the jungle floor, its descent slow and graceful, mirroring the pace of my own breath. Time seems to stretch, offering a glimpse of eternity in the simplest of things. My mind slows to match it, letting me just be in the moment and the flow.

Photography is like that: a tangible way to freeze time, to share moments of a story that speaks to the soul of the viewer, inviting them to experience the world through my eyes. Capturing a moment that would otherwise be lost—a fleeting expression, an unguarded interaction, a stunning natural scene that passes by in an instant—feels marvelous, both spontaneous and eternal. These are the moments I live for, the ones that tell the real story of my travels and experiences.

As the sun sets over the island, spreading a golden glow across the waves, I sit on the beach, letting the hum of the sea blend with the distant laughter of my friends. The last boat of the day disappears over the horizon, and I'm filled with gratitude for the time spent here. The island has become a part of us, woven into the fabric of our imperfect lives. Places like this always serve as a refuge for the soul.

Yet even in this serene setting, the pull of the unknown—the promise of the next challenge—calls to me from just beyond the limits of my perception. I gaze outward at the waves whispering their secrets and embrace the uncertainty of the future. Anticipation fuels my wanderlust.

Where will the journey lead me? I wonder. *What's next?*

CHAPTER 10

Hollywood: Breaking into the Business

Luck comes to those who stay busy while waiting.
– Szilvia Gogh

Eight middle-aged, somewhat out-of-shape police officers file into Aqua Adventures, immediately shifting their eyes to Greg, thinking he's their scuba guru. I can't help but grin, knowing they're in for a surprise. For the next ten days, *I* will be the one training the leaders of the Los Angeles Police Department's dive unit to become certified instructors.

Faced with some foreign female instructor half their size, the LAPD officers start out wearing the kind of condescending smiles that suggest they think this will be child's play. We dive headfirst into rigorous preparation for the instructor exam, and those smirks quickly fade as they realize the difficulty of what they've signed up for. The pool turns into a proving ground, where I take control and push each officer past his comfort zone.

Slowly but surely, I win the respect of these men as they grasp the intensity of the process and the skill it demands. The turning point comes when I demonstrate underwater skills they've never seen before: hovering motionless in perfect neutral buoyancy while solving complex equipment problems, executing flawless rescue scenarios while maintaining complete composure. When Officer Martinez struggles with mask clearing at depth, I don't coddle him—I make him repeat it until his technique is flawless.

"Underwater," I explain, "there's no room for 'good enough.'"

When Sergeant Thompson questions my safety protocols, I calmly walk him through the physics of nitrogen narcosis and decompression theory until he realizes I know more about underwater physiology than many doctors know about surface medicine.

By the third day, the jokes stop entirely. The officers start asking genuine questions instead of testing me. They seek my approval on their technique. When I critique their rescue scenarios, they listen intently instead of bristling. These are men accustomed to being the experts, the ones others look to for guidance and protection. But underwater, in my domain, they become students again—and they're professionals who recognize real expertise when they see it. The same qualities that make them good cops—attention to detail, respect for protocol, understanding that mistakes can be fatal—make them excellent diving students once they accept that I'm the authority here.

By graduation day, the shift is undeniable. The officers now look to me with deference. In a surprising gesture, they invite me on a high-stakes operational training dive at Castaic Lake, the largest state reservoir in Southern California. We join the SWAT team, local FBI agents, and members of the LA County Sheriff's Department there for a joint exercise, performing search and recovery drills among simulated explosions in zero-visibility waters.

With the LAPD training behind me, I fall back into the usual pattern: constantly chasing that next high, that next unforgettable moment. At age thirty-three now, I continually choose far-flung destinations and unusual dives, trying hard to test my skills and broaden my awareness. But the drive for something new has been burning within me like a fire, pushing me forward even when the odds seem stacked against me.

This desire is deep and unrelenting. Sometimes I think it's the reason my destiny brought me to California.

I want to break into the Hollywood stunt world.

* * *

"*Miami Vice*," Greg announced, hanging up his phone. It was a Tuesday morning at the dive shop, about three years ago, and his grin already told me that he'd landed something big. "They need a water safety team for a boat chase sequence—people falling overboard, fight scenes in the ocean. It's going to be epic."

My heart jumped. My interest in the mundane—organizing gear for that day's classes—was already flagging.

Managing a dive shop near Hollywood's major studios puts me in the orbit of stunt coordinators and performers preparing for underwater scenes. Every day is a chance to network and refine my expertise. I've built relationships with industry insiders like Wally Crowder, a legendary stunt coordinator, having trained his kids (and many other stuntmen's children) to scuba dive. For years, they have promised to help me get jobs, and I know these connections are the key to making my mark in the stunt world. But first I have to join the Screen Actors Guild.

Breaking into Hollywood is about more than just competence; you have to navigate the intricate world of the Screen Actors Guild. To work in films or TV, I need to be a SAG member. But to become eligible, I first need to work on a SAG production. It's the ultimate catch-22, a loop that only luck, connections, or extraordinary savvy can break.

Greg's offer for film work that Tuesday was exactly the kind of opportunity I'd been dreaming about. "When do we leave?" I asked eagerly.

The silence that followed felt like ice water down the back of my neck. Greg's grin faded. "Well, I'm taking the guys," he said, not meeting my eyes. "You know how it is—they've been with me for years."

Of course. It made sense. His long-time buddies had worked stunts and provided water safety at shoots with him for decades. I nodded, swallowing my disappointment.

"And since a couple of them aren't available," Greg continued, "I'm bringing Tim."

The words hit me like a slap. Tim was one of our regular clients, a guy I trained from zero experience to Rescue Diver over the previous year—a guy who still struggled with his buoyancy control and had maybe fifty logged dives to his name.

"Tim?" I couldn't keep the disbelief out of my voice.

"He's solid," Greg said defensively.

"Greg, I have way more experience than—"

"And he's available."

Available? While I—the one who ran his shop, who'd trained half his team, who had thousands of dives and years of water safety experience—stayed behind to teach pool classes and pick up the phone? I saw Greg as a father figure, and over the years we'd developed an incredibly close relationship—perhaps closer than he had with his own daughter. Why wouldn't he help me? I loved this man. But at times, I didn't like him at all.

"Someone needs to run things here, Szilvia." Greg's tone was final. "You're the only one I trust with the business."

He was already walking away to call the others, while I stood there surrounded by the scuba gear I maintained, following the schedule I organized, at the business I'd helped him take to the next level. And I realized something with crushing clarity: Being indispensable there meant being invisible everywhere else.

This was a cage with golden bars.

That was three years ago now, and as my hopes of breaking into the business have grown, so has my frustration. I have the ability, the experience, and the passion, yet I remain on the outside, looking in. Every film lights a spark of hope—and ignites the slow-burning fuse of frustration when I see the inspiring stunts, the daring moves, the performers living out my ambition. I know I'm capable, but the opportunity is always just out of reach.

Greg is passionate about stunt work, but the dive shop is his bread and butter. Relying on me to run the shop allows him to chase his own dreams and ambitions. By joining SAG, I would complicate that relationship. He could help me, but he doesn't want me to enter the movie world—it would throw a wrench into his own endeavors.

The pattern becomes clear over time. Every major Hollywood water job that comes through the shop becomes another reminder of the invisible ceiling above my head. The internal conflict is tough.

On one hand, I owe Greg gratitude for all the doors he's opened for me: He gave me a job and welcomed me into his family when I arrived in America with nothing other than two duffel bags, and has been my mentor ever since, teaching me much of what I know about diving.

On the other hand, I feel frustrated: Why should I hold back my dreams so Greg can keep living *his* ambition?

Torn between loyalty and the desire to move forward, I come to realize one thing for certain: My opportunity to work in the movie business will not be a result of Greg's help. Despite mixed feelings, I must carve my own path in the stunt world, even if it means facing a difficult choice.

When my break finally comes, I'll be unstoppable.

Beyond my exceptional diving background in ice diving, wreck diving, and precision buoyancy, my unique edge lies in being a petite woman— perfect for doubling female actors in underwater scenes. Standing at five foot four inches and weighing 120 pounds, I match the typical leading lady size; combined with my resemblance to certain stars, this could open new doors. It's a niche I'm perfectly suited for.

I feel confident that this rare combination of attributes will clear the way to joining SAG and stepping into the career I've been dreaming of. It's just a matter of time.

One day, the usual hum of activity at Aqua Adventures is interrupted by the arrival of a talent scout in search of girls who can swim in the ocean for an upcoming Axe commercial.

My life is about to change forever.

* * *

The commercial's plot is simple and absurdly entertaining: A skinny dude on the beach sprays himself with Axe deodorant, and suddenly he's the center of an inexplicable frenzy. Good-looking women, driven wild with desire, charge toward him from every direction—on land, through the forest, and from the middle of the ocean.

I'm cast as one of the blue bikini–clad women, representing the fearless group who swim through the icy waters of the Pacific. There's also the red bikini brigade, running on the beach in a scene reminiscent of Pamela Anderson's iconic *Baywatch* moments, and the green bikini group, charging through a dense forest. It's a spectacle of epic proportions, designed to showcase the supposed virility and power of Axe deodorant.

The job sounds straightforward enough—swimming in a bikini isn't exactly rocket science—but there's a catch: The water temperature at this time of year hovers around a brisk 50°F, and we'll be swimming in it all day long. This isn't just a quick dip. It's a grueling endurance test amidst the frosty, unforgiving Pacific Ocean.

The day starts early, with fifty women packed onto a chartered boat in blue bikinis, ready for the challenge ahead. As we prepare for the commercial shoot, the air buzzes with chatter and nervous energy. But as the hours drag on, the mood shifts.

Waiting between takes, the relentless rocking of the boat starts to take its toll. By noon, the bitter, uncaring ocean begins to claim the inevitable victims. Some are overcome by seasickness, others by exhaustion or the creeping chill of hypothermia. I watch girl after girl drop out, and fear creeps into my bones with the cold.

What if I can't last?

What if this is just another door slamming shut?

My hands are numb, and my lips are blue. But giving up now somehow means accepting that I'll never be more than the girl who runs someone else's dive shop.

By the end of the day, the winds have picked up and the swells have grown larger. The boat that once held fifty eager participants is nearly empty. Only two of us remain—a junior lifeguard and me. My lips are purple by now, and I can't feel my fingers, but something fierce burns inside me.

This is what I've been training for my entire life, I think. Not the commercial, but this refusal to quit even when everything in my body screams to stop.

The junior lifeguard and I prepare for what feels like the thousandth take, floating beside each other, shivering uncontrollably. Her teeth are chattering as soon as she opens her mouth to speak.

"So I'm definitely getting my SAG card from this?" she asks the stunt coordinator.

My heart stops. SAG card? From *this*?

"Absolutely," he replies. "What you two are doing out here—staying in fifty-degree water all day—no current SAG member could do this. It falls under the Taft-Hartley provision."

The words split the air like a lightning bolt. Taft-Hartley is the golden key that unlocks SAG membership when you perform something extraordinary, something no existing member can do. But I never imagined it could apply to me, to this moment.

"Excuse me," I interrupt, my voice barely steady. "Does that mean—could I—?"

The coordinator looks at me with something like respect. "You've been out here just as long as she has. Same conditions, same performance. Yeah, you'd qualify too."

Suddenly, the freezing water, the nausea, the bone-deep fatigue—none of it matters. The world narrows to this single, impossible truth: I'm about to get my SAG card.

Three years of running Greg's shop while watching others live my dream. Three years of training people who got opportunities I couldn't even audition for. Three years of being told I wasn't ready, wasn't connected enough, wasn't male enough for this industry. And now, floating in the wintry Pacific Ocean in a blue bikini, half-dead from cold but very much alive with possibility, I'm about to break through the wall that has kept me on the outside for so long.

"I need to make this official," the coordinator says, pulling out paperwork as we pull ourselves back onto the boat. "What's your full name?"

"Szilvia Gogh," I manage, wrapping my windbreaker around my shaking frame. Even saying it feels surreal—my name, about to be written on a document that changes everything.

As he scribbles notes, I think about my father, who died at age thirty-nine while chasing his dreams of building something better. I think about my mother, who sacrificed everything so I could pursue my own dreams despite her own grief and loss. I think about that fourteen-year-old girl standing over my father's grave, promising herself she'd never settle for a small life.

"Congratulations." The stunt coordinator hands me a form. "Welcome to SAG."

The paper is soggy from my wet hands, with the ink slightly smeared, but it might as well be made of gold. I stare at it through tears I didn't realize were falling—tears that have nothing to do with the cold and everything to do with the moment a dream stops being a dream and becomes reality.

* * *

Luck doesn't just strike out of the blue. Growing up, I was told many times by my parents to work hard and create my own opportunities, because they aren't likely to just pop up right in front of me. My mantra became: *Luck comes to those who stay busy while waiting.*

I believe we can create our own luck—and we need to. All it takes is thinking outside of the box, again and again: adaptability and perseverance. Add a sparkle of defiance for good measure. After all the hard work and frustration—all the staying busy while waiting, building my own future through a combination of willpower and willingness to try new things—I've finally made my own luck. This is it—the opportunity I've been waiting for. I've broken into SAG.

But it's really just the beginning.

In the world of stunt work, it's not easy to get regular jobs. Connections and trust are everything. I continue working at the dive shop, which has put me in the perfect position to build my reputation over the years.

I've encountered some of the biggest names in the industry, from stuntman Alex Krimm—known for his stunts in *Point Break, Black Panther: Wakanda Forever*, and *The Mandalorian*—whom I trained to become a scuba instructor, to Kris "Freeze" Jeffrey, a former Malibu lifeguard with credits on *Baywatch, Top Gun: Maverick, Jungle Cruise, Mission: Impossible* and various other water-based films. As I begin this new quest, their support is invaluable. Familiar faces from the dive shop help make my transition smooth.

Wally Crowder—best known for *Captain America: Civil War, Furious 7*, and the classic film *Grease*—is the first to hire me for water safety, on the TV show *Desperate Housewives*. Holding a position in water safety is like being a lifeguard—a tough task with huge responsibility. It's my job to foresee, prevent, and fix anything that could go wrong in or around the water.

As an experienced scuba instructor, I've dealt with anxious beginners and overconfident thrill-seekers, which gives me an edge in evaluating readiness and ensuring safe performance. I teach the actors quick scuba basics, like avoiding the dangerous mistake of holding their breath during an ascent —which can cause the air in their lungs to expand as the surrounding water pressure decreases, potentially rupturing theirs lungs, like a balloon pops when overfilled, a potentially fatal condition. My role requires staying close enough to intervene without ever being in the shot—like an invisible guardian of the set.

Figuring out camera blocking—where cameras will be positioned and how actors move through scenes—is a steeper learning curve for me. Deciphering the on-set language can be tricky too: When someone calls out, "Martini shot!" they mean the last shot of the day—no actual drinks involved. "Back to one" means everyone returns to their starting positions. "Checking the gate" is industry-speak for examining the camera for stray hair or debris interfering with the frame. But I'm catching on.

My reputation grows, and soon I'm working on TV shows like *Dexter, Agents of S.H.I.E.L.D., Scorpion, Euphoria, Chicago P.D.*, and *Obi-Wan Kenobi*. Each job sharpens my proficiency, increases my set etiquette, and builds my credibility.

My financial reality expands alongside my reputation. I've been making twenty dollars an hour at the dive shop, working eight-hour days. SAG day rates start at eight hundred dollars—but that's just the beginning.

Meal penalties kick in when production runs long without proper meal breaks, adding another fifty to seventy-five dollars to my paycheck for each one. Location fees compensate for working away from our hometown, often adding hundreds of dollars per day. If we're filming underwater sequences in Catalina's kelp forests or diving in San Pedro harbor's frigid waters, those "stunt adjustment" bonuses can double my daily rate. Plus, any work beyond eight hours pays overtime at time-and-a-half, after eleven hours on set, we make double time and if they need me for specialized safety work, that bumps me into even higher pay categories. With a single day on set, I can earn what I'd make in two weeks at the dive shop. For the first time in years, I can save money instead of just living paycheck to paycheck.

Three months after establishing myself on television sets, I am ready to get eaten by piranhas.

The call comes from Tanner Gill, a renowned stunt coordinator known for his work on *The Bucket List, Sons of Anarchy, Spider-Man,* the *Mission Impossible* series, and other major films. He is the diving operations coordinator for the upcoming remake *Piranha 3D*, and offers me the role of stunt double for actor Dina Meyer. This is the moment I've been working toward—a dream turning into reality.

CHAPTER 11

On Set: Making Movie Magic

Build upon what impresses you.
and forget what everyone else thinks.
– Yohancé Salimu

Stepping onto my first real movie set feels like floating on air, despite the strict union rules and precisely coordinated schedules. We're filming *Piranha 3D* at Lake Havasu, Arizona, a spring break hotspot—the perfect setting for a movie filled with entertaining chaos, bikini-clad extras, and wild parties. With laughter, music, and water splashing everywhere, the atmosphere is charged.

For my first few days in this new world, we're filming at a massive man-made lake inside a rock quarry—a marvel of engineering, with intricate cave systems, steep walls, and scattered boats designed to look as real as any natural lake. I am the only woman on the water team of about twenty men. It fills me with pride yet reminds me of the stark reality of the patriarchal nature of the stunt performance industry.

In almost a decade of working around film industry people in California, I have met only two female stunt coordinators and trained just a handful of stuntwomen who wanted to add scuba diving to their resume. But after years in the diving community, I am used to being the only woman in what is pretty much a boys' club. It may be 2009, but the professional diving world remains overwhelmingly male-dominated, with women making up only a small fraction of certified instructors. I've always had to work twice as hard as the guys to be appreciated half as much, so this part of the film business feels like nothing new.

It still irritates me, though not as much as it did in the early years of my career. By now, I have spent over ten years as a full-time dive instructor, and my confidence has grown. With four thousand dives under my belt and eight hundred students certified under my tutelage, from beginner to Divemaster and Instructor levels, I know that I'm really good at what I do.

To be honest, ten years ago I knew almost as much as I do now about diving, and I've always been a very responsible, safety-conscious instructor. But people just take a thirty-three-year-old woman more seriously than a younger woman. Is the world sexist and ageist? Hell, yes! But I cannot change that old-guard mentality. What I *can* change is how I perceive things. As an eternal optimist, I choose to look at the bright side: I am here. I got the job.

On set, I'm surrounded by friendly faces—people I've trained and known for years. Nino Neuboeck, a talented German camera operator, introduces me to all the right people and makes sure I'm well taken care of.

My dive setup for the movie is impressive: a scuba tank with two smaller prop tanks attached to the sides—designed to look like backup air supplies for the film's storyline. I'm also equipped with the latest full-face mask that allows for clear communication through built-in radio systems, and with a double-hose regulator—making it look like I am using a technical diving rebreather. Enhanced with powerful lights that can illuminate my face for the cameras in the murky lake depths, this configuration represents the cutting edge of underwater cinematography equipment. But my confidence takes a hit during what should be the simplest scene: a back-roll entry into the water—from a boat.

I've done this move hundreds of times. Freeze, doubling for actor Ricardo Chavira, executes it effortlessly. But performing in front of cameras, with renowned camera operator Pete Zuccarini and director Alexandre Aja watching, I struggle. Everything feels out of the ordinary. Under scrutiny, my familiar moves become clumsy.

"Again," Pete calls after my third attempt.

Once he is finally satisfied, we move on to another scene at depth. Hearing the underwater communication system as we are swimming frantically is hard enough, but understanding the director's commands through my tight neoprene hood makes everything harder. I can barely make out the mumbled directions from the surface, so I do my best to follow Freeze, who seems to know what's going on.

That familiar inner voice from childhood whispers, *Maybe you're just not good enough.*

I push it down. I *am* good enough.

I can do this, I tell myself.

As the days progress, I begin to grasp the way of things. Movie shoots are in a constant state of flux. Directions shift rapidly. The scenes I master in rehearsal can change on a dime. It's a lesson in adaptability—one I'll need to use throughout my stunt career.

During breaks, Mike Cameron—James Cameron's younger brother, who is serving as our on-set safety diver—shares enthralling stories about working on *The Abyss* and *Titanic*. His tales remind me that I'm now part of a legacy of water work in Hollywood.

The work is demanding but exhilarating. We film complex cave sequences where I follow Freeze, witness his savage piranha attack, and frantically back out. To my surprise, being a stunt performer requires acting skills I never expected to need. I'm not just executing moves—I'm telling a story with my body.

The biggest challenge comes when the director decides to rewrite my death sequence on the spot.

In filmmaking, scenes are rarely shot in the order they appear in the final movie. Instead, they're recorded based on logistics—what location is available, which actors are on set, and the availability of the crew. So, despite all my practice for what was in the script for today—me getting chased by piranhas and dying alongside my buddy in a cave—everything changes on a dime.

Earlier, watching the crew tape a scene using a mannequin as my lifeless body, face down in the water, I noticed something odd: The dummy wasn't wearing the full-face mask I had been drilling with. When I point this out, instead of reshooting that earlier scene to fix the inconsistency, the director decides to rewrite my death entirely. Now, after losing her gear in a final, desperate struggle, throwing away her full-face mask, my character dies in the cave as the piranhas tear into her in a frenzied swirl of bubbles and blood.

Alexandre Aja, who's been dubbed the "Fellini of horror movies," has a reputation for creating impressive scenes of terror. His fans will love this scene for sure.

The new direction is intense: I have to kick and thrash against the ferocious, sharp-toothed fish, all while removing my life support headgear and holding my breath. Then, with the last of my strength, I'm supposed to crawl out of the tunnel, gasping for air.

I show a calm face, but inside I'm freaking out. This is going to be way harder than the scene I've been practicing. Now I wish I'd said nothing and just chosen the "easy way" to film what I've been practicing. But of course, that was never a real option for me.

The sunlight that had poured through the cave's two entrances disappears as camera operators position themselves, their bulky equipment blocking every ray of natural light. What was once an underwater cavern with gentle illumination becomes a tomb of absolute blackness.

Freeze squeezes my arm reassuringly as we hover in the middle of this liquid darkness. Around us, Pete and the other camera operator focus their underwater lights, creating harsh, artificial beams that slice through the water but somehow make the shadows even deeper, more menacing.

The director shouts, "Action!"

Still underwater, Freeze and I immediately begin our death dance. After a few calculated flutters and jerks to simulate the piranha attack, I force myself to take the deepest breath of my life. Then, going against every survival instinct I possess, I frantically pull off my full-face mask and throw it away, along with my regulator.

The moment the seal breaks, ice-cold water floods my face. The cave fills with a violent explosion of water rushing upward in a silver torrent, creating a chaos of sound and motion. Suddenly, I can't see anything. The camera lights are diffused and scattered by thousands of bubbles rising through the water all around me.

With no gear and only the air in my lungs—air that's already starting to feel finite and precious—I begin my theatrical escape. But navigating in this watery pandemonium is like being inside a washing machine. The stirred-up silt creates a brown-black cloud that clings to my skin.

The trick to breath-hold diving is slowing the heart rate and staying calm. Freaking out burns oxygen fast. So even as I perform submerged desperation for the cameras—flailing my arms, kicking frantically against invisible attackers—I force my mind into a meditative state.

Relax, I tell myself as my lungs begin to burn. *There's no real danger. The safety divers are watching.*

My lungs are screaming now, the carbon dioxide buildup creating a fire in my chest. The urge to breathe is becoming overwhelming—not the gentle suggestion of a meditation exercise, but a primal, desperate need.

Finally, I see it: the faintest suggestion of light ahead. I claw my way toward it, my movements becoming genuinely frantic now as my air supply dwindles. The moment I breach the surface, I explode into the air with a gasp that's part performance, part genuine need for oxygen.

"Cut! That's a wrap on Szilvia!"

Relief washes over me in waves, but so does something else: profound satisfaction. I've just survived something that pushed me beyond my limits, that demanded everything I had to give.

And I gave it all.

* * *

Working on *Piranha 3D* has been one of the greatest challenges I've faced in a long time, urging me out of my comfort zone in ways I never anticipated. What makes this experience particularly special is the incredible people I've had the privilege of meeting and working alongside. As the production winds down, I just hope I've done well enough to leave a lasting impression.

Six months later, my hope is satisfied. Word about my cave performance has traveled through the tight-knit stunt community, and the best opportunity of my career arrives: I'm cast as the double for Drew Barrymore's water scenes in her upcoming movie *Big Miracle*. It's an intriguing transition, from the intense, blood-soaked sets of *Piranha 3D* to collaborating with a Hollywood icon—my favorite actress from my childhood.

It feels like the universe is once again aligning in my favor.

Inspired by the real-life events of 1988, when three gray whales became stranded in ice off the coast of Barrow, Alaska, the movie follows the efforts of a local news reporter (played by John Krasinski) and a Greenpeace volunteer—Drew's character—who work to bring attention to the whales' plight and coordinate a massive rescue effort. After a straightforward start to this project, things get complicated.

Now, there are four of us in the running for the same role as Drew's stunt double. To make the selection process even more dramatic, the director decides on an unusual approach: an in-water audition.

In the world of stunt performers, relationships sometimes speak as loud as reputation and performance. Camaraderie and long-established trust reign supreme. But as a female stunt performer with ice diving experience, I have a unique edge. This time it's about proving who's the best for the job, not who knows whom.

The four of us gather by the pool for what becomes a spectacle of talent and nerves. Each contestant is introduced on camera, and while we all share a similar physique to Drew's, our experience levels vary dramatically.

When my turn arrives, I slip into the water with a focus that channels my years of training. The cold is a familiar embrace, and I descend with smooth precision. I feel the intense scrutiny of the director and camera crew but remain composed, demonstrating my command over the situation. After all, I have been ice diving since I was a kid.

Ice diving is more than just a skill; it's an art that demands control and finesse. The other contestants, using rented dry suits, flounder in their attempts. Their unfamiliarity with dry suit diving becomes apparent as they struggle with buoyancy and control. After several tries, it's clear that my competitors are quite literally out of their depth.

As I wait for the director's decision, my heart pounds so hard, I'm sure everyone can hear it. When he finally announces my name, triumph and relief flow through me.

After a few months of intense preparation, I head to the airport, ready to embark on a journey to Alaska. Meeting the incredible stunt team and hearing their wild anecdotes fills me with exhilaration. Tanner, who advocated for me to be chosen as Drew's double, takes me under his wing again, sharing all he knows about movie jargon and set etiquette.

To reduce potential environmental harm, we won't be filming under real glacial conditions. Instead, we use a local aquarium for the under-ice scenes so we can control visibility and lighting while avoiding the unpredictable dangers of real ice. I step into a brand-new TLS350 scuba dry suit, custom-fitted to my exact measurements—a satisfying choice of high-tech gear to support me in subzero waters.

The shoot itself involves intricate choreography to mimic the difficulty of breaking through ice to save the three whales. As with the "piranha" in Arizona, the whales are CGI creations, but the emotional connection we create with these invisible creatures becomes very real on-screen.

One key scene requires me to reach out and gently touch the mama whale. Hovering in freezing water for hours, I keep repeating this heartfelt action as though connecting with an imaginary friend. Every movement has to be perfectly controlled as I interact with the invisible CGI whale. It's so bizarre! I am not a trained actress, yet as a stunt professional, I have to convince the audience of my deep emotional connection with creatures that aren't really there.

Another critical scene involves freeing the baby and mama whales trapped beneath the ice. This "save the day" moment is filled with suspense and urgency, adding drama to the storyline. The cold aquarium water and simulated glacier environment help create the illusion of the whales' desperate situation, and intricate choreography mimics the difficulty of breaking through the ice. The actors perform maneuvers that highlight the intensity of the situation, long before CGI whales are added in post-production. The combination of underwater shots and special effects creates a gripping, emotional moment for the audience.

By seven p.m., I'm in desperate need of a long, hot bath to defrost my limbs. The experience, though strenuous, is immensely rewarding. Even Tanner, known for his reserved nature, takes a rare moment to compliment my performance.

When Drew Barrymore comes on set, we learn that she is committed to performing many of her own stunts. Her presence is warm and magnetic, and her willingness to dive into frigid waters speaks to her dedication. Far from Hollywood glamor, she is surprisingly down-to-earth. Our conversations reveal a delightful connection as we bond over our shared Hungarian heritage and love for travel.

During a break between takes, as we're warming up with hot tea, she notices the tiny elephant pin on my dive bag. "Oh my God, is that from Thailand?" she asks, her eyes lighting up. "I was just there last year!"

Soon we're chatting about eating our favorite Thai dishes and riding motorcycles through rice paddies, but most of all about the way Thailand gets into your soul and never leaves. We discover we both have vision boards plastered with the same dream destinations—surfing in Costa Rica, swimming with whale sharks in the Maldives, trekking through Patagonia.

Spending time with Drew is like meeting a childhood friend who understands me completely. She has a gypsy soul too, and recognizing it in each other creates an instant bond that makes the freezing water and grueling hours feel like an adventure we're sharing rather than hard work we're enduring.

"People think I'm crazy," Drew admits. "Like, 'You're successful in Hollywood, why would you want to sleep in a tent in the middle of nowhere?' But there's something about travel, about putting yourself in completely unfamiliar places …"

"It changes you." I finish.

* * *

The stunt jobs keep coming, and my reputation as a reliable water specialist grows. Each project brings new challenges and builds my credibility in the industry. I've moved to Venice Beach so I can finally afford to live closer to the ocean. Isn't that why I stayed in California in the first place?

The move actually came after I bumped into Joel, the owner of a nice little dive shop, Deep Sea Adventures, who asked me to come work for him. My time at Aqua Adventures was starting to feel played out: With the sense of challenge dwindling and everything running on autopilot, I'd started to feel bored and unmotivated. So the offer of a manager/course director position with more money and insurance benefits—in the heart of Venice Beach—felt like good timing.

Of course, after years of working with Greg, I wanted to end things on good terms. I gave my notice but stayed until the end of summer, not wanting to leave him in the middle of the busy high season. Now, in my new apartment overlooking the beach, I can enjoy the smell of the ocean and the view of palm trees every morning with my coffee. Though I miss the clubhouse vibe at Aqua Adventures, I love the new dive shop's atmosphere. I was ready for a change.

My next major stunt project comes eight months after returning from Alaska: I'll be working on the TV series *FlashForward*, in a dramatic sequence that features an entire bus plummeting off a bridge and sinking into water. My character is central: the hero who saves the trapped passengers.

The scene is being filmed in a controlled pool environment, which offers better visibility than other options. Inside the flooding bus, I'm wearing business attire—a tight-fitting knitted skirt, blouse, and a blue blazer.

Getting wet while fully clothed is a weird feeling. The water brushes my legs, hips, abs, chest and shoulders as it fills the space super-fast. I keep my eyes open, scanning the bus, as the water rapidly rises from my chin to the top of my head.

In this moment, I must act quickly and decisively. As the motorcoach floods, pushing the passengers against the confines of the vehicle, my role is to take charge, to become the beacon of hope amidst the turmoil. Pumped up and ready to save the day, I position myself near a window, my heart pounding as I prepare for the next crucial action.

With a powerful kick, I shatter the window, creating an escape route. Then I begin to push the trapped passengers through the opening, one by one, with movements that are fueled by adrenaline but still calculated and precise. Anxiety mounts as the bus continues to descend and the water surges around us, a maelstrom of swirling currents and limited visibility.

The bus is now completely filled with water; I am holding my breath. Yet I remain focused on guiding the passengers to safety, keeping my heart rate slow to retain enough air to save everybody. I can only see blurs, but that's enough.

Pushing the last passenger out, I prepare for my own escape through the window, swimming through the dark water while fighting against the rising pressure and the disorienting currents. It's time to look up and start kicking. My heart races as I break through the surface, gasping for air and welcoming the relief of escape.

I look back at the bus, fully submerged now, and feel that delicious blend of triumph and exhaustion. All the meticulous planning and execution has brought this impressive stunt to life. The crew's cheers and applause signal the end to another exhilarating shoot.

What makes this project special is that among many familiar faces, I'm also working with Greg, who is finally seeing me as a professional peer in the film industry. The irony isn't lost on me: It took proving I didn't need his help to eventually gain his respect.

Six months after *FlashForward* wraps, another grand opportunity arrives: *Sinister* with Ethan Hawke. This horror film presents a completely different challenge—a pulse-pounding scene where a serial killer binds my character and her family to lounge chairs and drags them into a pool at night. This is no ordinary shoot. It's a high-stakes, high-intensity scene that pushes the boundaries of stunt work, demanding precision, preparation, and an unwavering focus on safety.

The set for this harrowing sequence is dark and foreboding, under a night sky shrouded in ominous mist. Flickering lights cast long shadows across the pool. The air is thick with tension as the crew hustles to prepare for this complex, nerve-wracking stunt. The gravity of the scene is heightened by the fact that we're not merely acting out a simulation, but immersing ourselves in a scenario that feels all too real.

Our lounge chairs are rigged with industrial-strength duct tape, painstakingly applied to remain secure throughout the stunt yet allow us to escape the bind in an emergency. Given the inherent risks of being submerged while restrained, this elaborate setup ensures that every precaution is taken. Hookahs are strategically hidden under our lounge chairs, where we can reach them in case we run out of air while underwater. Each stunt performer is paired with a dedicated safety diver who stands at the ready, their presence a reassuring constant amidst the jumble.

The cameras roll, starting with the unsettling sound of the serial killer's footsteps and the eerie creak of the chairs being dragged toward the pool. The sight of the victims bound tightly and heading toward their watery doom will surely send shivers down the spine of anyone watching the film.

When my chair is pushed into the pool, the shock from the frigid water is immediate. My every movement now is calculated, every breath deliberate. The pressure of the duct tape against my skin feels unnatural combined with the resistance of being under the pool surface. Visibility is limited, yet we remain fully aware of our surroundings carefully executing the sequence of events with intense focus and with confidence in the crew's vigilance. Despite the inherent danger and the adrenaline rush, there's a profound glee in implementing every fastidious detail. In the scene's final cut, the interplay between the haunting score and our frantic underwater thrashing is chilling.

Once filming wraps, my sense of relief is matched only by the feeling of accomplishment. The intensity of the shoot and the teamwork it required are all part of the thrills and challenges of working in the stunt industry, where each project pushes me to new heights as I further hone my craft.

The reality of working in Hollywood also comes with a darker side. While getting that SAG card was a significant step forward, it's no guarantee. Only about 10 percent of those in the guild are actually working at any given time—a harsh reality that's well known throughout the industry. No matter the project, the atmosphere on set is often charged with ambition. Networking is part of the daily grind—stunt performers show up where their friends work, just to schmooze with coordinators who might hire them for the next job—but so is backstabbing.

Securing roles often depends more on who you know—or better yet, on who knows you—than on talent alone. This insularity makes breaking into the business incredibly challenging for outsiders. I feel an immense sense of accomplishment as I get called back for jobs one after another. A handful of stunt coordinators start calling me first for water jobs—a validation of my skills, professionalism, and attitude.

Most stunt people have well-rounded résumés, including fights, high falls, and horse work. I consider taking stunt driving classes to diversify my career. But then I realize: I have no desire to be set on fire or compete with twentysomethings. Rather than spread myself thin, I decide to focus on my niche: water work.

Of course, I'm always eager for that next call, perhaps even the offer to work on something spectacular. I would love to be a full-time scuba stunt performer and water safety coordinator—an exciting job with insanely high compensation compared with my typical instructor positions. But I am not willing to hustle or bulldoze in order to get there. I build relationships through work and let my experience speak for me. I don't kiss ass, and I don't pretend to like people I don't like. That's just not who I am.

I have seen this industry ravage the personal lives of too many colleagues. Long shoots away from home strain relationships, and many marriages fall apart. The constant travel, odd hours, and unpredictable schedules make it nearly impossible to maintain close connections. Not having a family or even a serious, long-term partner makes me fortunate, I suppose.

I'm happy in the movie industry as long as I can engage with the vigor of stunt work without getting sucked into the darker aspects of Hollywood, and as long as it adds to the valuable lessons I've been learning all my life about resilience, integrity, and staying true to myself. While I may not fit the mold of the typical industry player, I feel better about carving my own path guided by thoughtful ambitions and long-held principles.

Balancing my involvement in the film world with my other pursuits—and with a healthy dose of self-awareness and humility—allows me to maintain both stability and fulfillment. It's an approach that savors the best of what the film world offers while remaining grounded in my values. This balance helps me preserve my free spirit and prioritize my principles in life.

CHAPTER 12

Antarctica and South Africa: Pioneering New Adventures

It is not the strongest of the species that survives, nor the most intelligent.
It is the one that is most adaptable to change.
– Leon C. Megginson

One winter day, sitting at an outdoor lunch with Hilaire Brosio—who has become a close friend over the years since we met on that Channel Islands outing—a revolutionary idea takes root. Why not merge our talents and explore the world … without spending a dime?

Much of the planet may be blanketed in snow, but we're basking in the warmth of Southern California in shorts and T-shirts at a restaurant not far from the dive shop. Our weekly conversations have become a sacred ritual, filled with deep discussions over delicious Italian food. We explore our shared obsession for scuba diving, traveling, and beach outings while also unraveling life's complexities and the latest issues in our lives.

After his two-year paid sabbatical came to an end, Hilaire transitioned into camera work and producing network TV shows. Now we want to build a business together, where exotic travel destinations and tours would provide us with a free vacation in return for producing stylish video and online content that helps market their offerings. It's 2011, and this is a novel idea.

Our free-wheeling, free-loading vagabond concept sounds simple enough when spoken aloud over a few glasses of California wine. "Szilvia, I think we can make this work," Hilaire ventures.

We decide to go for it.

To make time for these trips, I strike an agreement with Joel to take unpaid vacation from Deep Sea Adventures. I like working at the new dive shop, but I've never been cut out for the two-weeks-off-per-year mentality. To me, time has always been more important than money. I plan to take several months off each year to negotiate for jobs and get our new business off the ground.

Soon enough, however, this far-reaching dream becomes a nightmare of rejection, financial strain, and crushing self-doubt. The first harsh lesson comes immediately: Nobody wants to give away free trips to unknown content creators.

Our initial approach is embarrassingly naive. We walk into our first travel trade show with my homemade portfolio of diving photos and Hilaire's demo reel, expecting operators to jump at the chance to work with us. Instead, we're met with polite dismissals and barely concealed eye rolls.

"And you are … ?" asks a representative from a luxury safari company, glancing at our makeshift presentation materials with barely disguised disdain.

"We're travel content creators," I explain enthusiastically. "We can provide professional marketing materials in exchange for—"

"Do you have any published work? Magazine credits? A media kit with circulation numbers?"

The answer, humiliatingly, is no. We have the passion, the equipment, and a website that gets maybe fifty visitors a day. In the professional travel industry, we're nobody.

We press on, visiting booth after booth, but the rejections pile up like an avalanche of humiliation. Resort after resort, tour operator after tour operator, the response is always the same: "We work with established travel writers from Condé Nast and National Geographic. What can you offer that they can't?"

What we can offer, we learn, is apparently nothing that matters to them.

After that first disastrous travel show, I sit in my car in the parking lot, fighting back tears of frustration. We've just been turned down by forty different operators in one day. One woman from a Maldives expedition company actually laughed when I mentioned Miss-Scuba.com, asking if it was "some kind of hobby blog."

The financial reality hits even harder than the rejections. To create the kind of professional content that might impress these operators, we need equipment that costs more than most people's cars. The camera housings alone run eight thousand dollars each, and we need multiple setups to protect cameras in different shooting conditions. Underwater lighting systems, backup equipment, travel cases designed to survive airline baggage handlers treating them like soccer balls—the list seems endless, and each item carries a price tag that makes our stomachs churn.

Hilaire drains his savings account buying a professional underwater camera setup, telling himself it's an investment in the future of our company. We're burning through money faster than we can possibly earn it back, with no guarantee that any of this will even work.

The equipment arrives in a mountain of cardboard boxes that takes over Hilaire's entire living room in Redondo Beach. As we unpack each piece—cameras, housings, strobes, arms, clamps, sync cords—the magnitude of what we're attempting becomes crushingly apparent. This isn't just expensive gear; it's a commitment to a lifestyle that could bankrupt us both.

"Maybe we should start smaller," I suggest one evening as we sit surrounded by instruction manuals and equipment that we're still learning to use. "Create local content. Build up a portfolio first."

I can see the doubt creeping into Hilaire's eyes—the same doubt that's been eating at me for weeks. We can't deny the facts: The competition in the travel content creation business is without mercy. Established photographers have relationships built over decades, expense accounts that dwarf our entire budget, and most important, the credibility that comes with years of published work.

We're competing not only against other content creators, but against people who can afford to travel to expensive faraway destinations—no free trips necessary. How can we contend with travel bloggers whose trust funds allow them to spend months in exotic locations, producing content without the pressure of needing immediate returns? Or professional photographers who can afford to take artistic risks because they're not gambling their rent money on every shoot?

Months of rejections follow, and the breakthrough—when it finally comes—is about desperation as much as strategy.

"We need to stop positioning ourselves as wannabe travel writers," I point out to Hilaire, "and start leveraging what makes us unique." I'm more than just another scuba instructor with a camera—I'm a PADI Course Director with a brand, Miss Scuba, and a substantial following in the diving community. And Hilaire is more than just another videographer—he's got legitimate industry credentials from working with major record labels and television networks.

We completely reframe our pitch. Instead of asking for free trips in exchange for generic travel content, we start offering specialized marketing packages targeted at specific audiences. For dive operators, I can provide tantalizing content that reaches serious divers, not just casual travelers. For adventure travel companies, Hilaire can create promotional videos with the high production values of network television.

The shift in our approach transforms everything, but it also raises the stakes exponentially. Now we're not just promising pretty pictures—we're promising measurable results. We're guaranteeing precise deliverables, audience reach numbers, and social media engagement metrics. The pressure to perform feels like a stranglehold.

Our first "yes" comes from a small dive operator in the Philippines that is desperate for marketing help. This isn't a glamorous trip to Galapagos or Madagascar—it's a modest package to a middle-tier resort that's struggling to compete with the luxury properties. But it's a start, and more important, it's validation that our concept can work.

The relief of that first acceptance is overwhelming, but it's immediately replaced by a new kind of terror: What if we can't deliver? What if the content we create doesn't meet the operator's expectations? What if we've oversold our abilities and we end up destroying any chance of building credibility in this industry—or worse, destroying my credibility in the scuba world? Diving is a relatively small community. If word gets out that I am a flake or delivering mediocre a product, it could ruin more than what we can gain with a few free trips.

Every piece of equipment we pack for that first trip represents money we can't afford to lose. Every shot we film has to work, because we don't have the budget for do-overs. The financial pressure transforms what should be an exciting creative adventure into a high-stakes business proposition where failure won't just be disappointing—it's potentially catastrophic.

As we prepare for our first professional content creation trip, I realize Hilaire and I have crossed a line we can't uncross. We're no longer just friends who love to travel and dive. We're business partners whose financial futures are tied to our ability to justify the trust—and money—that operators are investing in us.

The weight of that responsibility is both terrifying and exhilarating. We've moved beyond the safety of steady paychecks and traditional career paths into the uncertain world of entrepreneurship, where success means everything and failure means starting over from scratch—if you can.

* * *

As the months pass, Hilaire and I dive together in numerous countries. We explore shipwrecks in Sudan. We sail on a luxurious dive yacht and swim with the majestic marine life around Komodo Island in Indonesia. We hobnob with tiger sharks in Fiji against the glorious backdrop of an abundant coral reef. The internet is still in its relative infancy, and social media is far from an omnipresent phenomenon. Armed with six Pelican cases of camera equipment and a deliberate selection of lights, microphones, and dive gear, we are capturing the underwater world in ways that few have attempted.

Through Miss-Scuba.com, which I originally created to bring together adventurous women from around the world, I document our travels using Hilaire's photos and videos, writing blog posts and dolling up to serve as the on-camera host for the Adventures with Miss Scuba vlog. Being a competent diver sets me apart, boosting our production value over that of content providers that hire pretty models who are not necessarily water people. Each post brings our journeys to life, and together we produce short music videos, full-length DVDs, and travel articles that share our experiences with readers. In return for professional marketing content, resorts and destinations open their paradises to us, free of charge.

Hilaire's transition from marketing rock bands to behind-the-camera work, paired with my scuba and networking expertise, ensures we're delivering powerful promotional content to a targeted audience. Travel operators are delighted with the results, and in return, we pull off legendary adventures that would have been financially impossible for us otherwise. We are carving out our niche with determination and innovation, laying the groundwork for a global trend that will soon explode.

Then, a once-in-a-lifetime opportunity presents itself: diving in the frigid waters of Antarctica. Oceanwide Expeditions has invited us to document the maiden voyage of its ship the *Plancius* on a basecamp expedition to Antarctica. This excursion is the culmination of years of hard work and determination, a chance to capture a part of the world most people only dream of seeing.

With just two weeks' notice, we scramble to gather all the gear we need in six checked bags and four stuffed carry-ons—a mission in and of itself. This isn't your typical dive outing—we're preparing for the extreme cold, which requires specialized trekking and scuba equipment, everything from underwater camera housings and lights to dive gear with environmental sealing and layers of extra-warm clothing. Thankfully, my sponsorship with Patagonia makes it easier to gear up for the freezing conditions.

Our first stop is Buenos Aires, the capital of Argentina. With its charming buildings and picturesque avenues, Buenos Aires resembles an old European city. Indoor and outdoor cafes abound, hopping with well-mannered, fashionably dressed locals. We spend a late summer evening dining along the city's river walk, savoring fabulous Argentinian Malbec. Later, strolling the cobblestone streets, we stumble upon a spontaneous couple tango dancing, surrounded by smiling pedestrians. It's like a scene from a romantic movie.

The next morning, we board a three-hour domestic flight to Ushuaia, a beautiful Patagonian city that lies between snow-capped mountains and the sea. It's the planet's southernmost city, known to many as *Fin del Mundo*: the End of the World. Young mavericks, families, and elderly couples fill the streets of this popular South American vacation destination, wandering in and out of mountaineering stores, wine shops, and resort hotels. Though we notice few North Americans or Europeans, Ushuaia strikes me as the next "it" place for adventurous travelers in Patagonia.

After a day of hiking and browsing the outdoorsy shops, we are ready to board our vessel for the Antarctica journey. Originally built in the mid-1970s as a Russian ice-breaker, the *Plancius* boasts a plush observation lounge and an extensive library. Rooms are spacious, equipped with ample storage and flat-screen TVs. The bar in the observation lounge becomes my go-to spot for swapping stories and sipping hundred-year-old Scotch over three-thousand-year-old glacier ice. The espresso machine quickly becomes my best friend, as I aim to participate in every activity offered. How often does such an opportunity arise in life?

Just as I'm becoming accustomed to such luxuries, we leave the relative shelter of the Beagle Channel, and I start to learn what the seasoned crew meant by the "price of admission to see Antarctica." We have entered the notorious Drake Passage, one of nature's finest gauntlets, where the rewards of extravagance are quickly replaced by a test of human endurance that pushes every passenger to their breaking point.

The first hint of what's coming arrives when the ship's movement changes from a gentle rock to an ominous roll that sends unsecured items sliding across surfaces with increasing violence. The weather report crackles over the intercom, its colorless tone contradicting its words: *Category 11 storm, sustained winds at seventy knots, wave heights thirty-seven to fifty-two feet.*

"All passengers are advised to remain in their cabins," the captain announces. His voice carries a forced calm that doesn't fully mask his concern. "Repeat! All passengers must remain in cabins until further notice." A coffee cup skitters across a table, crashes to the floor, and shatters—the first casualty in what soon becomes a thirty-six-hour war between human will and the raw fury of the Southern Ocean.

By hour three of this daunting storm, the civilized veneer of our expedition ship begins to crack. The dining room, until recently a social hub of excited chatter about penguin sightings and iceberg photography, transforms into a chamber of misery. Tables that should be laden with gourmet meals instead hold strategically placed sick bags and towels to absorb the constant spillage as plates and glasses slide back and forth with each violent pitch of the ship.

That first evening, I make the mistake of attempting to eat dinner in the ship's galley with a few other brave souls. The lamb looks delicious, but as I lift the fork to my mouth, the ship lurches so aggressively that I'm thrown sideways and only just manage to thrust my free hand down and keep my chair from falling over. The meat flies off my fork and splatters against the wall three feet away. Around me, other passengers clutch their stomachs, their faces taking on a greenish pallor.

The sound becomes the worst part—a relentless cacophony of mechanical stress and human suffering. The ship's hull groans and creaks like a living thing in pain, punctuated by the explosive crashes of waves that hit with the force of freight trains. Through it all, incessant retching echoes from the bathroom stalls and cabin corners where passengers have given up any pretense of dignity.

By the thirty-two-hour mark, when the storm begins to show signs of exhaustion at last, those of us who are still functional are bonded by a shared trauma that feels military in its intensity. We've seen each other at our absolute worst—heaving, terrified, reduced to crawling on hands and knees when the ship's motion becomes too vicious for walking.

When the captain finally announces that passengers can move freely about the ship again, the calm seas and silence feel almost supernatural. The absence of crashing waves and groaning metal seems too quiet, like the aftermath of an explosion that leaves your ears ringing.

The first glimpse of Antarctica through the clearing clouds hits with an emotional impact amplified by everything we've endured to reach it. The pristine white mountains and impossibly blue icebergs aren't just beautiful—they're redemption, proof that we've paid that price of admission and emerged triumphant on the other side of one of the most hostile waterways on Earth.

When it's time for our first scuba dive, I can hardly believe it. Though I've dreamt of diving in polar waters for my entire life, I never thought the day would actually arrive.

Diving in Antarctica requires more gear than most places I've visited. Each diver needs two environmentally sealed regulator sets to prevent freezing, a dry suit, and several layers of undergarments, and most divers opt for dry gloves and a thick hood. Keeping my head and hands warm is crucial to maintaining my core body temperature as I descend in the 32°F wet environment.

While the giant, submerged whale bones are impressive, the floating icebergs are my favorite part. Ten stories tall, these shiny white sculptures are intimidating at first, but soon I'm transfixed by their ever-changing walls. Instead of smooth as I had imagined, the ice is textured with uniform dimples—created, as our dive guide explains, by sunlight reflecting through the ocean's surface.

After dinner one evening, we head ashore for the ultimate adventure—camping on the Antarctic ice. As we step onto the frozen landscape, the cold bites at our cheeks, but it doesn't dampen the excitement. Above us, the sky stretches out, blanketed in stars so bright and vast, this must be another world. We stand in awe for a moment, taking it all in, before retreating into our small, igloo-like tents. Inside, wrapped in sub-zero sleeping bags, we feel surprisingly cozy, even as the wind outside howls and rages, reminding us just how wild and remote this place truly is.

At four a.m., we're jolted awake—not by alarms, but by the chattering of penguins, their voices breaking the eerie stillness of the night. We venture out eagerly into the fresh snow, our breath freezing in the crisp air. Our surroundings are otherworldly, bathed in the pale glow of early morning. We capture photo after photo of the vast, untouched environment, feeling like explorers on another planet. An hour later, the warmth of the ship's cabin and the aroma of breakfast welcomes us back to reality, as though we're returning from a walk on the moon.

Blessed with blue skies and sunshine, we opt for a kayaking excursion along the coast, paddling for hours among drifting ice slabs. Away from the tumult of civilization, I revel in the grand view, reflecting deeply on Antarctica and life in general. My thoughts and senses are uncluttered here, more finely tuned than ever.

Then, without warning, the world transforms before my eyes. A massive iceberg—easily the size of a skyscraper—begins to roll with thunderous cracks that echo across the water like gunshots. I freeze in my kayak, paddle suspended midstroke, watching in breathless awe as this ancient giant slowly turns upside down, revealing its hidden underwater cathedral of translucent blue ice. The sound is primordial—deep groans and sharp fractures that seem to come from the planet's very core. Water cascades from newly exposed surfaces in spectacular waterfalls, and the iceberg settles into its new position with a final, earth-shaking sigh.

In that moment, witnessing this raw display of Mother Nature's power, I understand what Thich Nhat Hanh means when he writes about impermanence. After gradually forming for thousands of years, this iceberg has transformed in mere minutes. Everything changes, constantly. The ice that seems so solid and eternal is actually in constant motion, just like our lives.

The silence that follows feels sacred, broken only by the gentle lapping of water against my kayak and the distant calls of penguins. This is meditation in its purest form. Sitting here in my tiny vessel, dwarfed by forces beyond human comprehension, I feel the Buddhist teaching of interconnectedness settle into my bones. I am not separate from this ice, this water, this moment—we are all part of the same magnificent, ever-changing whole.

When we reluctantly return to basecamp, Hilaire and I spend hours completely captivated by the gentoo penguins—curious and bold little creatures that waddle right up to us without a hint of fear. It's March, late summer in Antarctica, and the penguin chicks in this protected sanctuary are in the middle of a transition that's as awkward and comical as it is endearing: Some have not yet shed their fluffy down feathers and look like mismatched bundles of fluff, while others have started donning their sleek, grown-up winter coats and already resemble miniature versions of their parents.

Dynamic encounters with nature continue to enrich our eleven-day journey across the peninsula. The weather shifts constantly—clear blue skies turn to snow, then wind, and suddenly back to sunshine. "You don't take a trip to Antarctica," our expedition leader grins. "Antarctica takes *you* on a trip."

On our return through the Drake Passage, the seas are serene, the sky is blue, and I take pleasure in gazing at the horizon, with no land in sight in any direction. Two humpback whales glide toward our ship, their massive bodies cutting through the water with a grace that takes my breath away. They stay with the *Plancius* for hours, swimming alongside us like curious relatives or old friends. Every few minutes, one rises to the surface, sending a misty spray from its blowhole into the air, and the sound of its breath ripples through the great stillness. Before they depart, one rolls onto its side, waving a giant fin in the air as if to greet us—or wish us a good journey home.

* * *

Back in California, barely a week passes before I begin preparing for a three-week trip to Africa with Hilaire. Africa Tours has invited us to document and promote luxurious destinations, from upscale accommodations to stunning diving experiences and thrilling jungle excursions.

Our journey starts in Umkomaas, along Aliwal Shoal, a scuba lover's haven that is a magnet for both international travelers and local divers. On our first dive we explore the Cathedral, a vibrant, rocky reef populated by about ten ragged-tooth sharks, also called sand tigers. Despite their fearsome appearance, these sharks are docile. But nature has more tricks up its sleeve than wildlife alone.

Diving in these chilly waters from sturdy zodiacs is a far cry from the comfort of warm-water boat dives. What the brochures don't tell you is that South African scuba diving is essentially combat diving disguised as recreation. The conditions here don't just challenge your skills—they actively try to kill you.

"Eight-to-twelve-foot faces," our divemaster announces one morning as if he's discussing lunch plans. "Twenty-to-thirty-foot swells behind the break. It's going to be sporty today."

Sporty. That's the South African euphemism for conditions that would shut down diving operations anywhere else in the world. The other local divemasters, weathered men who've been launching boats through these surf breaks for decades, assess the conditions with the grim expressions of soldiers preparing for battle. The swells make my stomach drop just looking at them from shore. The zodiac itself looks reassuringly robust until you realize it's going to be launched directly into waves that tower above our heads—essentially, a high-speed rubber missile that we're about to ride through a washing machine.

"Whatever you do," the divemaster shouts over the roar of surf that sounds like continuous thunder, "don't let go of your gear! And when I say hold on, I mean with everything you've got! People have been thrown out of the boat. Some of them, we found …"

His comment, though intended to be light-hearted, sends ice through my veins. But there's no time to process that fear. The zodiac's engines scream to life like jet fighters taking off from a short runway, and suddenly we're accelerating directly toward walls of white water that look like they could crush buildings.

Wave after wave punishes our inflatable boat, until the simple act of getting to the dive site becomes an extreme sport unto itself. I put on my scuba mask, which improves my line of sight somewhat and doubles as safety goggles protecting me from an unwanted saline eyewash. My hands are cramped and my knuckles white from gripping the safety lines so hard. Salt water has forced its way into every tiny crevice in my wetsuit. We haven't even reached the site, and I'm already becoming hypothermic.

When we clear the surf break and reach the relatively calmer waters beyond, the silence feels unnatural. But we're still dealing with swells that lift and drop the zodiac twenty feet at a time. And underwater, the conditions don't improve.

The surge from the surface waves creates an underwater commotion that slams divers, with bone-crushing force, into both rocks and each other. The wave action kicks up sediment, reducing visibility to arm's length. How are we supposed to shoot a marketing video about amazing dives that persuade people to spend their hard-earned money to come here?

After twenty minutes under the surface, disaster strikes: My regulator fails completely. This is the moment every diver trains for but hopes never to experience: complete equipment failure in dangerous conditions. Tumbled about in the currents and unable to see much of anything, I manage to locate Hilaire and signal for air sharing, but the relief is short-lived. The shared regulator system, designed for calm water emergencies, becomes almost unusable in the surge. Every few seconds, the current rips the regulator out of one of our mouths.

The ascent takes forever. We fight our way up through currents that seem determined to drag us back down. When we finally surface, the zodiac is nowhere to be seen. The swells that seemed manageable from the boat's deck now tower above us like moving mountains.

When the zodiac does show up to rescue us, the remedy feels as dangerous as the emergency itself. Getting back into the vessel requires that we time the swells perfectly and haul ourselves up over the side while wearing full scuba gear that now seems to weigh twice as much as it did this morning.

The sprint back to shore provides no relief from the chaos—like riding a rocket into a blender. When the zodiac accelerates to highway speeds as if trying (unsuccessfully) to outrun the breaking waves, we get caught by a massive breaker that picks up the entire boat and hurls it forward like a javelin seeking dry land.

Back on solid ground at last, I stumble out of the boat, my legs shaking from adrenaline and exhaustion. That wasn't diving—it was survival.

"Good dive?" Our divemaster chuckles at our shocked expressions as he helps drag the zodiac up the beach. "Conditions were pretty calm today."

His cheerful assessment is more of a prediction: The next morning dawns with an eerie stillness. The ocean that tried to kill us less than twenty-four hours ago now extends outward as flat as a sheet of polished glass.

"This is why we do it," he says as we slide over the surface, gesturing toward water so clear, we can see the bottom. Gone is the grim-faced warrior, transformed into a relaxed dive guide with a devil-may-care grin. "Days like this make all the chaos worth it."

Instead of being hurled into the water by the furious motion of the boat, I slip into the ocean with gentle grace. The moment my head dips below the surface, a profound peace settles over me like a comfortable blanket. I descend through water so tranquil and clear, it barely seems to exist.

The reef reveals itself in layers of increasing wonder. Purple and pink hydrocoral formations cover every surface, spreading across the reef like a springtime meadow, their delicate structures swaying in the gentlest of currents. This underwater garden rivals even the most pristine tropical waters—a powerful reminder of diving Hin Daeng and Hin Muang in Thailand's Andaman Sea but with a temperate twist that makes it uniquely spectacular. The colors are deeper, more complex, like an oil masterpiece when you've only ever seen watercolor paintings.

The dive unfolds like a meditation in motion. We drift along the reef with the current, barely fin-kicking, letting the ocean carry us through room after room of this underwater temple. Then, emerging from the blue distance like a vision from a dream, comes the marble ray.

The creature appears with the slow majesty of a flying carpet, fluttering its eight-foot wingspan. It seems to be made of living ocean, with movements so graceful that they must be choreographed. For ten minutes that feel like hours, the ray performs its underwater symphony for our small group of onlookers.

When we finally begin our ascent, it's with genuine reluctance. Breaking the surface feels like waking from the most beautiful dream.

"This is the real South Africa," the dive leader says as we motor slowly back to shore. His usual professional demeanor has been replaced by the satisfied smile of someone who has just shared something sacred. "Yesterday was about surviving the ocean. Today was about understanding why we love it."

* * *

Our journey through South Africa continues with adventures that deepen our appreciation for the natural world and leave us with memories to last a lifetime: braving the swinging bridge at Oribi Gorge, observing crocodiles and hippos on a cruise through the St. Lucia wetlands, diving among the world's southernmost coral reefs at UNESCO World Heritage site Sodwana Bay. Showering in a tree house with a view of the Rocktail Bay coastline—while staying at a shabby chic lodge nestled between jungle and dunes, with miles of untouched beach in sight—infuses me with a heart-pounding sense of freedom.

After a full week of diving, we embark on our first safari at Hluhluwe-Imfolozi Park to seek the Big Five—African elephant, black rhinoceros, cape buffalo, lion, and leopard. Our encounters with these magnificent creatures, from a rhino mother and her calf to a pride of lions with blood-smeared faces from their recent kill, showcase nature's raw beauty and power in unforgettable technicolor. Bidding farewell to this remarkable country, both Hilaire and I carry with us the spirit of adventure and our earnest gratitude for the experiences that continue to shape us.

The financial risks we've taken, the equipment we've invested in, the rejections we've endured—all of it feels like the right choice once our success starts mounting. We are building the foundation of a new business model and partnership.

Yet as I've traversed the globe while working with Hilaire, our friendship has deepened beyond shared dives and our growing business. Countless moments spent together—late-night conversations under starry skies, spontaneous escapades in unfamiliar cities, the simple joys of discovering new cultures—have strengthened our bond. What began as a connection rooted in our mutual passions has evolved into something more intimate and enduring. We're becoming more than best friends—we're each other's anchor in a constantly shifting world.

I'm starting to realize that the true treasure isn't just the jaw-dropping dive sites and thrilling adventures, but sharing life's most breathtaking and priceless experiences with someone I care about deeply.

CHAPTER 13

Thailand and Nepal:
Finding My Soulmate

I love you not only for what you are,
but for what I am when I am with you.
– Elizabeth Barrett Browning

No one is surprised when our grandiose Antarctic and African adventures do nothing to slake our thirst for globe-trotting. Our next destination is a perennial favorite of mine but new to Hilaire: Thailand, where I will host a group of divers in the Similan Islands, a national park.

My love for the people, culture, and food (not to mention the massages) of Thailand runs deep. Over the years, however, I've learned that Asia can take some getting used to. So, I ease Hilaire into our exciting monthlong journey by starting in Hong Kong, where we enjoy the seamless blend of convenience and style that this sparkling city offers, from its user-friendly metro system to its renowned bespoke tailoring to its bustling dim sum restaurants.

Next, a few days in Vietnam offer a fascinating glimpse into local life, despite the country's challenges with poverty and air pollution. Hanoi overwhelms my senses from the moment we step off the plane—the air thick with humidity and tinged with exhaust fumes, incense from street-side shrines, and the smoky aroma of pho broth simmering in countless sidewalk kitchens.

The city pulses with constant motion: motorbikes weaving through narrow alleys in impossible numbers, their horns squawking in a concerto of urban chaos that never stops. Vendors squat on tiny plastic stools, calling out in rapid Vietnamese while chopping fresh herbs and grilling meat over glowing charcoal braziers. The Old Quarter's streets are a kaleidoscope of colors—crimson lanterns hanging from ancient buildings, emerald silk scarves fluttering in shop doorways, golden Buddhas gleaming behind clouds of sandalwood smoke.

Every step brings new textures: the smooth worn stones of temple courtyards, the rough brick of colonial French architecture, the sticky heat that makes my clothes cling to my skin. The taste of Vietnam lingers on my tongue—sharp cilantro, fiery chilies, the tangy sweetness of fresh spring rolls, and strong Vietnamese coffee that jolts me awake so I can face the sensory assault of this crowded, colorful, utterly alive city.

Reaching Thailand, we immerse ourselves in the ethical elephant and tiger sanctuaries of Chiang Mai before traveling south to explore the kinetic city life of Bangkok and concoct traditional Thai dishes in hands-on cooking classes. Then, after three weeks of travel, we finally reach the dive portion of our trip with high hopes.

My vivid memories from living in Thailand more than a decade ago—diving in the Andaman Sea, its warm waters alive with colorful reef fish, graceful leopard sharks, curious octopi, and prehistoric-looking turtles—come bubbling to the surface. I remember the Similan Islands as the crown jewel of diving landscapes, expecting the underwater equivalent of the Sistine Chapel, a celebration of nature's greatest works of art. But the reality that greets us is so far removed from that expectation, it feels like arriving at a funeral.

The first dive is a punch to the chest. As we descend through water that should be transparent blue but instead carries an ominous, milky tinge, the reef structure comes into view like a postapocalyptic hell. Rather than vibrant coral formations, these are skeletal remains—bleached, white bone structures that reach toward the surface like the stiff fingers of drowning victims.

The silence is devastating. In place of all the subtle sounds of a living ecosystem, from the constant chatter of reef fish to the clicking of crustaceans, there is only the hollow echo of my own breathing amplified in this subaquatic graveyard.

I hover above what our dive guide identifies as a table coral formation that, in healthy times, would have been twenty feet across and home to hundreds of fish. Now it's a crumbling monument of calcium carbonate, its surface covered not with colorful polyps but with a brown, slimy algae that moves listlessly in the current like tattered funeral shrouds. The reef where I once led wide-eyed tourists on magical undersea journeys has become a cemetery marking the demise of everything I thought was permanent and protected.

It's the death of a world I once called home.

Tears mix with seawater inside my mask. Entire coral cities that once teemed with life now stretch before us as ghost towns at the bottom of the sea. It's like returning for the holidays to your childhood home only to find it burned to the ground, with nothing but charred remains where rooms full of memories once stood.

I'm completely unprepared for the overwhelming emotional impact of this environmental damage, but the real horror comes on our seventh dive, as we explore a site named Paradise Reef. We're barely forty feet down when the water around us erupts in a violent burst and every molecule in my body screams with alarm. The explosion isn't visible—it's pure sensation, a pressure wave that hits like being inside a bass drum when someone strikes it with a sledgehammer.

Dynamite fishing.

The sound travels through the water with a clarity and power that no land-based detonation could match. Within seconds, the aftermath becomes visible as fish, stunned and killed by the blast, sink rapidly through the water column like a macabre snowfall—whole fish, half fish, pieces of fish, all drifting down in a ghastly parade of destruction.

The reef section where the blast occurred—hundreds of yards away from our dive site, thankfully—is completely obscured by a cloud of sediment and debris. Even from this safe distance, the underwater shockwave had been powerful enough to rattle our masks and send vibrations through our bodies. Through the murk drifting toward us, we see the white flash of more dead fish surfacing, and the dark silhouette of the fishing boat as it moves in to collect its grisly harvest.

They're fishing with bombs inside a national park, in protected waters—a former paradise in more than just its name—in broad daylight, with complete impunity.

My first instinct is to rage at the casual destruction of an ecosystem that has taken centuries to develop. But this pure, burning fury quickly gives way to something much worse: helplessness. There is no way for me to stop this. What exactly am I supposed to do? Confront armed fishermen? File a complaint with authorities who are either complicit or powerless?

We surface from that dive in grave, agonized silence. The tour operator, a cheerful Australian woman who has been running trips to the Similans for fifteen years, has tears in her eyes too.

"It's gotten so much worse," she says quietly. "Five years ago, you'd hear dynamite maybe once a week. Now it's daily, sometimes multiple times per day. The authorities know about it, but the fishermen have bigger engines and faster boats than the enforcement vessels. By the time anyone responds, they're long gone."

The reality of this environmental wasteland begins to crystallize in my mind. This isn't random vandalism—this is organized, systematic strip-mining of the ocean, conducted with industrial efficiency and protection from prosecution. The national park designation that should protect these reefs has become meaningless.

Over the remaining days of our trip, the psychological toll becomes almost unbearable. Each dive should be a festive occasion of the Andaman Sea's wonders but instead becomes a shocking education in the speed of human destruction and a solemn documentation of immeasurable loss. I am hosting a group of divers from California who had heard me speak passionately about Thailand's underwater beauty for years and begged to join me on this adventure. We came to create content that would inspire others to experience this subaquatic glory, yet we're leaving with footage that serves as a requiem for worlds that have already vanished.

The professional crisis, too, becomes clear. How do we produce content that fulfills our contractual obligations without fundamentally misleading potential visitors? Do we document the reality and destroy the tourism that provides the only economic incentive for reef protection? Or do we focus on the few surviving healthy patches and pretend the devastation doesn't exist?

In the end, I choose honesty over profit, writing a blog post on Miss-Scuba.com that tells the truth—the whole truth. I describe the beauty that remains alongside the heartbreaking reality of what the world has lost.

Diving in Thailand now feels like visiting a museum—beautiful in its way, but hollow with the echo of everything that's been lost. It's heartbreaking to know that for most visitors, those who never experienced these reefs in their prime, this degraded version will seem normal, perhaps even impressive.

Will I go back to Thailand someday? I don't know. There was a time when I called it home, a place filled with cherished faces and moments, where I could see myself retire and live out my days. But something has shifted—it's no longer the same, and perhaps neither am I. I want to keep the Thailand I loved intact, untouched in my memory, a refreshing phase in my life that I can revisit anytime in my mind.

The next time Asia calls, I will be drawn to explore different parts of the continent, new stories and cultures, fresh landscapes and ventures. Thailand will always be a part of me, but maybe it's time to see what else the world has in store.

* * *

Returning to California, I realize that Hilaire and I have accomplished something unprecedented over the past year of remarkable travel. Long before the term *influencer* bursts onto the scene, we have pioneered a model of travel content creation that will eventually become an entire industry. In just a few years, social media mavens will jostle for attention with smartphones and drones, but we are among the first to fuse travel, adventure, and influence into a sustainable lifestyle.

But perhaps more important, this journey is teaching us both something profound about the nature of our partnership, both professional and personal. Working together in the most challenging conditions—from the violent seas of South Africa to the heartbreaking devastation of Thailand's reefs—we're discovering that we function not just as effective collaborators, but as a team whose combined strengths exceed the sum of our individual abilities.

To me, this has been about more than just taking the next career step or pioneering travel content creation. We've learned to trust each other completely, to rely on one another in any situation, to invest in our shared personal and financial gain. Going out on a limb professionally has given us something even more precious: each other.

The world we've been documenting, from the pristine wilderness of Antarctica to the tragic decline of coral reefs in Thailand, has become not just the subject of our work, but the backdrop against which our own love story unfolds.

I'm in love with Hilaire, I realized not long after our first trip together, to produce content for that small resort in the Philippines. Suddenly everything made perfect sense, but the path from friends to lovers seemed complicated at first. Although we'd been close friends for years, the spark was there from the start—an undeniable chemistry that crackled beneath our easy camaraderie. Was it foolish to risk all that for romance?

Plus, our timing came with a callous sense of humor: We were never single at the same time. Whenever I broke up with a boyfriend, Hilaire was deep in a relationship. When he finally became available, I was dating someone who seemed perfect for me. Although these other relationships always ended up leaving us restless and unfulfilled, we'd danced around each other in this frustrating pattern for years.

I would watch Hilaire with other women and feel a stab of jealousy I couldn't quite name. He would see me with other men and grow distant, our usual banter becoming strained. Our mutual friends noticed the tension.

"You two are idiots," Eo told me one afternoon while we were diving with Hilaire and his latest girlfriend. "Everyone can see it except you."

But that was part of the problem: Everyone could see it. The pressure from our friend group became suffocating. Some rooted for us like we were characters in their personal romantic comedy, while others shook their heads in warning.

"You're both too stubborn," Greg told me bluntly. "Two alpha personalities like you would kill each other within a month. You'd compete over everything—who's the better traveler, who knows more about cameras, who can plan the perfect trip."

His words stung because there was truth in them. Hilaire and I were both fiercely independent and accustomed to being the one in charge, to calling the shots in our respective fields. Rather than merging our lives, we'd be setting out on a collision course.

What if we tried romance and it crashed and burned? Hilaire wasn't just any friend—he had become my perfect travel companion, the one person who shared my wanderlust and matched my pace. We could spend weeks together in remote locations without getting on each other's nerves. Finding that kind of compatibility is rare, maybe once-in-a-lifetime rare. What if the sexual chemistry killed the friendship? What if we discovered we're better as companions than lovers? The thought of losing him entirely—losing our adventures, our easy conversations, our shared dreams—was far more painful than the idea of staying single forever.

My fear was paralyzing. After my realization, for months of exquisite agony, I stood by as Hilaire dated a woman who was everything I'm not: conventionally pretty, a homebody, content to let him take the lead. She didn't dive, didn't share his passion for remote destinations, didn't understand why he'd want to spend three weeks filming in dangerous locations.

Everything about her was safe. She wouldn't challenge him or compete with him … or potentially destroy the life he had carefully built.

When they finally broke up, I was in the middle of my own relationship disaster, with a real estate agent who wanted me to be more "conventional" and less "obsessed with dangerous hobbies." He loved how different I was from the American women he'd dated, yet he wanted to change everything about me.

The breaking point came one rainy Tuesday evening, after another fight with my boyfriend about my "reckless" diving career. I was sitting in my car outside his house, gathering the courage to drive away for the final time. Hilaire had been single for three months. I'd been miserable in my relationship for six.

My hands shook as I dialed Hilaire's number. "Want to grab dinner?" I suggested, trying to sound casual.

"Sure. Everything okay?" he asked. "You sound weird."

I took a deep breath. "I need to tell you something."

We met at our usual Italian place, the one where we'd shared countless lunches as friends. But that night felt different. The air crackled with possibility and terror.

"I broke up with him," I said without preamble.

Hilaire's face didn't change, but I caught the flicker of something in his eyes. "I'm sorry. What happened?"

"He wanted me to be someone I'm not." I fidgeted with my napkin, avoiding Hilaire's gaze. "And I realized I've been trying to fit into relationships with people who don't really get me."

"And … ?" The word hung between us, loaded with years of unspoken tension.

"And I think I've been an idiot." I finally looked up at him. "We've been idiots. Let's give it a shot."

The silence stretched so long, I started to panic. What if I'd misread everything? What if he really did see me only as a friend? What if I'd just destroyed the most important relationship in my life?

"Szilvia, I have been waiting for this moment for a very long time," Hilaire said at last, his voice careful.

I released the twisted napkin, then the breath I was holding in. And then I started to rattle off all the worst outcomes I worried about. "But what if it doesn't work? What if we're terrible together? What if we wish we'd stayed friends? I can't lose you."

Hilaire laughed, though I could hear nervousness in it. "What if we're amazing together and we've been wasting all this time being scared?"

"Our friends think we'd kill each other."

"Our friends don't know everything." He reached across the table and took my hand. The simple touch sent electricity through my entire body.

"Okay," I said. "Let's give it a shot. But if this goes badly—"

"It won't."

"But if it does, we promise to find our way back to friendship." I thrust my hand across the table. "Deal?"

"Deal."

Most couples remember their first kiss; we're going to remember our first business negotiation about love. It was so absurd that we both started laughing as our hands met across the table. Even as we shook on it, both of us knew there was no going back.

It took no time to settle even further into life together, and after a while, I moved into Hilaire's home in Redondo Beach. And a year or so later, as we're packing away our cameras and diving gear from Thailand, it occurs to me that in the process of building something new together, we are also building the foundation for a life together.

Every destination we've explored, every challenge we've overcome, every success we've celebrated together has added another layer to our relationship, which is growing into something neither of us expected when we first sat down for those sacred lunches near the dive shop, dreaming of making adventure pay for itself. I realize that the most valuable discovery from our travels isn't captured in any photograph or video. It's the knowledge that I've found my perfect travel companion, creative partner, and—though I am only beginning to understand it—life partner.

Soon it becomes clear: Hilaire and I want to spend the rest of our lives as a couple. Our perfect friendship has survived the beautiful, terrifying leap into love.

Now we'll find out whether it can survive the leap into marriage.

* * *

As our love story continues to unfold, we're eager to formalize our commitment and begin the next chapter. But what should be a joyful planning process quickly becomes diplomatic warfare over geography.

My family in Hungary has strong opinions about where we should marry. "You should come home," my mother insists during one of our weekly Skype calls. "Your grandmother is ninety-five years old. She may not live to see another wedding in the family."

The guilt is nothing to sneeze at. But then Hilaire's father chimes in: "It makes more sense to do it in California, where you both live. Why should everyone here have to travel halfway around the world?"

The logistics make my head spin. If we marry in Hungary, Hilaire's elderly relatives can't make the journey. If we marry in California, most of my family and childhood friends can't afford the trip. We're caught between two continents, two cultures, and two sets of expectations.

After weeks of agonizing phone calls and sleepless nights, we settle on California—but that only opens a new can of worms.

"Well, if it's going to be in America," my sister says, "you need to invite at least the Hungarian family who live there—cousin Andrea, cousin Csaba ..."

"And obviously all our diving friends," Hilaire adds, making a list. "Greg, Eileen, Eo, the whole Aqua Adventures crew ..."

"What about the Miss Scuba community? We can't invite some and not others ..."

"And my NBC colleagues ..."

"And the jewelry clients who've become friends ..."

Within days, our intimate ceremony has ballooned into a 150-person production. Every name we add reminds us not to exclude someone else. Every phone call brings hurt feelings or obligations we hadn't considered. The stress is sucking all the fun out of planning what should be the best day of our lives.

"This is insane," I tell Hilaire one evening, staring at guest lists scattered across our kitchen table. "We're planning this wedding for everyone except us."

The breaking point comes when my mother calls, upset that we haven't invited my father's side of the family—relatives I haven't spoken to in years. "But they'll expect an invitation," she insists. "What will people think?"

"I don't care what people think!" I finally explode. "This is supposed to be about Hilaire and me, not about managing everyone else's expectations."

That night, Hilaire and I make the radical decision to uninvite *everyone*.

"Let's start over," he suggests. "Just us. Just witnesses. Just what *we* want."

We rip up the guest lists. The relief is immediate, but so is the self-reproach. And the phone calls are dreadful.

"You're having a wedding without your own family?" my mother asks, her voice small and hurt.

"Mom, we're not having a wedding without family. We're having a wedding that is *just* family—Hilaire and me, starting our own family."

Karen, a diving instructor friend of ours, agrees to officiate, and Eo (on my behalf) and John (Hilaire's friend), will serve as witnesses. That's it. Five people who truly matter in our lives, on a beach that holds meaning for us. But then, three days before the ceremony, the weather forecast appears: one hundred percent chance of rain.

Rain. In Southern California. In November.

It never rains here—that's why I live here, why everyone comes here for destination weddings. The irony is cruel.

"Maybe it's a sign," I tell Hilaire, staring at the dark clouds gathering outside our window.

"A sign of what?" he asks.

"That we should have done this in Hungary. In a church. With a hundred and fifty people and a proper reception."

He takes my hands. "Do you want a hundred and fifty people and a proper reception?"

"No."

"Then it's not a sign. It's just weather."

But I'm spiraling. "What if it pours? What if we're standing on the beach getting soaked? What if the photos are ruined? What if—"

"Then we'll get married in the rain," he says simply. "And it will be our story."

The morning of our wedding, I wake to the sound of heavy raindrops on our roof. The beach, usually crowded with joggers and surfers, is completely deserted. Gray clouds hang low over the ocean, and the wind whips sand across the empty shoreline.

"This is perfect," Hilaire says, and I think he's lost his mind.

"Perfect? It's a monsoon!"

"No, look." He points out the obvious. "It's ours. The whole beach is ours."

He's right. The rain has given us something money can't buy: complete privacy. No curious onlookers, no competing photo shoots, no distractions. Just us and the raw beauty of the ocean.

I put on my bohemian silk dress, a kaleidoscope of colors that mirrors my gypsy spirit—deep purples, blazing oranges, electric blues. It's completely impractical for a beach wedding, and I love it. Hilaire looks devastating in his sharp Italian suit, a true gentleman even facing a storm on our wedding day.

We slip on our rain boots—bright printed ones with flowers, which I bought as a joke—and head to the beach. Karen, Eo, and John are waiting, huddled under a lifeguard tower, laughing at the absurdity of it all.

As we walk along the beach, something miraculous happens: The rain stops. Not gradually, but all at once, as if someone has turned off a faucet. The clouds part just enough to let a shaft of golden sunlight break through, illuminating the wet sand so it sparkles like diamonds.

"See?" Hilaire whispers as we take our positions. "Perfect."

The ceremony is intimate and heartfelt, with the sound of waves as our soundtrack and the scent of rain-washed air as our perfume. When we kiss, the sun breaks through fully, warming our faces and turning the gray morning into something luminous.

Our wedding photos capture us laughing in our rain boots, dancing on the soaked sand in front of an iconic, turquoise-blue California lifeguard tower, completely ourselves in a moment we'd almost let others define for us. The threatening storm becomes our blessing—the thing that cleared away everything unnecessary and left us with exactly what we needed for this new beginning.

It's far from a grand production, but it's perfectly us. No family drama, no diplomatic guest lists, no one to please but ourselves. Just two people who chose each other, standing on a beach, promising to weather whatever storms come next.

* * *

Instead of pouring our savings into a big, traditional wedding, Hilaire and I invest in a meaningful experience together: a honeymoon trip to Nepal. We share a deep love for exploration and experiencing different cultures, and Nepal promises a journey filled with majestic landscapes, spiritual encounters, and the chance to trek in the Himalayas. Choosing Nepal over a lavish wedding reflects our principles and priorities: to seek experiences that enrich our souls rather than conforming to societal expectations.

Once we arrive in Kathmandu, our senses come alive amidst the city's radiant energy. Wandering through narrow alleys, we stumble upon a hidden gem—a small shop brimming with silver treasures. Among the trays of intricate jewelry, our eyes are drawn to two simple silver rings, designed to spin like ancient prayer wheels and adorned with the revered mantra *Om mani padme hum*. The phrase, often translated as "Praise to the jewel in the lotus," is one of Buddhism's most sacred mantras, believed to contain the essence of compassion and wisdom.

Each syllable carries deep meaning: *Om* represents the body, speech, and mind of Buddha. *Mani* (jewel) symbolizes the enlightened mind of compassion. *Padme* (lotus) represents wisdom growing from the mud of suffering, just as the pure lotus emerges from murky water. And *hum* signifies the unity of wisdom and compassion that leads to enlightenment. Tibetan Buddhists believe that reciting this mantra, or spinning it on prayer wheels, purifies negative karma and cultivates loving-kindness toward all beings.

As I hold these two rings, thinking about the journey that brought Hilaire and me to this moment—through the challenges of friendship, the risks of love, the adventures that tested and strengthened our bond—the symbolism feels perfect. Like the lotus rising from mud to bloom in beauty, our relationship has grown from the uncertain ground of *What if we ruin our friendship?* into something pure and strong.

"For husband and wife," the old man says with a knowing smile, "special price. Ten dollars. Both."

Ten dollars for our wedding rings. It's so absurd, we start laughing, but we know these rings aren't just jewelry—they need to become something more.

We find a Buddhist monk in a small temple tucked away in a quieter corner of the city. In a serene courtyard adorned with fluttering prayer flags, he performs a ceremony that feels more sacred than anything we could have had in a grand cathedral. The monk blesses our rings, our union, our journey together. When he places the rings on our fingers, they're warm with intention.

In a breathtaking twist of fate, we encounter the same holy Sadhus who grace the cover of our *Lonely Planet: Nepal* guidebook—a serendipitous moment that transforms a simple encounter into something extraordinary. We visit the sacred temple of fertility, where our conversations about starting a family take on deeper significance. But our ultimate adventure is trekking to Poon Hill.

At four a.m., guided by dim headlamps, we ascend through darkness toward the mountain summit. As the first light breaks over the horizon, prayer flags stretch across the sky, and a sense of tranquility washes over us. In this celestial setting, with hot chocolate warming our hands against the chill, we feel an absolute connection—to each other, to nature, and to the spiritual essence of the Himalayas. We take in the panoramic view, knowing the significance of this experience is etched into our souls forever.

After our epic journey through Nepal, filled with moments of awe and connection, we return home to a warm embrace from Eo and Paul, who generously host a wedding party for us in their enchanting garden, nestled among fragrant orange trees. The setting feels mystical, with twinkling lights adorning the branches, creating a canopy of soft illumination under the evening sky.

Amidst the glow of lanterns and the rustle of leaves in the gentle breeze, we dance under the stars, grateful for the love and support that surround us. This garden party, filled with warmth and sincerity, becomes the next episode in our love story, marking the beginning of a new, wild ride.

CHAPTER 14

Southern California: Becoming a Home-Based Gypsy

The moment a child is born, the mother is also born.
– Rajneesh

As Hilaire and I navigate life together, our time amid the peaks of the Himalayas and the colorful streets of Kathmandu stays with me, and a subtle shift occurs—a transformation I never saw coming. This fresh perspective alters my life's course in ways I never imagined.

For years, I have reveled in the thrill of travel, the rush of diving into new adventures and dreams, the determination to chart my own path without ties or responsibilities. In all that time, the idea of having children felt distant, almost repellent given my pursuit of freedom and exploration. But now, at age thirty-five, everything changes. Deeply immersed in my relationship with Hilaire, who shares my love for adventure yet grounds me in ways I never knew I needed, I find the thought of settling down and starting a family no longer feels daunting or restrictive.

It isn't a sudden epiphany but a gradual realization that echoes through quiet moments and shared dreams. I begin to see beyond my own desires and aspirations, to envision a future where our lives intertwine in new and meaningful ways. Having children with Hilaire resonates as a natural progression—a choice born from love and a deep connection.

I embrace the idea of becoming a home-based gypsy, blending the adventurous spirit that defines us with the warmth and stability of creating a true home. I imagine our future children as part of this vibrant tapestry, raised with a sense of wonder and curiosity, nurtured by the same love for exploration that has shaped our lives. This profound desire humbles me and fills me with a sense of purpose I have never known. I understand, finally, what my mother spoke of: a burning desire not just to create life, but to nurture it, to share in its joys and challenges, and to forge a legacy rooted in love and adventure.

As I journey onward with Hilaire by my side, I embrace this realization with open arms, knowing that our path forward will be as unpredictable and exhilarating as the adventures that brought us together. But to my shock, getting pregnant does not come easy.

Both Hilaire and I have lived lives filled with daredevilry and vigor. Now, the reality of our past experiences comes into sharp focus. Hilaire, twelve years my senior, once embraced the rock 'n' roll lifestyle to the fullest, touring with iconic bands like AC/DC and Metallica, where fast living was part of his job. Years of late nights, travel escapades, and the highs of live music have left their mark, not just on our memories but on our bodies, too.

Despite our youthful exuberance and zest for life, the road to conception becomes a lesson in patience and resilience. We navigate doctor's appointments, medical advice, and the emotional ups and downs that accompany this deeply personal journey. Each month brings a mix of hope and disappointment as we wrestle with the uncertainties of fertility and the weight of our own histories.

Our process leads us down the costly and emotionally turbulent path of in vitro fertilization, or IVF. A cycle begins, filled with daily injections, monitoring appointments, and a delicate balancing act of hope and anxiety.

Each step forward feels like a rickety rope bridge, swaying between thrill and fear. Yet through it all, our bond grows stronger. We lean on each other for support, finding solace in shared moments of vulnerability and determination. We confront the challenges head-on, drawing strength from our love and the vision we hold of a future family.

Choosing the doctor with the best IVF success rates proves challenging. We finally select a doctor renowned more for his clinical skill than his bedside manner. During our first consultation, I notice amateur underwater photos on his desk. To my surprise, he's an avid diver like us. Thanks to our common love for the ocean, amidst charts and treatments in that sterile medical environment, we connect on a personal level.

When my phone rings with the news, I'm teaching scuba diving at a private client's pool, where the aquamarine waters shimmer under the California sun. Somehow, the call feels weighty before I even answer. My student watches me, unaware of the monumental news being delivered. My heart races with eagerness and disbelief. Tears well up in my eyes, mirroring the happiness flooding through me.

Against the odds, our doctor's expertise and a bit of fate have aligned: We've defied statistics and expectations, achieving success on our very first attempt.

In that moment, surrounded by the echoes of splashing water and the faint scent of chlorine, the world stands still. Gratitude washes over me, mingled with the incomprehensible realization that our IVF journey has reached its goal, bringing us this precious, life-changing gift.

* * *

The news of our pregnancy fills us with exhilaration and relief. Hilaire and I delight in this moment, suddenly realizing how much things are about to change.

As I progress through my pregnancy, an indescribable glow of euphoria and contentment envelops me. Each day deepens my connection to the miraculous journey of creating life, and I savor every moment. The gentle fluttering of our baby's kicks fills me with love and wonder—a cherished reminder of the new life growing within, a constant source of amazement and anticipation.

Preparing for our little one's arrival becomes a beautiful, bonding experience for Hilaire and me. Despite the bliss of early pregnancy, life continues to bring both challenges and opportunities. Each morning, my heart brims with a smile, not just from the glee of carrying our baby, but also from the influx of stunt-related job offers coming my way.

I'm still managing daily operations at Deep Sea Adventures. Acutely aware of the need to prioritize my health and safety, I carefully vet each SAG opportunity, ensuring that it aligns with my commitment to my well-being and that of our unborn child. When a casting director reaches out about divers needed for a major brand's ad campaign, I'm intrigued. And when I learn that the shoot will take place in a studio with no water involved, my enthusiasm skyrockets.

The casting process is rigorous, with thousands auditioning. But soon I receive the spine-tingling news: I've been selected for the role. I'll be featured in the new billboard advertisements for Nissan.

On the day of the shoot, the studio buzzes with energy as the crew prepares for the commercial. The set is carefully designed, with a sleek, turquoise Nissan at its center. Once we start, I'm fitted with a harness and wires over my wetsuit. The director explains the scene: I'll be suspended, creating the illusion that I'm floating out of the trunk of the blue-green vehicle and swimming toward a school of colorful fish, which will be added later through CGI.

The project wraps, and I'm tickled to learn that the billboard campaign spans major US cities from Beverly Hills to New York. The completed billboard—bold and bedazzling, a striking fusion of Nissan and my own personal journey—fills me with a deep sense of pride.

Once I discover I'm pregnant, I stop diving, but my connection to the ocean evolves as I focus more intensively on managing Deep Sea Adventures. Deep down, however, I know that after our kid is born, I will not want to be away from my newborn.

Alongside my work at the dive shop, Gogh Jewelry Design has continued to thrive, evolving from a passion project into a flourishing business. What began as a creative outlet has grown into something much bigger. The realization is strange but honest: I'm ready to transition from focusing on somebody else's scuba business to running my own company.

Thankfully, the pregnancy is smooth and relatively comfortable. My days are sprinkled with yoga, blissful swims, and brisk, energizing walks. Staying active is a priority, and even as my belly grows, Hilaire and I continue in-line skating on the boardwalk and hiking in nearby national parks, savoring these moments before our little one arrives.

Convinced we're having a girl, we settle on the name Sophia, imagining our future with her. When we learn the baby is in fact a boy, our elation shifts and we start hunting for the perfect name. Hilaire suggests something Italian, and I love the idea of something timeless with cultural depth. After much debate, inspiration strikes: Enzo, after the legendary freediver Enzo Maiorca, made globally famous by the film *The Big Blue*. This beautiful name resonates with both of us, capturing our love for the sea and the pursuit of excitement. Also, *Enzo* is hard to butcher—with names like Hilaire and Szilvia, we understand that this is a factor.

In the final month, my body transforms—heavy and stretched, accommodating this new life. I feel like a giant whale. Each day brings physical challenges, but the water becomes my sanctuary, where the heaviness lifts, and I find peace and relief, floating weightlessly.

Eileen, my wonderful scuba friend, throws me a baby shower. Walking into the teahouse, I'm greeted by my friends, all beaming with joy—for me. Surrounded with the generosity, love, and blessings of friends I've made since I moved to America, I'm deeply touched. I never imagined being part of such a sisterhood. Despite always seeing myself as the tomboy type, I now have way more female friends than male ones. And I like it.

Many of my yogi friends swear by their doula, and I want that steady emotional support during childbirth. But when I discover our insurance won't cover the cost—fifteen hundred dollars—I feel discouraged. Although I connect with a few doulas, disappointment soon sets in: The first is booked, and the second cancels due to burnout. With no doula in sight and my due date approaching, I rethink my approach.

Instead of giving in to frustration, I channel that money into weekly prenatal massages, offering both physical relief and calm—moments of peace amid the hectic final weeks of pregnancy. While it isn't the plan I originally envisioned, it's a plan that works for me. Sometimes the best support comes in unexpected forms.

A week before Enzo's due date, I'm at a gem show, navigating the aisles with an enormous belly that seems to brush against everything, each step slow and deliberate. Although it feels as if I'm carrying the weight of the world along with my soon-to-be-born son, the trip is worth it. December is always a whirlwind for my jewelry business. Each crafted piece feels like a bit of myself that I'm sending out into the world, and I want each one to be perfect. My holiday orders are piling up, and I'm on the hunt for the perfect beads to fulfill them before Enzo arrives.

I get home, drained but with adrenaline from the day still buzzing through me. The clock ticks closer to nine p.m., and after a long day of crafting, I finally wrap up my work just as Hilaire walks through the door. He's been working tirelessly for NBC, balancing roles as a camera operator, producer, and editor for shows like *1st Look* and *Open House*.

Just as I stand up to get ready for bed, there's a sudden, unmistakable rush as my water breaks. In an instant, the calm of the evening shatters.

We spring into action, grabbing our things and heading out the door. Despite the urgency, I can't help but ask Hilaire to make a quick detour to the post office so I can drop off the completed orders. It's absurd! But that's me: unable to bear the thought of leaving anything unfinished.

We arrive at Harbor City Kaiser Permanente hospital at eleven p.m., and the atmosphere shifts to one of preparation. Being scheduled to give birth suddenly feels serendipitous; from the start, I unexpectedly receive the kind of care and support I've been longing for. The nurse asks me to rate my pain and inquires about my birth plan. She chuckles at my hopeful naïvety in counting on my vision of a "quick and easy" birth, knowing full well that labor rarely goes as planned.

I quickly toss aside the exercise ball we brought, as the pain is too intense to meditate or perform relaxing breathing exercises—like the worst period cramps I've ever had, multiplied by ten. There's no point in waiting: I'm going to want that epidural eventually, so why not get it now? The nurses agree, and by midnight, the epidural is in place.

The relief is almost immediate, and I can breathe again. Hilaire and I settle in, both of us drifting off to sleep while the monitor quietly tracks Enzo's progress.

Five hours later, to everyone's surprise, I've progressed far faster than expected. The nurse wakes me up, saying, "It's time to have a baby!"

The room buzzes with quiet preparation as the staff prepare for delivery. When a homeopathic midwife arrives, I feel a wave of relief. I didn't want to deliver with a stranger wielding a scalpel; I wanted someone to guide me through the natural, sacred process of birth. But with Kaiser, you don't get to pick your doctor. Whoever is on duty the day of your baby's arrival is going to help deliver your bundle of joy.

As each contraction arrives, I push or hold back in response to the midwife's directions as Hilaire stays by my side, holding my leg. I decline the mirror, not sure I want to witness by body tearing as Enzo's head crowns. Hilaire, ever the adventurer, sees everything—images I'm sure he'll never forget.

At 6:28 a.m. on December 7, after both an eternity and just a moment, our Enzo is born. His first breath seems to fill the room with a sense of awe. They place him on my belly—healthy and beautiful, weighing 7.7 pounds, all covered in slime—and for a moment, time stands still.

He is perfect.

Without hesitation, he latches onto my breast, nursing like a champ within minutes. His hair is dark and thick, a full head of it, and his eyes are a deep, captivating blue. His tiny hand grips his father's finger, inspiring love and amazement in Hilaire's eyes as he looks down at our son.

This moment is indescribably powerful—the three of us together, skin to skin, sharing in the magic of this golden hour. It's a moment of pure connection, a bond that feels ancient and unbreakable, as we welcome our child into the world and into our hearts.

* * *

Newborns can't see much in their first days, but Enzo already knows us. He senses us, recognizing our voices after months spent listening to us from the warmth of my belly. When we speak, he turns his tiny head toward the sound, his unfocused eyes searching for the familiar presence of his parents. It's a small, miraculous thing—this connection that transcends sight.

Since insurance covers it, Hilaire and I decide to take advantage of an extra night in the hospital to learn from the nurses and get some rest before parenthood fully hits. The nurses show us things no book or class can fully prepare us for: how to swaddle Enzo, interpret his cries, and navigate the basics of newborn care. I reflect on the months of preparation, the baby classes, the decisions we made. Now, with Enzo in my arms, all I feel is gratitude for this little life we've brought into the world.

At home, Enzo sleeps peacefully in a bassinet next to me while I work on jewelry orders for the holiday rush, music playing softly in the background. It's our way of blending our old life with the new, making space for him without losing ourselves. Physically, I'm recovering well. Enzo is healthy, and we're all adjusting to this new life together. We're only at the beginning, but I know it's going to be the greatest journey of our lives.

When Enzo is just a week old, our family of three starts taking long, leisurely walks on the beach—a ritual to introduce him to the world while keeping our spirits high. From the beginning, Hilaire and I agree on keeping parenting as stress-free as possible. A little dirt on the pacifier? It's good for the immune system.

Hilaire reluctantly resumes his busy work schedule. His steady job at NBC provides our safety net, and his unwavering support reminds me that we're navigating this delicate balance together. Enzo and I are on our own for the long days now, and walks on the beach or around the block do wonders for both of us. The fresh air calms the baby, and it gives me a chance to clear my mind, to step away from the well-meaning parenting advice descending on me from all directions.

As if adjusting to life with a newborn isn't enough, we also dive head-first into house hunting. Our small home in Redondo Beach is cozy, but we need more space for our growing family. After months of searching, we finally find a place we both love and can afford—a new home that feels just right for this next phase of our lives.

My mom comes from Hungary to visit her first grandchild, and I'm on cloud nine. We take a road trip to San Francisco when Hilaire is hired to video Robin Williams' house for a TV show. As we drive back to Southern California, I stare out the window at the sun setting over the Pacific, feeling blessed. Moments like these are truly precious.

Throughout my time at home, bonding with Enzo, the thought of returning to work at Deep Sea Adventures fills me with dread. I've loved every second I've spent with him—his sweet gurgling, his adorable smiles, the way his tiny fingers curl around mine. I keep thinking of Hungary, where new mothers can stay home for two years with pay. In America, many get only two weeks. I stretch my leave to three months, unpaid, wishing desperately for more time.

Joel kindly offers to let me bring Enzo to work at Deep Sea Adventures, but the reality isn't ideal. Enzo spends most of his time trapped in his bassinet on my desk while I handle clients, and I have to retreat to the changing room to breastfeed. It's not the nurturing environment I'd envisioned for either of us.

When Joel suggests I leave Enzo with Rhonda, his housekeeper, while I work, it seems like a reasonable solution. My son is well cared for and bottle-fed, but I can't shake the feeling that I'm missing everything that matters. I drop him off at Joel's house at ten a.m. and pick him up at seven p.m. The separation feels like a physical ache.

Hiring Rhonda allows me to focus on running the dive shop and my jewelry business, knowing Enzo is in capable hands. Rhonda is warm and attentive, and Enzo adores her. But as the months pass, I start noticing the heartbreaking details—how Enzo reaches for Rhonda when he's upset, how he claps excitedly when she walks through the door—and barely notices in passing that I am leaving for work.

It's the moment I'm not supposed to see that breaks me completely. I'm running late to pick up Enzo from Joel's house. Through the kitchen window, I see my son take his first real tumble—a stumble that sends him sprawling across the patio. For a split second, my heart stops.

This is it, I think. *This is when he'll need his mama.*

But instead of crying for me, instead of looking around for the comfort only a mother can provide, Enzo reaches for Rhonda. She scoops him up and kisses his scraped knee, and within seconds, he's giggling again. The ease of it, the natural way he turns to her for comfort—it's like watching someone else's child.

I stand frozen outside that window, feeling like an intruder in my own son's life.

What am I doing? I wonder. I'm working full-time in Venice Beach with the diving operation, and the money I make barely covers the cost of someone else raising my child. And to be honest, my heart is no longer in it. I'm burnt out from managing other people's dive centers.

Maybe I need an exit strategy. I've been building up my jewelry business from home, selling through Whole Foods and Amazon. Is it time to leave Deep Sea Adventures to become a full-time mom and entrepreneur?

The thought stirs up a tempest of emotions. Stepping away from the dive shop would mean losing the structured environment where I thrive—the camaraderie, the sense of purpose, the daily interactions that energize me. I worry that the isolation of working from home would creep in, making me question whether I'd made the right choice. And even with Hilaire's safety net, relying solely on my jewelry business feels financially precarious.

But what's the point of it all? What is worth missing Enzo's every milestone, watching him prefer another woman's comfort, sacrificing these precious early years—for what? To break even? To pay someone else to be the mother I'm supposed to be?

My heart tells me this is the path I need to take. Being present in my son's life—in my own life—is worth any risk. I need to stop making life possible for someone else and start building something that's my own.

Everything has to change.

CHAPTER 15

Malta and Spain: A Balancing Act

Grief is the price we pay for love.
– Queen Elizabeth II

Too much time has passed since my last scuba dive, an outing to Catalina Island. I'm settling into my new routine of managing the jewelry business from home, but amid the chaos of life's major changes, I yearn for the solace of the underwater world.

As much as I want to savor Enzo's childhood, I don't quite fit in with the other stay-at-home moms. Their conversations revolve around nap schedules and organic snacks, while I take a more laid-back approach. I have little interest in dissecting sleep training methods or debating the merits of various baby products and parenting manuals. I have no intention of becoming one of those helicopter parents, even when he gets older. I'll be more likely to watch him from the corner of my eyes, content to let him run free, explore the world, and get dirty while my mind drifts elsewhere. I love being his mom, but I don't entirely belong in this world of constant baby talk.

I decide to seek out occasional stunt work and start teaching private diving lessons again. My first client after pregnancy is one of my favorites: Michael Wolper, whose father produced *The Undersea World of Jacques Cousteau*. Michael grew up spending time on Cousteau's ship, the *Calypso*. He is a free-spirited ocean lover, just like me, which is why we get along so well. I trained all of his kids, his brother's kids, and several friends he referred to me over the years. Teaching his wife to dive now feels like reconnecting to that legacy and camaraderie.

Stepping back into the water brings an overwhelming sense of relief and joy. The Pacific Ocean greets me with unusually clear visibility and vibrant marine life, making my return feel like a warm embrace. But even as I try to find my rhythm, life has other plans.

Soon after Enzo was born, Hilaire's father was discharged after a routine surgery only to be rushed back to the hospital with sudden complications. He suffered a heart attack and was clinically dead for several minutes before being revived. Hilaire arrived just in time to witness his father's heart stop three more times before he slipped into a coma.

I was holding on to hope that Enzo's only grandfather would regain enough strength to see his grandson grow up. But after several months in the hospital, Hilaire's father passes away, leaving Hilaire physically and emotionally drained—and an orphan, as his mother passed away from cancer just before we met.

Now I'm hoping that what once made us so happy will cure our current blues. We both love to travel and want to instill that same passion in Enzo, so he'll see the world as a place to explore. We want him to grow up feeling like traveling to faraway places is an essential part of life. When Enzo's passport arrives, it opens up the door to many adventures.

Our first family trip is to Malta, where my mom, my sister, and my friend Eo join us. Traveling with an infant takes things to a whole new level, and not just because of the free airline travel for children under two years old. We do our best to work around his sleep schedule, though it doesn't always go as planned. I tell myself that every new experience will help

Enzo acclimate to various environments and make him more adaptable to constantly changing plans.

Hilaire and I set our sights on Gozo Island and the Blue Hole—one of my all-time favorite spots in Malta. The landscape is just as breathtaking as I remember, with rocky formations framing the sparkling azure waters. I shed the cumbersome wetsuit in favor of a shorty, reveling in the warm embrace of the sea.

We descend into the Blue Hole, where the chimney-like entrance plunges fifty feet before opening into the vast sea. I am overtaken by awe and respect, yet beneath its beauty lies the stark reality of this technical dive spot. Each diver must navigate the intricate passageways with precision, because there is only one way in and out: a swim-through that leads from the surface to the open ocean. It is one of the most magnificent and dramatic seascapes in the big blue.

But that day, misfortune strikes, shattering all my thoughts of tranquility. An Englishman runs out of air and shoots up too quickly from 120 feet, and his buddy desperately follows him in a reckless ascent. The chaos escalates when a sixty-three-year-old Austrian man becomes separated from his group and is later found unconscious, floating on the surface. Strong winds ground the rescue boats, so helicopters are called in, their whirring blades slicing the air.

We soon learn that all three divers lost their lives—a tragic reminder of the dangers that humans face beneath the waves. Each heartbeat echoes in my chest, absorbing the terrible news. The serene seascape I longed to escape into is now overshadowed by the weight of loss. Our peaceful dive day has quickly transformed into a somber indication of the ocean's unpredictable power and the tragic consequences of unpreparedness. I just want to go back to our apartment.

On the journey back, a rare, foreboding Maltese rain begins to fall. Traveling the slick, oily roads, we encounter ten accidents in just forty minutes. Most involve motorcycles and scooters, but just a block away from our destination, two cars collide right in front of us. We mount the sidewalk, narrowly avoiding them, and then take break from driving for a while. By the time we arrive at the apartment, Hilaire and I, and pretty much everybody in our vehicle, are ready for a shot of vodka.

After a less-than-relaxing vacation in Malta, I look forward to spending a week in Hungary, where both of my grandmothers cherish their time with Enzo. This trip also marks a long-awaited reunion with my childhood friend Nóra and two other diving companions from the BHG Scuba Diving Club: Reni and Vica. All of us are excited to meet each other's kids.

We eat a picnic lunch spread out on a checkered linen blanket by a lake we used to compete in. Vica's toddler is fast asleep in her stroller—it's well past naptime, but she'd rather let him sleep naturally after our morning hike than rush home to maintain a rigid schedule. Reni, who nurses her baby as we catch up on the years that have passed since we last saw each other, is unfazed when he fusses during our animated discussion.

"He'll adapt," she says with a shrug, adjusting him to her other arm so she can sketch our route on a napkin.

When Nóra's son scraped his knee on the rocky path earlier that morning, Nóra simply rinsed it with water from her hiking bottle, gave him a quick hug, and pointed out a butterfly nearby. Within minutes, all the kids were back to exploring, mud-streaked and grinning. These women haven't shrunk their worlds to fit around their children—they've simply expanded their adventures to include them.

Amidst these joyful moments, and perhaps intensified by them, I struggle with a sense of uprootedness. The easygoing nature and adventurous spirit of old friends makes me wish they lived closer. I meet so few mothers like this—laid-back, fun-loving, deeply connected to the outdoors—in the US.

My home country was once the center of my world, but after living abroad for nearly half my life, I no longer feel like I belong in Hungary. I am not familiar with today's Hungarian music trends and don't get the most current slang. Over more than a decade, I've built a good life in America.

But I will never feel truly American. I did not grow up watching TV here, so I do not understand references to certain events and older movies my Californian friends talk about. Now that I have a child, this feeling of being caught between worlds is even stronger. My identity has become a mosaic of all the places I've lived and the experiences I've had, but I long for a place where I feel fully at home.

* * *

A year after returning from Hungary, the renovation of our new house in Redondo Beach is underway, with workers coming and going at all hours, hammering, sawing, and banging. Living and working under these conditions, I find it hard to relax. Hilaire and I hardly get any time alone together, not even for a date night. We're always tired and impatient with each other and frustrated with life in general. I think of that saying: *It takes a village.* But where is this village when you need help?

To regroup and recharge, we set out for a family trip to Spain.

We arrive in Barcelona past midnight, and the lively local atmosphere draws us in right away. Instead of renting a car, we walk everywhere, soaking up both the Picasso exhibition and the mild November weather. We savor delicious ham, cheese, and fresh bread, all perfectly complemented by a Spanish gin and tonic. Enzo quickly falls in love with the local food, deciding right then and there to abandon baby food altogether.

Our plan is to explore Spain by train, a mode of travel convenient for parents and ideal for a curious little boy. En route to Madrid, Enzo stays wide awake, mesmerized by the changing scenery and the gentle rhythm of the ride. In the heart of the city, we feast on tapas and visit the Prado Museum, where Bosch's psychedelic art leaves a lasting impression. Hilaire thoughtfully crafts our daily itinerary so Enzo can roam a nearby park in the mornings before dozing off, and we can seize the afternoon naptime for cultural stimulation and a bit of adult conversation.

In Sevilla, we marvel at rich ambiance and the ornate, Moroccan-inspired decor. But Granada, with its Egyptian-style architecture and mouth-watering gyros, steals our hearts. We climb the basilica tower for sweeping views, explore the stunning palace gardens (a must for any *Game of Thrones* fan), and linger over tea beside fragrant jasmine bushes. Staying at the Alhambra is magical for us all, stirring up Enzo's joyful energy and savored moments over coffee and wine, deep conversations, and laughter.

Traveling in Europe brings its own unique charm and effortless elegance, whether in the cuisine, the art and architecture, or the people themselves. This carefree escape feels like the perfect reset before the holiday season—a refreshing pause to enjoy each other and experience the warmth, beauty, and charm of Spain.

The following Tuesday at seven p.m. Hungary time, I'm looking forward to sharing my impressions with my mother on our weekly video chat. It's only ten a.m. in California, and I'm shattered from another sleepless night. Maybe it's jet lag—Enzo was up every few hours, and I feel like I'm moving through fog. But this is our routine, and I love the way Mutti's face lights up each week when she sees her grandson.

I settle into my office chair with Enzo in my arms, his sweet jabbering filling the space as I dial. I'm already smiling, anticipating that virtual hug from my mom, the way she'll coo at Enzo through the screen and tell me what a good job I'm doing as a mother.

But when her face appears on my laptop, my stomach drops. Her expression is somber, heavy. Gone is the usual sparkle that lights up her eyes when she sees us.

"Szilvia," she says.

Something hollow in her voice makes me grip Enzo tighter. I know immediately that bad news is coming. I just have no idea how devastating it will be.

"I had a biopsy last week," she continues, her words careful and measured. "Of a lump I found in my breast."

The words don't compute at first. I stare at her pixelated image, Enzo still gurgling innocently in my arms, oblivious to the bomb that's just been dropped.

"The pathology results ..." She pauses, and my world tilts. "It's malignant. And it's spread to the lymph nodes under my armpit."

Cancer.

Mutti has cancer.

I freeze with my breath caught somewhere between my lungs and my throat, choked by the magnitude of what I've just heard. But I'm sure I heard wrong. This can't be happening. I've just had a child—I can't become an orphan now. Mutti has desperately wanted a grandchild for decades, and she finally has Enzo.

How can this be happening?

I take a deep breath, forcing my mind into survival mode.

What's next? How can I fix this? There has to be a way to fix this.

"Okay," I hear myself saying, though my voice sounds foreign. "Okay, Mutti. We're going to figure this out. What did the doctor say? What are the treatment options?"

But even as I ask the practical questions, even as I try to be strong for her, a terrifying thought creeps in: I could lose her. Just like Dad. Just when Enzo needs his grandmother most.

That night, after Hilaire falls asleep, I lie in bed with my hands pressed against my chest, feeling for lumps that might not have been there yesterday. My breasts are still heavy with milk, tender and swollen, making it impossible to know what's normal and what might be deadly.

Is this lump from nursing? Or is it something more sinister?

Each night becomes the same ritual: lying in the dark, checking and rechecking, feeling for changes, for threats, for the thing that might take me away from Enzo the way it took Dad from me. I finally have everything I want in life, and now this specter of genetic destiny looms over it all. I calculate obsessively: Dad died at thirty-nine. I'm thirty-eight.

Does that mean I only have a year? Should I be planning for the worst?

Enzo sleeps peacefully beside me, his tiny chest rising and falling with complete trust in the unspoken promise that I'll be there when he wakes up.

What if I can't keep that promise?

* * *

My mother dives into a whirlwind of alternative treatments, from Chinese medicine to Brazilian telepathic healing and even a grapes-only diet.

Suddenly, everyone is an expert, bombarding Mutti with advice on what to eat, what to try, what to avoid. My cousin Andi insists she abandon chemo altogether, a suggestion I strongly oppose. But the real nightmare begins when we try to navigate the Hungarian healthcare system.

Free healthcare sounds like a blessing until you realize what "free" actually means in Hungary: outdated equipment, overworked doctors, and a system so overwhelmed that it fails to serve consistent information or empathy. When the MRI shows cancer has spread to Mutti's bones, the doctor, exhausted from a twelve-hour shift, delivers the news with clinical detachment: "Bone metastases. We'll need to start aggressive daily chemotherapy for three weeks, then a week off. Fifty-fifty chance of success."

Csilla calls me, crying, to break the news. While Enzo naps beside me, I frantically Google survival rates and find that each statistic is worse than the last.

For weeks, I exist in this new reality. I research bone cancer treatments, alternative therapies, anything that might give us hope. I plan how to get Mutti to America for better care, even though we can't afford it. I calculate how many jewelry sales I'd need to pay for experimental treatments.

Then Csilla calls again. "They did a PET scan." I hear something different in her voice. "The results are ... confusing."

The PET scan shows no bone involvement. None. The cancer is in her breast and lymph nodes only. Either the MRI was completely wrong, or Mutti somehow healed miraculously through all those grapes she's been eating and telepathic healers she's been trying.

The relief is so overwhelming, I actually vomit. Enzo wakes up crying, startled by the sound, and I'm sobbing and laughing as I pick him up, telling him his grandmother might be okay after all. But my relief is short-lived.

"Her doctor says we should trust the PET scan," Csilla continues. "But the chief oncologist thinks the MRI was probably right and the PET scan missed something. They can't agree."

How can they not know? How can two tests, done a week apart, show completely different realities? In America, this would mean more tests, second opinions, clearer answers. In Hungary, it means shrugging doctors and conflicting advice from overtasked specialists who barely have time to review the files.

So which is it? Is Mutti going to live or die?

The uncertainty becomes torture. Every day brings new confusion, new contradictory information. One day, the nurses are optimistic. The next, they're preparing us for the worst. The emotional whiplash is unbearable—hope in the morning, despair by evening, back to hope the next day.

The endless cycle of hope and despair around my mother's treatment reminds me of something I've read in Thich Nhat Hanh's writings about impermanence. *This too shall pass*, he teaches—but the wisdom applies to both the good news and the bad. The relief when her PET scan showed no bone involvement passed just as quickly as the devastation when the MRI suggested otherwise. Learning to hold both hope and despair lightly, without grasping too tightly to either, becomes its own form of survival.

Mutti's treatment drags on, with no clear prognosis, and a question haunts me daily: Should I go home for an extended visit?

Every night, after Enzo falls asleep, I stare at my laptop screen, researching one-way tickets to Budapest. The cursor hovers over *Book Now* as I imagine being there to hold Mutti's hand through chemo … drive her to appointments … be the daughter she needs right now.

Then reality crashes in like a cold wave. I have a baby who is still nursing, still needing me every few hours. How could I take him there now—exposing him to hospitals, to the stress and chaos of a medical crisis, to a country where his father can't easily visit because he is working full time and has no vacation days left for this year? I see it in Hilaire's eyes when I bring up the possibility: the fear that if I take his son to Hungary now, he might lose us both to distance, to a family emergency that could stretch for months, maybe years.

"You don't want Enzo in that situation," he says gently, desperately. "And what if something happens to you? What if you get sick too?"

I hate it, but he's right.

Leaving Enzo behind is equally unthinkable. What mother would abandon her nursing baby? It feels like an impossible choice, between the person who gave me life and the person I gave life to. But trying to parent from six thousand miles away would be even worse than trying to daughter from the same impossible distance.

The cruel mathematics of an international family crisis become clear: Moving my mother here for treatment would bankrupt us. But staying here while she suffers feels like a betrayal of everything she sacrificed for me. I'm trapped in this netherworld of partial presence, where every video call becomes both lifeline and torture device. Mutti's face grows gaunt. Her energy fades. And all I can do is watch through a screen.

"Maybe you should go," Hilaire finally says as I pace our bedroom for the third night this week. "Take Enzo. I'll visit when I can."

We both know what that really means. His job can't accommodate extended international travel. If I go, he'll be alone. Our family will be split across continents during some of the most crucial months of our son's life.

There's no good choice. Every option betrays someone I love: Stay, and I abandon my mother in her darkest hour. Go, and I risk my son's health and his bond with his father. The guilt is eating me alive. I'm failing everyone who matters most.

My visit to Hungary for the holidays brings some precious moments, particularly introducing Enzo to the winter white of a snowed-in Budapest. I do my best to savor moments of joy: Enzo meeting his new cousin Hanga, long walks in the Hungarian countryside. But the shadow of Mutti's illness looms over everything.

At a family gathering, I catch up with my cousin Noémi, who is just a year older than me and has three beautiful daughters. To my surprise, she was recently going through a divorce when cancer upended her life completely, too. I have not spoken to her in years and had no idea about these difficult milestones in her life. She initially decided against a mastectomy, terrified of losing her sense of self, her femininity. But after a year of hoping natural remedies might save her, she has no choice now but to begin chemotherapy.

Pesti Nagyi, my maternal grandma, is also struggling with deteriorating health. In the hospital for a month now, she can't even sit upright and is gasping for breath. She doesn't recognize anyone, doesn't want to eat or drink, and sleeps all the time. Her skin has thinned so much, it's practically translucent. It's awful to see her like this, and I hope she doesn't linger too long in this in-between world.

Mutti makes it through her surgery and is recovering well. Back at home, she receives visitors every day, cooking for them instead of just serving them a bag of chips or letting them bring food to her. Typical.

But her chemotherapy isn't working. The ultrasound shows the tumors haven't just failed to shrink—they've grown. Another devastating scan shows cancerous tumors everywhere: her ribs, her spine, even her skull. A week later, an X-ray shows nothing. We're stuck between contradictory results, teetering between relief and dread—again.

Grandma dies one Wednesday at age ninety-seven, without Mutti ever telling her she has cancer. But Grandma knew. They didn't talk about it, but a mother can sense these things.

When I accompany Mutti to her next chemo session, I ask whether she might be strong enough to visit California next month, when this round of treatment will be over. The doctor stares at me, bewildered. "The treatments will continue indefinitely—as long as they're effective," he explains. "There is no end date."

Once a week ... forever.

The floor shifts beneath me as finality settles in like cold steel. All this time, I'd clung to hope of a finish line. Now I'm left wrestling with the truth: We are trapped in this rhythm of waiting, wondering how much time we have left.

I take Enzo back to California and try to maintain an optimistic outlook, but it's hard to see good in this situation. This year has worn me out: My hair has gone gray. My face is wrinkled from stress.

In the new year, just a month after my last visit, Csilla insists I should come back home as soon as possible if I want to see Mutti alive again. I think she's being dramatic, but I buy a plane ticket anyway.

Deep down, I know she's right.

* * *

The mammography room feels colder than usual, or maybe it's just me. I've done this only once before—the ritual disrobing, the awkward positioning, the mechanical compression that squeezes the breath from my lungs. The technician's previous chatter has dried up into clipped, professional silence.

"Hold your breath," she says, her voice carefully neutral.

The machine whirs and clicks. I stare at the ceiling tiles, counting the small holes in each square, focusing on anything but the uncomfortable pressure flattening my breast against the cold metal plate. My heart hammers against my ribs—can the machine pick that up too?

"Breathe normally. We're going to do a few more views."

A few more views? That doesn't seem normal.

My stomach starts to churn, but I force a smile when the technician glances my way. As she adjusts the paddle again, the gel feels like ice water spreading across my skin. Each compression sends shooting pains through my breast, but I grit my teeth and stay still.

Minutes stretch toward infinity. The technician steps behind her protective barrier, and I hear the familiar buzz of the X-ray—once, twice, three times. With each exposure, the knot in my stomach tightens.

"You can get dressed now," she finally says, avoiding my eyes. "Someone will call you."

"Everything look okay?" I ask, trying to keep my voice light.

She pauses at the door, her hand on the handle. "I'm not an expert. The radiologist will review everything and be in touch."

The way she says it—like she's reading from a script—makes my mouth go dry.

Two hours later, my phone buzzes.

"Ms. Gogh? This is the imaging center calling. We need you to come back in for some additional views."

I sink onto my couch, my legs suddenly unreliable. "Additional views?"

"We found some areas of concern that need further evaluation. Can you come in Tuesday for a biopsy?"

Areas of concern. The phrase echoes in my head as the room seems to tilt sideways. I grip the arm of the couch, my knuckles turning pale. "How many areas?" My voice sounds strange, like it's coming from somewhere far away.

"Three distinct masses. Dr. Harrison will explain everything when you come in."

Three. The number lodges in my throat like a stone. I try to swallow, but my mouth has gone completely dry. "Tuesday," I repeat numbly. "But I'm supposed to fly to Hungary tomorrow to see my mother. She's … she's very sick."

"I understand this is difficult timing, but these seem to be solid masses, not cystic. The biopsy really can't wait."

Solid masses. The phone slips in my sweaty palm. The clinical language doesn't soften the blow—if anything, it makes it worse. In the background, the clock on the table ticks on, each second marking time I might not have.

"Okay," I whisper. "Tuesday."

Tuesday arrives like a death sentence. The biopsy suite is smaller than the mammography room, more intimate in its sterility. Dr. Harrison is a woman in her late sixties with silver hair and kind eyes behind wire-rimmed glasses. She has performed thousands of these procedures, her hands steady and sure. I see something in her expression that makes my chest tighten.

"We're going to numb the area first," she explains, her voice gentle but professional. "You'll feel a pinch, then some pressure."

The needle slides in, and I flinch at the sharp burn of the lidocaine. My heart is beating so hard, I'm sure everyone in the room can hear it. The assistant adjusts the ultrasound probe, and suddenly there they are on the monitor: three dark shadows in the grainy gray landscape of my breast tissue.

They look malevolent. Predatory.

"Try to stay very still," Dr. Harrison murmurs as she positions the biopsy gun.

The first sample sounds like a stapler firing. The vibration travels through my entire body, and I bite down on my lower lip to keep from crying out. Even through the numbing, I can feel the violation of the needle piercing deep into my flesh, claiming pieces of me.

Snap. Another sample. *Snap.* And another.

I focus on breathing, on not moving, on anything but the sound of my tissue being harvested for judgment. Dr. Harrison's brow furrows slightly as she studies the ultrasound screen. That tiny crease between her eyebrows tells me everything I don't want to know.

"How long until I can call for results?" I ask when it's finally over, pressing the gauze firmly against the tender spot.

"Usually a week. We don't typically give results over the phone ..."

Something in my expression stops her. Maybe it's the desperation I'm trying so hard to hide, or the way my hands are shaking despite my efforts to appear calm.

"You're traveling to see your mother?" she asks softly.

"She's dying. In Hungary. I may not get another chance to say goodbye."

Dr. Harrison studies me for a long moment, her professional mask slipping just slightly. "What's your flight schedule?"

"I leave tomorrow morning."

She nods slowly. "I'll see what I can do about expediting the results."

Perhaps the doctor senses that I'm the type of person who prefers to face challenges head-on. Whatever the reason, I'll be grateful to have all the facts as soon as possible. I've reveled in the thrill of the unknown all my life, but this is one time when I would rather not be left in suspense.

CHAPTER 16

Diving Inward: A Completely Different Journey

Never, never, never give up.
– Winston Churchill

Thursday morning, Budapest. The plane touches down at Ferenc Liszt International Airport, and I'm already reaching for my phone before we reach the end of the runway. The Hungarian countryside rushes past the small window—golden fields and red-roofed villages that should feel like coming home but instead feel like entering purgatory.

I'm wheeling my suitcase through the terminal when my phone buzzes with a California number: Dr. Harrison, calling from halfway around the world to deliver news that couldn't wait.

My blood turns to ice. "Hello?" My voice is barely a whisper.

"Ms. Gogh, it's Dr. Harrison. I told you I'd call if I could expedite the results."

The terminal noise fades to a distant buzz. People stream around me, hurrying toward customs, toward their families, toward their normal lives. I stand frozen in the middle of the flow like a rock protruding from a river.

"Time is of the essence here, and I didn't want you to spend another day not knowing." Her voice is gentle but direct—the voice of a woman who has delivered this news too many times. "All three biopsies came back positive for invasive ductal carcinoma."

Cancer.

The word arrives in my mind with such force, I stumble backward. The walls of the airport terminal seem to close in. The fluorescent lights are too bright, the air too thin. My free hand reaches out instinctively, grasping for something solid to hold onto.

"I need you to understand—this is aggressive, and it can't wait. You need to start treatment immediately. Not in a week. Not in a month. Now."

"But my mother … " I start, and then stop. What am I going to say? That I can't have cancer because my mother is already dying from it? That our family has already used up its quota of tragedy?

"I know this isn't what you wanted to hear, especially now. But these cancers—they don't wait for convenient timing. Every day matters."

My legs give out, and I sink onto a nearby bench, clutching the phone with both hands. Around me, loved ones reunite with laughter and tears of joy. A little girl runs into her father's arms. An elderly couple embraces after what must have been a long separation.

Life is continuing normally while mine implodes.

"What do I do?" I whisper.

"Come home. We need to get you in for staging immediately—MRI, CT scans, blood work. The sooner we know what we're dealing with, the sooner we can fight it."

Fight it. The words spark something deep in my chest—not hope exactly, but something fiercer. Defiance.

"How long do I have?" I ask, making my voice stronger than I feel.

"With treatment, with the right approach—this is very treatable. But time is critical."

I thank her and put the phone down on my lap, closing my eyes as the weight of the decision presses down on me. Spend these last precious moments with my dying mother, or save my own life? It's a choice between past and future, between goodbye and hope.

When I open my eyes, I'm already reaching for my phone to change my flight.

* * *

I have twenty-four hours.

Twenty-four hours to say goodbye to my dying mother before I fly back to fight for my own life. The universe's timing couldn't be more sadistic.

At the hospital, Mutti looks smaller than when I left just a month ago, her skin paper-thin and translucent. The morphine has dulled her pain but also stolen the sharp wit I've always admired. When I take her hand, it feels like holding autumn leaves—fragile, ready to crumble at the slightest pressure.

"I have to go back to California tomorrow," I tell her, my voice carefully controlled.

She nods weakly, her eyes struggling to focus. "The diving?"

Maybe it's the shock, or the desperate need to share this unbearable truth with someone, or because she's the only person who could possibly understand. The words spill out before I can stop them.

"No, Mutti. I have breast cancer."

I say it simply, directly, the way she taught me to face hard truths. The words hang in the air between us like an arrow I can't call back.

For a moment, her eyes sharpen—a flicker of the fierce woman who raised me. I think she's going to cry, or rage, or pull me into her arms. I brace myself for her reaction, for the shared grief of our genetic curse—but what I really want is her to hug me and tell me that everything will be okay.

Instead, she blinks slowly and turns her head toward the window.

"The weather has been so strange this winter," she murmurs, her voice distant. "Zsuzsa was just saying yesterday how her garden is all confused …"

I stare at her, stunned. Did she not hear me? Did the morphine steal my words before they could land?

"Mutti," I try again, leaning closer. "I said I have breast cancer. Three tumors. I need surgery and—"

"Oh, that reminds me," she interrupts, her gaze still fixed on the gray sky outside. "You should take some of my jewelry back with you. The blue necklace—you always loved that one."

The dismissal hits me like a slap. I sit back in the uncomfortable hospital chair, feeling like I've just thrown myself against a wall. My cancer—the thing that's about to tear my life apart—doesn't even register on my mother's radar.

Or maybe it does, and she simply can't process one more piece of devastating news. Maybe her mind is protecting itself the only way it knows how: by refusing to let my diagnosis exist in the same space as her own approaching death. Maybe acknowledging my cancer would make her own fight feel even more futile. Or maybe the drugs have simply stolen her ability to hold on to the burden of new information.

But the effect is the same. I am alone with this knowledge, even sitting next to the one person who should understand it best.

I study my mother's face—the way the illness has carved deep hollows under her cheekbones, how her once-radiant eyes have dimmed to gray shadows. This is what cancer looks like in its final stages. This is where my journey might lead.

The irony is so vicious, it makes me dizzy. I've flown back and forth over the months, watching her fight and fail, fight and fail. I've held her hand through chemotherapy sessions, celebrated tiny victories, mourned devastating setbacks. I've become an expert in the language of oncology, the rhythm of hope and despair. And all the while, my own cells were turning traitor.

But something else gnaws at me, something that makes this diagnosis feel less like a cruel coincidence and more like a genetic death sentence already written in my blood.

Thirty-nine.

The number has haunted me all year, lurking in the back of my mind like a monster I refused to acknowledge. My father was thirty-nine when cancer claimed him, when his body turned against him with the same ruthless efficiency that I'm now facing.

I used to think it was just a horrible coincidence. Dad worked stressful jobs, breathed in chemicals, lived a life so different from mine. I told myself his cancer was environmental, occupational—something I could avoid through clean living and California sunshine. I convinced myself that geography could cheat genetics.

But now, sitting beside my dying mother at age thirty-nine myself, I feel the weight of my own diagnosis. This isn't someone else's life, and it isn't coincidence. This is an inherited burden, a terrible calculus of heredity. There's nowhere to run.

This is something I can't escape.

* * *

The plane cuts through the night sky, and I'm trapped between two worlds— the one behind me where my mother is dying, and the one ahead where I might follow her. Ten hours in this speeding metal tube, suspended between a desperate fate and a fight for survival.

It's unfair. It sucks. It's a cosmic joke so malicious that if I weren't living it, I wouldn't believe it.

I've spent my life overcoming challenges—losing a parent at a young age, leaving my home behind, building a career in a foreign country, learning to dive in ice-cold waters, performing stunts that terrify most people. I've faced down dangers that would paralyze others. Haven't I paid my dues to the universe? Haven't I earned some smooth sailing?

Instead, I get to watch my mother die from afar while my own body turns against me. I'm fighting a war on two fronts, with no time to process or prepare for either battle.

The number keeps echoing in my head like a death knell: *My father. Thirty-nine. Cancer. Dead.*

And now me. Thirty-nine. Cancer. Fighting for my life.

It can't be coincidence. The timing is too precise, too heartless to be random. Somewhere in my cells, in the DNA I inherited from a man I barely remember, a timer was set. A genetic bomb with a thirty-nine-year fuse.

Leaning back in my airplane seat, I think about my father's last months—the way cancer ate him alive, how the machines kept his body running long after his spirit had fled. Is that my future? Am I following a script written in my genetic code, destined to replay his tragedy at exactly the same age?

The passenger next to me is reading a romance novel, completely absorbed in someone else's happy ending. The man across the aisle is sleeping peacefully. Others are reckoning with the ordinary problems awaiting them back on the ground—work deadlines, mortgage payments, what to make for dinner. Normal problems. Manageable problems.

I would give anything for their problems.

The flight attendant dims the cabin lights, and most passengers settle in for sleep. But my mind refuses to rest, instead churning through the impossible mathematics of my situation: How long do I have if the cancer has spread? What are the odds of surviving when my genetic lottery ticket was clearly marked *LOSER*? How do I tell my two-year-old son that Mommy might not be around to see him grow up?

As we fly through the darkness toward Los Angeles, toward MRIs and oncologists and treatment plans, I grip the armrest so tightly, my hands begin to cramp.

It's another cruel irony: I'm flying away from death to face death. I'm leaving a beloved cancer sufferer behind to become one myself. I'm abandoning my role as the strong daughter to become the terrified patient.

Somewhere in the middle of this nightmare, I have to find the strength to survive what my mother cannot.

* * *

Two weeks later, my oncologist's office in Los Angeles feels like a courtroom where I'm about to receive my sentence. Dr. Lowe sits across from me with a manila folder that contains the scientific proof of my genetic destiny. His expression is carefully neutral—the practiced face of someone who delivers life-altering news for a living.

"Your BRCA2 test came back positive," he says simply.

The verdict is inconceivable even though I've been expecting it. BRCA2 positive, the genetic mutation that turns my own DNA into a weapon against me.

"What does that mean, exactly?" I ask, though I already know. I've been researching obsessively since my diagnosis, reading medical journals until my eyes burn, trying to understand the enemy living in my cells.

"It means you carry a mutation in the BRCA2 gene—the gene responsible for DNA repair. When it's faulty, like yours is, it can't fix the cellular damage that leads to cancer." Dr. Lowe opens the manila folder, revealing charts and statistics that look like a numerical death sentence. "You had approximately an eighty percent lifetime risk of developing breast cancer."

Had, past tense, I think, trying to wrap my head around the semantics of disease. *Because now I have it.*

"And ovarian cancer?" I ask, my voice barely a whisper.

"Your risk is significantly elevated. We typically recommend prophylactic removal of the ovaries and fallopian tubes, usually by age forty."

Forty is just a year away. I'm right on schedule for the demolition of my entire reproductive system. But it's the next piece of information that stops my breath entirely.

"We also tested your mother's sample," Dr. Lowe continues. "Hers came back negative."

The room tilts. "Negative?"

"Your mother doesn't carry the BRCA2 mutation. Which means ..." He pauses, letting me complete the devastating equation.

"It came from my father." The words feel like stones in my mouth.

He nods gravely. "The mutation can be inherited from either parent. In your case, it came through your father's line."

My father. Dead at thirty-nine from cancer. The same cancer that's now growing in my body at the exact same age. The chromosomal time bomb he passed to me along with his blue eyes and strong cheekbones.

"There's something else," Dr. Lowe says softly. "Given your family history—your father's death at thirty-nine, your current diagnosis at the same age—it's likely that his cancer was also BRCA2-related."

The room spins. My father didn't just die of cancer—he died of the same genetic predisposition that's now trying to kill me. We're linked not just by blood, but by a shared genetic flaw, a hereditary countdown timer set to explode at thirty-nine.

"What about my cousin—my father's niece?" I ask.

By the time Noémi had finally agreed to surgery, it was too late. The cancer had spread through her lymph nodes and into her organs. She had died just a few months after I last saw her, at age thirty-nine—the same shadow, cast over our family again.

Dr. Lowe makes a note in his file. "That would be consistent with a BRCA2 mutation running through your father's family line. The gene doesn't discriminate—it passes equally to sons and daughters, though it manifests differently."

Passes equally to sons.

I think of Enzo, barely two years old, playing innocently at home while his mother sits in this sterile office, learning that she might have sentenced him to the same hereditary fate. My father's legacy isn't just the cancer growing in my body—it's the potential cancer I might have already given to my son. The chromosomal Russian roulette that I played without knowing the gun was loaded.

The thought makes me physically sick.

The question isn't just whether I'll survive this cancer. The real question is whether I can break the family cycle, whether I can beat the thirty-nine-year deadline. Can I rewrite the genetic script that's been killing us Goghs off?

I walk out of Dr. Lowe's office carrying the weight of my father's DNA like a loaded weapon I never knew I possessed. But I also carry something else: the fierce determination to prove that genes aren't destiny.

* * *

While I'm attacking my diagnosis like a military campaign—scouting out every treatment option and interrogating multiple oncologists—my mother is in Budapest accepting hers like a prayer. She lights candles, visits healers, and meditates on crystal beds alongside her chemotherapy.

I approach cancer like I've approached every challenge in my life: with stubborn determination and the utter refusal to accept defeat. My mother approaches hers with resignation. "If it's my time," she says when I call, "it's my time."

The difference between us is heartbreaking and absolute. I'm planning to win; she's preparing to lose.

When Hilaire comes with me to the next oncologist visit to be my "boots on the ground," Dr. Lowe gives us some oddly comforting news amidst the storm of bad tidings: I have the "best" possible type of breast cancer, not the triple-negative kind that my mother has. If all goes well, I might just need hormone therapy and surgery to remove the three lumps in my breast.

Meanwhile, Mutti is getting worse. She's back in the hospital, where many people are visiting her: her friends, her sisters Éva and Zsuzsa, and of course, Csilla. I just wish she could either rally and come home, or fall asleep forever—anything to stop her agony. It's so hard to know she's in such pain when I'm not there physically to hold her hand and give her comfort and encouragement.

When her pain becomes unbearable, the doctor urges Csilla to come as soon as possible. They'll need to increase Mutti's morphine, so this is likely to be the last chance for a coherent conversation with our mother. I join over Skype, and as the screen flickers to life, I see Mutti— her fragile body trembling, her voice a faint moan. Csilla tells me she's ice-cold, her skin clammy. She is barely there.

With choked voices, my sister and I tell her that it's okay to let go, that she's given us everything, that we are both grown up and we'll be alright without her. We promise her that she doesn't need to stay in this pain for our sake. We urge her to go be with our father, to reunite with her own parents, waiting for her in heaven.

"Apu," she whispers.

I think she is referring to her own dad.

And then, "Leave me…" Her words slip away like fragments of a dream.

I say goodbye as her exhaustion overtakes her.

An hour later, Csilla's face appears on the screen again, streaked with tears, and I know before she speaks.

"She's gone," Csilla whispers.

The words sink in, but it's impossible to grasp. She's really gone. We'll never see Mutti's face again, never hear her laugh. Yet there's a strange sense of peace, a release from this nightmare, knowing her suffering has finally ended.

* * *

The next day, still in shock from Mutti's passing, I'm sitting in my oncologist's office discussing my surgical options. The timing is so merciless, it feels preordained by a malevolent universe.

For lesser ailments, I've always leaned toward Eastern medicine and homeopathic remedies, trusting in nature's healing and energy work. But faced with the brutal reality of cancer, I can't take chances. Dr. Lowe is explaining my options. I could go with a lumpectomy and radiation, but the thought of cancer lingering, waiting to resurface, is intolerable.

I refuse to live in fear. I insist on taking control. So, I choose the alternative: a double mastectomy.

Choosing to follow my oncologist's plan is in stark contrast to my mom's approach—searching for a miracle but never really believing she'd survive. But I can't afford to gamble with my life. I mourn the loss of my cousin, yet I'm grateful for the harsh lessons of her experience. I am determined to watch my son grow up. The protocol may feel cold and clinical, but I plan to follow it. This is about survival.

Both of my breasts will be removed, with implants to follow. It's a drastic decision, but it means no radiation, no constant worry for the rest of my life, no looking over my shoulder for cancer's return. And with an eighty percent chance of developing ovarian cancer, there's no question: My ovaries have to go, too. I'm not just fighting the enemy this time. I'm making sure I never have to fight it again.

Hormone therapy is the first step, and cruelly, it throws me into menopause overnight. My body, once familiar and predictable, becomes a foreign battleground. Waves of heat leave me drenched, as if I'm burning from the inside out. Routine tasks become Herculean feats, my energy sapped by all-encompassing fatigue. I'm living in a body and mind I barely recognize.

The fact that I can't bear more children, can't give Enzo a sibling, is hard to swallow. The emotional upheaval of this sudden plunge into menopause makes it even more bitter. My moods swing from stable to irritable with little warning, each day a roller coaster that I can't seem to get off. I grapple with sudden bouts of anxiety and a heartrending sense of sacrifice and loss. Everybody, including me, is getting on my nerves. I yearn for the comfort of my former self.

In the middle of this hormonal chaos, we fly to Hungary, where Csilla and I plan a memorial that reflects Mutti's vibrant life. Everyone wears something turquoise, her favorite color, and we play Café del Mar–style music instead of traditional funeral music. My sister and I give a eulogy we wrote together to celebrate our mother's spirit. I decide to reveal my own diagnosis only to Csilla for now, wanting this moment to be about Mutti.

The irony is crushing: I'm burying my mother while secretly carrying the same disease that killed her. I'm comforting others in their grief while writhing in my own terror. I'm promising that she's at peace while knowing that my own war is just beginning.

Onboard the jet back to California with Hilaire and Enzo by my side, the daunting reality of my seven-hour surgery settles heavily on my chest.

The night before surgery, I lie in bed, staring at the ceiling, my mind scouring every possible outcome. I touch my breasts over and over, memorizing them. Today they feel warm and soft and alive. Tomorrow they'll be gone—cut away and discarded as medical waste. These parts of my body that fed my son, that Hilaire has kissed a thousand times, that have been with me since I was thirteen years old—soon they'll exist only in memory.

The pre-op instructions sit on my nightstand: *Nothing to eat or drink after midnight. Remove all jewelry. Shower with antibacterial soap.* Such clinical language for the dismantling of my body.

At five a.m., I shower with the special soap that smells like disinfectant and tears. I scrub my skin until it's raw, knowing this is the last time I'll shower with my original body.

The procedure itself is grueling. Two skilled surgeons work in tandem, each focused on their crucial task. One meticulously removes the breast tissue, while Dr. Burrell, my plastic surgeon, steps in immediately to place the temporary expanders.

These expanders will be gradually filled over the next few months with saline, using a surgical needle. Once four rounds of chemotherapy are behind me and I've recovered enough physically, they will be replaced with permanent implants.

This journey is projected to span almost a year.

* * *

The first sensation after surgery isn't sight or sound—it's pain. Pure, white-hot agony that radiates from my chest like lightning bolts. I try to take a breath and immediately understand that breathing will never be the same. My chest feels ransacked, compressed, like a concrete slab pushing down on my ribs.

My eyes flutter open to harsh fluorescent lights that stab into my skull. Everything is too bright, too loud, too much. A nurse leans over me, her face floating in and out of focus like I'm underwater.

"How are you feeling?" she asks, her voice coming from the end of a long tunnel.

I try to speak, but my throat is scraped raw from the intubation tube. Only a croak comes out. My mouth tastes like metal and anesthesia, like I've been sucking on pennies for hours.

Then I see the tubes.

Three plastic lines emerge from my body like alien appendages: two snaking out from the surgical tape near my ribs, and one—*dear God!*—poking out from my left inner thigh. They lead to clear bulbs that hang like grotesque ornaments from my hospital gown, slowly filling with pink-tinged fluid that I realize, with horror, is coming from inside me.

I try to sit up and instantly regret it. The pain slams into me with such force that black spots dance across my vision. It feels like my chest has been split open with an axe—which, I suppose, it has.

"Easy," the nurse says, gently pressing me back down. "You just had major surgery. You need to rest."

Rest. As if rest is possible when your body has been carved up and reassembled like a jigsaw puzzle.

Over the next hours and days, the tubes become my constant companions, my plastic tormentors. They tug at my skin with every breath, every tiny movement. Once I'm up and about, the drainage bulbs dangle from safety pins attached to my gown, swinging with each step like liquid metronomes marking time in my personal hell.

The worst is the thigh tube—a constant reminder of the tissue that was harvested to rebuild what cancer took. Moving my leg pulls at the incision, sending shooting pains into my hip as each motion tugs at the metal wire joining my flesh and the tube. I become obsessed with protecting this tube, walking with a strange hunch like I'm cradling a wounded animal.

At night, I wake up in a panic, tangled in plastic hoses twisting around me like constrictor snakes. *Have I pulled something loose?*

The sound of fluid sloshing in the bulbs makes me nauseous, a constant *glub-glub-glub* as my body drains itself. The nurses empty the bulbs three times a day, measuring the fluid output like some science experiment. "Looking good," they say cheerfully, pouring my bodily fluids down the sink. "Good drainage is what we want to see."

But *I* don't want to see it. I don't want to know that my body is literally leaking, that pieces of me are being collected in plastic containers and measured and recorded and disposed of.

Despite the relentless agony, a sliver of hope pierces through the haze of pain. The surgeons' findings offer a small relief: Nothing abnormal is discovered in my lymph nodes. The pathology report confirms the cancer has not spread beyond the areas removed. For now, I am free from the shadow of cancer's advance. It's a fragile, tentative victory, but a victory nonetheless—a glimmer of faith amid the despair.

Four days after surgery, Dr. Burrell comes to my hospital room to remove the bandages. "Ready to see your new chest?" she asks with practiced optimism.

Not really, I think, knowing I'll never be ready for what's next. But I nod anyway.

The adhesive strips away skin cells, making me wince with each pull, as the doctor peels away layers of gauze and tape, revealing what lies beneath. Finally, she removes the last layer, and I see myself.

The first thought that crosses my mind is: *This isn't my body.*

Where my breasts used to be, there are now two alien mounds— swollen, bruised, completely foreign. The skin is stretched tight over the temporary expanders, giving me the appearance of a poorly constructed mannequin. And the color is all wrong—deep purple bruises bloom across my chest like violent flowers, fading to yellow and green at the edges. But it's the scars that steal my breath.

Two long, vertical lines cut from my nipples to the base of my breasts, parallel to each other like railroad tracks, held together with surgical staples that glint in the harsh hospital light. The metallic fasteners look grim and industrial—like something you'd use to hang drywall, not repair a human body.

"The swelling will go down," Dr. Burrell says, but her voice sounds distant, muffled. "And we'll adjust the shape as we expand them."

I can't stop staring. This chest—these unrelated objects attached to my body—feel like props, like special effects makeup for a horror movie. I want to peel them off and find my real breasts underneath.

When I tentatively touch the skin, I feel nothing. The nerve endings have been severed, leaving a dead zone. It's like touching someone else's body while looking down at what should be mine.

"Will I ever feel anything again?" I whisper.

"Some sensation may return," she says carefully. "But it will be different."

Different. Such a gentle word for such a heartless reality.

My body has been permanently altered, and I'm left to wrestle with the isolation of feeling so out of sync with my own self. Stability, vitality … how did I take these things for granted?

But even as I struggle, I remind myself of why I'm enduring all this. It's not just about surviving. I am reclaiming my life. I am fighting for my future. I am holding on to the hope that on the other side of this blistering tempest, I'll discover some semblance of normalcy—and a chance to rebuild.

CHAPTER 17

Santa Catalina and Ireland: Staying Afloat

When you come out of the storm, you won't be the same person who walked in.
That's what the storm is all about.
– Haruki Murakami

I'm going to the pool today, for the first time in an eternity—six weeks at least. My body is stiff and my arms heavy, as if they've forgotten the simple joy of movement. I feel powerless, like a puppet being controlled by invisible hands.

Ever since the surgery, when I look in the mirror, the person looking back isn't me. It's someone who's been through a war and barely survived. My chest looks like a construction site, all swelling and bruising, held together with industrial staples. But this isn't reconstruction—it's a crude approximation of what used to be.

In the shower, I avoid looking down and just focus on washing my hair, my arms, anything but my chest—the red, angry scars, the skin pulled tight over artificial lumps that bear no resemblance to the breasts that once lived there. Water runs over the numb skin, and I feel nothing.

This lack of sensation is the strangest sensation of all—the profoundly disturbing disconnect between what my eyes see and what my nerves feel. Water is hitting my chest, but it might as well be falling on a marble statue. And stepping out of the shower is worse. I just stand there in front of my reflection, naked and mutilated and trying not to cry.

After the surgery, getting the rest I needed became a strategic campaign, a frustrating, daily dance of taking tiny steps forward, only to stumble back. Every time I started to feel a hint of relief, impatience clawed at me, daring me to push a little harder, do a little more. Back at home, with no nurses to keep me in line, Hilaire stood firm—my unyielding rock, managing everything with Enzo and reminding me, gently but firmly, to slow down. But the pain, searing and relentless, kept catching me off guard.

Skipping painkillers, even once, was a mistake that left me curled up, gripping the edges of our bed, forced to rely on the meds again, no matter how much I hated the heavy, foggy haze they brought.

The painkillers brought a second nightmare, too: constipation. Every trip to the bathroom was a battle, triggering flare-ups of hemorrhoids that felt almost worse than the leftover surgery pain itself. Desperate for a way out of this loop, I started weaning off the meds by trying THC and CBD gummies, hoping to dull the constant, gnawing ache without adding another layer of misery.

Then, one day, a new drama: After snagging the drainage tubes one too many times on cabinets, door handles, every damned obstacle in the house, one of them came loose and pulled out. I was in the kitchen making coffee when I felt the tug, sharp and immediate. Looking down, I saw the tube dangling free and pink fluid leaking from the hole, spreading across my shirt. And then came the pain, instant and blindsiding, shooting from the hole in my side up into my shoulder.

"Come in immediately," the nurse said when I called Dr. Burrell's office. "Don't wait." An ultrasound showed the problem—a dark pocket of liquid building up in my chest cavity.

"We'll need to drain this manually," Dr. Burrell explained, pulling out a medieval torture device and pushing it between my ribs, unleashing the deep, visceral wrongness of metal puncturing my chest, searching inside me, probing for the pocket of fluid. The relief was immediate but disgusting, as the dark fluid flowed into the syringe and she withdrew a full cup of liquid from inside my body.

Three days later, I went back to do it again. The fluid buildup was still substantial, so the doctor decided to insert a fresh tube. Even through the numbing medication, I sensed the pressure of the scalpel blade cutting through skin and muscle. The wet, tearing noise of the incision made my stomach turn. As Dr. Burrell threaded the plastic line through my chest wall, I felt it slithering inside my torso like a fat, pulsing worm.

"Almost done," she said, the concentration evident in her voice as she pushed harder.

Then something gave way inside my chest—a pop felt more than heard, creating yet another new kind of pain, sharper and more urgent than before—and the tube finally lodged where it should.

"This one should stay put," Dr. Burrell said, first securing its position with wire thread, sewing me to the tube, and then double-taping it in place.

But as I sat up, something felt different. The tube didn't just drain fluid—it throbbed with each heartbeat. Every breath sent a sharp reminder of the plastic pipeline running from my chest to the outside world.

Weeks dragged on, and the fluid refused to stop draining. The tubes were unbearable, tugging at my skin, sometimes slipping loose during the night and soaking our bedsheets. Every twinge, every leak—I just wanted them *gone*.

I tried to spend as much time as possible outdoors, even just lying on the terrace lounge chair—to get some fresh air. On better days, I walked along the beach near our home.

Hilaire's frustration was palpable. Why couldn't I just rest? He was right, and I tried to listen, to hold back, to keep still. But every time I began to feel a bit better, the restless energy inside me conquered any sense of caution, and I found myself outside pulling weeds or attempting gentle yoga, pushing my body harder than I should.

This endless cycle of pain, frustration, and longing for my old life has been a riptide, and I'm struggling to stay afloat.

At a post-surgery check-up with my oncologist, Dr. Lowe presented me and Hilaire with updated results from additional testing. The "personality" of my cancer—something called an Oncotype DX score—had come back at 51, pushing me into the high-risk category.

"I know we discussed surgery and hormone therapy," the doctor said, his voice careful and measured. "But these results change everything. This is one of the most aggressive types of cancer we see. I'm recommending four rounds of chemotherapy—just to make sure we eliminate every last cancer cell that might be lurking in your system, waiting to resurface when you least expect it."

The words hit like a physical blow. Chemotherapy. The thing I thought I might avoid had become unavoidable. The image of my mother, weakened and sick from her treatments, flashed through my mind. But I also thought of my cousin Noémi, who waited too long, trying gentler approaches while cancer spread through her body.

"I won't take any chances," I told him. "I want to watch Enzo grow up."

The gravity of this recommendation—treatment every three weeks, for a total of four sessions—means my long-awaited reconstructive surgery is on hold until the chemo is complete. I'm left in limbo, where every day stretches on, filled with uncertainty.

The weight of it all, of this nothingness, threatens to crush me. So, I'm doing the only thing that has ever brought me weightlessness and peace: I'm returning to the water.

As I slip into the pool, I can barely achieve a proper stroke. Each attempt to move my body feels like a slog as I toil against my own limits. But I push through the struggle, desperate to reconnect with that lost part of myself, the part that's been on hold while the war against cancer takes center stage. As I move from lap to lap, my muscles start to loosen. The water, so familiar and comforting, begins to wrap around me, easing the tension in my body and mind. It enfolds me in its soothing embrace, a balm to the wounds of the past weeks.

I wasn't surprised by the results of my cancer's "personality test." On a scale from 1 to 100—where anything below 10 means no chemotherapy is needed, and above 30 indicates a strong need for it— my score of 51 jumped off the page. This result stands as one of the highest ever recorded by my doctor, a stark warning about the severity of my situation. But here, amidst the rhythmic splash and glide, I am reminded of who I am beyond the illness and the struggle. Each stroke becomes more relaxed, less stiff, as I reclaim something precious. The initial resistance melts away, replaced by relief … and freedom.

The water is my sanctuary, a place where the weight of my worries dissolves. I lose myself in the rhythm of my strokes, feeling the joy and weightlessness that swimming brings. In this tranquil space, I find a fleeting but unadulterated sense of joy. Swimming becomes more than just exercise; it's a rediscovery of a piece of my soul, a moment of serenity amid the chaos—a sign that despite everything, there are still moments of pure happiness.

* * *

At my first round of chemo, sitting in a comfortable leather chair with my feet propped up, I try not to think about the poison slowly dripping into my vein, try not to wonder whether it will eliminate every last, tiny cancer cell before it kills me. I listen to an audiobook to pass the time while creating beaded bracelets for my store, and everything feels okay at first. The pain doesn't start until that night, and when it does, I start throwing up.

The next day is a blur of nausea and sleep, but I manage a walk with Hilaire and Enzo, grateful for small moments of peace.

A week later, my next trial begins innocently enough: a few strands of hair on my pillow when I wake up one morning. Nothing alarming—everyone loses hair, right? I brush it off the bed with a swipe of my hand and continue with my morning routine. But there's no denying it when I run my fingers through my hair a week or so later, and an entire section comes away in my hand like autumn leaves surrendering to winter.

The sight stops me cold. I stare at the dark strands wrapped around my fingers, my scalp suddenly tingling with awareness of what's coming next.

I become obsessed with catching every falling strand, as if I could somehow collect each hair and put it all back. I check myself constantly, running my hands through my hair in the car, in the grocery store line, while playing with Enzo. Each time, more hair comes away. Each time, my heart sinks a little deeper.

Hair is everywhere now: Settling on my shoulders like dark drifts of snow. Scattered across the bathroom counter. Clinging to Enzo's clothes after I hug him. Clogging the shower drain in thick, accusatory clumps.

I start wearing darker colors to hide the upsetting evidence. I buy lint rollers and keep one in every room of the house. I braid my hair tightly, desperately, as if I could force it to stay attached through sheer will. But every morning, my pillow tells the truth: I'm losing the battle.

The itching is unbearable. My scalp is on fire, every follicle screaming as it prepares to let go. I scratch until my nails come away bloody, but relief never comes. My hair isn't just thinning—it's abandoning ship. My head is rejecting every strand, pushing them out like foreign invaders. What was once thick, lustrous hair now looks like it belongs on a neglected doll.

I try to fluff and arrange it to hide the bare patches, but it's useless. Every movement sends more strands floating to the floor. I'm leaving a trail of myself wherever I go.

Though it seems like a lost cause, Hilaire persuades me not to shave it all off immediately. I schedule a haircut, aiming for a look inspired by Charlize Theron in *Mad Max: Fury Road*, but deep down, I'm still bracing for the inevitable loss.

"Very chic," the stylist says as she works. She clearly has dealt with chemo patients before, and doesn't comment on the hair that comes away in her hands as she washes what's left, but we both know we're just buying time.

The pixie cut looks cute for exactly three days before the relentless shedding makes it look patchy and desperate.

Enzo keeps staring at me with confusion. "Mommy hair?" he asks, reaching up to touch the strange, sparse covering on my head.

I have to turn away before he sees my tears.

* * *

After my second chemo session, the weight of it all becomes too much to bear. My eyebrows have petered out, my eyelashes are falling out one after another, and my remaining hair is thin and erratic, like I have some terrible skin condition that's ejecting each hair from its follicle. The itching has intensified, too: I can't sleep, can't concentrate, can't think about anything else.

That's it, I decide one afternoon. *The hair has to go. All of it. Now.*

While Enzo naps and Hilaire works in his home office, I lock myself in the bathroom and turn the shower on full blast. Then, with shaking hands, I pick up the razor usually reserved for my legs.

The first pass is the hardest. I start at my temple, where barely any hair still exists, and cut a clean path through what remains.

"Just hair," I whisper to myself, cutting away swath after swath. "It's just hair."

But I know that's a lie. This isn't just hair—it's my femininity, my identity, my illusion of invincibility. Hair is deeply personal, not just an accessory. Losing it is a symbol of this monstrous struggle, and letting it go is another painful step in this process. Each pass of the razor reveals more of the reality: I am sick. I am bald. I am fighting for my life.

The loose hair falls away, mixing with the water and swirling down the shower drain like dark tears. I watch it disappear and feel something inside me break. All those years of braiding, styling, washing, conditioning—all of it reduced to debris vanishing into the sewers.

When I step out of the shower, completely bald, the shock is physical. My reflection looks alien to me. The woman in the mirror has my eyes, my nose, my mouth, but she's a stranger wearing my face.

My scalp is pale white, almost translucent, and the shape of my skull is fully exposed—every bump, every contour, every asymmetry that hair once concealed. The skin feels smooth and strange under my tentative fingers—soft and vulnerable, like a baby's head. This is what I looked like when I was born, I realize: completely bald and completely defenseless.

Without hair to soften the transition, my head sits on my shoulders like a cue ball balanced on a baseball tee. I look skeletal, diminished, like cancer has already started consuming me from the outside in.

The absence of eyebrows and eyelashes makes it worse. My whole face looks blank, unfinished, like a portrait someone forgot to complete. Without the frame of hair, my features seem to float in an ocean of pale skin. I try different expressions in the mirror, searching for one that looks normal, recognizable.

Smiling? It just makes the baldness more obvious.

Frowning? No, it makes me look sick.

There's no angle, no expression, no lighting that makes me like what I see. I look like an alien.

Working up the courage to show Hilaire and Enzo, I walk into the living room where they're watching TV now, with the towel still wrapped around my head like a turban.

"Ready?" I ask, my voice barely a whisper.

Hilaire nods, muting the television. The silence feels enormous.

I unwrap the towel slowly. The fabric falls away, and for a moment, neither of us says anything.

"It looks like …" I start, then stop, touching my bare scalp self-consciously.

"Like what?" he asks gently.

"Like I'm wearing a white swimming cap," I moan. "Like I'm about to dive into a pool. Except the pool is cancer treatment, and I can't surface for air."

Hilaire doesn't try to tell me it looks good. He doesn't lie and say it doesn't matter. Instead, he reaches out and runs his hand over my bare scalp with infinite tenderness. "Your head is perfectly shaped," he says finally.

"Like a soft balloon," Enzo adds, stroking my bald head with his chubby hands. Such a funny comment, one that only a two-year-old could make—not particularly comforting, but true and real.

I catch sight of myself in the reflection of the dark TV screen: a bald woman crying while her husband and child stroke her head. The image is so far from any future I'd ever imagined for myself, I almost can't believe it's real.

This is what cancer looks like, I think. Not a brave, inspiring survivor with perfect makeup and a designer headscarf, but this—a woman mourning her hair in her living room.

I consider wearing a wig or a headscarf, but nothing seems right. I've never liked hats and scarves, and now they feel even more out of place. I'm a scuba instructor and stuntwoman, always in motion and immersed in my dynamic world. Wearing a wig feels foreign, uncomfortable, restrictive, and utterly impractical.

I cling to the notion of this bald cancer summer as just one of the many changes I'm going through, a temporary part of a bigger journey. Though it's hard to shake the sweeping sadness that comes with seeing a part of who I am disappear, I tell myself I can make it through. My spirit is still strong, no matter what my body looks like now.

Having decided not to hide what I'm going through, I post a few pictures on Facebook, showing a side of my life that is not so pretty and happy. I refuse to put on a brave face and pretend that everything is okay while I secretly suffer. That's just not me.

Nor is seeking sympathy. I just want to be real and transparent, to share these raw, unfiltered moments as a way to get through them. I want others to see the truth of my struggle, not just a polished version. Inviting friends, acquaintances, and even strangers into my world feels like a way to bridge a gap, to let them know that it's okay to talk about hard things and connect on a deeper level.

As I scroll through the comments and messages, the genuine support and empathy are both comforting and humbling. People have a great capacity to care about others, and my openness creates a space for understanding. It's a small but powerful way to make sense of my journey and to find solace in the connections I'm building along the way.

I think about how different my approach is from my mother's.

While I'm broadcasting my journey far and wide, she hid her chemotherapy behind wigs and silence. She kept her diagnosis secret from almost everyone—including her own mother—and tried to maintain the illusion that everything was normal.

During infusions, I make art. She endured them in quiet resignation.

I document every side effect, every moment of fear and triumph. She suffered privately, protecting others from her pain.

Neither approach is right or wrong. They're just different philosophies about how to face down mortality.

When my white blood cell count crashes, the doctor prescribes an injection that leaves me curled up and clutching myself in excruciating pain that radiates through my bones. Michael Wolper's wife, Alison, helps me with several physical therapy sessions, free of charge. Her specialized technique—fascia massage, or myofascial release—targets the deeper layers of connective tissue beyond the muscles, aiming to restore natural flexibility and ease. She untangles the tight spots and dissolves the tension that has built up over time in the spider web of fascia connecting every part of my body. Her kindness and gentle hands soothe not just my muscles but some deep ache inside me.

I make an effort to stay active every day, swimming, walking, in-line skating, or taking a family hike, depending on how much energy I have. The fresh air, the movement, even the afternoon nap that follows—all of it helps me feel better, bit by bit.

One day, a kind woman tells me about the Look Good Feel Better program, and though I've never cared much for makeup, I crave any touch of normalcy and decide to go. I arrive at the conference room in a shared-space office building to find a circle of women, all at different stages of this terrible journey, yet each radiating a fierce will to keep going. The warmth in the room instantly makes me feel less alone.

The makeup artist shows us how to fill in our thinning eyebrows and hide the bruising under our eyes. Then she hands each of us a bag of luxury cosmetics: Christian Dior, Estée Lauder. I'm speechless at the generosity, the thoughtfulness behind it all. Putting on such high-end makeup feels like taking back a piece of myself for just a moment. My face lights up in the mirror. For the first time in a while, I see me.

I hadn't realized how much these little things would matter. It's more than just makeup—it's an omen. Despite cancer's relentless grip, I'm still here, still worthy of feeling good, still able to find small joys in the reflection looking back at me.

After that, I decide to get eyelash extensions. Sitting in the salon chair, I feel a mix of emotions as the technician carefully applies each lash. It's a strange sensation, lying there with my eyes closed, knowing that when I open them, I'll look a bit different—hopefully a bit more like the person I remember.

When she tells me to open my eyes, I can't help but laugh. My eyelashes are dramatically long and fluttery, an absurd contrast against the stark ivory of my bare scalp. Still, it brings a smile to my face. In the midst of all this change, these bold yet delicate lashes feel like a small triumph, a reminder that even facing loss, I can find ways to reclaim myself, to see some beauty in the struggle.

* * *

The third round of chemo hits me the hardest yet. The morning after the infusion, I'm throwing up constantly. A few days later, I'm still so weak, I can't do anything—and my childhood diving friends Nóra and Vica are coming all the way from Hungary to cheer me up and celebrate my fortieth birthday.

Their arrival is a true blessing. We have barely seen each other in the past twenty years, but the moment they walk through the door, it's like no time has passed. These aren't just any friends. They're the girls I grew up with, the ones who know and share my origin story. We fall right back into our old rhythm, laughing and chatting like the carefree teenagers we once were.

Every day of their visit, Nóra and Vica cook and bake delicious treats, transforming our kitchen into a refuge of love and care. They squeeze a whole bag of bright, sun-ripened oranges, filling every glass with fresh juice packed with the vitamin C my immune system needs. They whip up a pot of my favorite lentil soup, rich and aromatic, the kind that warms you from the inside out. And then, as if to prove that sweetness can still exist in this strange, painful season, they bake donuts from scratch, flooding the house with the heavenly scent of warm, sugary dough. For the first time in weeks, it feels like home again.

Their visit becomes a steadying anchor, a chance to grab hold of life outside the walls of hospitals and clinics. We roam through downtown LA, savoring every corner, every sunbeam. When the ocean calls to us, we spend an afternoon at Venice Beach watching surfers and street performers, our laughter mingling with the waves. We wander through the charming coastal streets of Manhattan Beach, Redondo Beach, Hermosa Beach, stopping at tiny cafés and breathing in the sea air, letting it clear the heaviness from our hearts.

One day, we visit the South Coast Botanic Garden, an oasis of resplendent blooms and green expanses. Surrounded by flowers, I find a quiet joy. Each petal, each leaf whispers that life, however fragile, persists in beauty. Then I show them my favorite yoga spot in the park, beneath a massive oak where we stretch and breathe together. And then, in one of the most healing experiences of all, we let ourselves melt in the warmth of a Korean scrub spa. The steam envelops us, washing away the weight we've been carrying. For a few moments, we are just bodies—softened, soothed, and reminded of what it feels like to simply be here, alive, together.

We cram so much into their visit, talking endlessly about everything and nothing, reliving old memories and making new ones. Having them here to mark my fortieth birthday feels like a quiet victory, a moment that carries great meaning. I breathe a huge sigh of relief and step out from under the emotional weight of being thirty-nine. My family's "danger zone" is a heavy legacy, like the infamous age of twenty-seven that haunted music legends like Jim Morrison, Jimi Hendrix, and Janis Joplin. Now here I am, beginning a year I wasn't sure I'd ever see, holding onto the people and experiences that make me feel grounded, alive, and deeply grateful.

Not long after Nóra and Vica return home, I am happy to pay forward that gratitude in a cause close to my heart, as I host our annual scuba diving event with the A Chance for Children Foundation. This tradition, supported by my circle of diver friends, allows us to give kids from underserved communities a glimpse into the beauty of the underwater world. As I guide them through their first underwater breaths in the pool, I can see that they don't care or even notice that I'm bald. They simply see someone opening a door to a whole new world—an escape, a thrill, and a memory they can carry with them forever.

Working alongside Tai Collins, the founder of A Chance for Children, always fills me with admiration and hope. Her organization was born from a powerful moment in the early '90s when Greg Bonann, creator of *Baywatch*, rescued two inner-city kids who couldn't swim and were swept into deep waters by rip tides while he was working as a lifeguard. This experience inspired Greg's vision for a "Baywatch-themed camp," which became reality when freelance writer Tai Collins offered her help, leading to the creation of the Chance for Children Summer Camp.

Despite her success, which has earned her a beautiful beachside home in Malibu, Tai's life focus remains on helping at-risk youth in Los Angeles who face poverty and gang violence. With gangs recruiting children as young as seven and millions lacking after-school options, her camp and year-round outreach programs provide a vital lifeline by exposing kids to the beach, teaching them swimming, and creating joyful memories while giving them productive outlets to dream big and set goals.

Her story of resilience and generosity truly inspires me, as she channels her energy into improving the lives of disadvantaged children. She has become my role model for how I want to live my life.

Teaching underprivileged kids to dive is vastly different from instructing privileged ones. For at-risk children, an hour underwater can be a life-changing event. Many have never been to the beach or owned a swimsuit, yet they eagerly jump into the pool with smiles on their faces and excited thumbs-up signals.

Watching the kids' faces light up at the wonder of breathing under-water, their wide eyes taking in the hidden universe beneath the waves, is an experience like no other. They marvel at the sunlight dancing through the water, grinning through their masks and overcome with awe, and I'm reminded of why I fell in love with diving all those years ago.

* * *

My fourth and final round of chemo proves to be the most brutal. From the first moment of infusion, the familiar onset of weakness creeps over me. Each session seems to carve out a deeper exhaustion than the one before, leaving me drained and frail as my body surrenders to the harsh reality of the treatment.

Discomfort is a constant companion, gnawing away at me. My days are a blur of bed rest, helplessness, and grappling with pain from head to toe. My throat and stomach burn, and I can barely complete simple tasks without collapsing. Only watermelon offers a brief respite, its cool sweetness a moment of pure, focused bliss. Then the effect wears off, plunging me back into a dim haze of nausea and vomiting.

When my false eyelashes fall out and the expander in my right breast deflates again, these worries seem like small, insignificant details amidst the larger struggle. I find solace in holding on to a single thought: *One day soon, this battle will be behind me.*

After weeks of feeling drained, I muster the energy to embrace some-thing that brings me joy: organizing a Miss Scuba program for the annual PADI Women's Dive Day, an event that fuels my spirit and provides a welcome distraction from fatigue. We gather a fantastic group of twenty women and set off eagerly for Santa Catalina Island—my refuge, the place where I first fell in love with California diving and where the in-person Miss Scuba community was born.

Returning here feels like coming full circle. This island witnessed my transformation from someone running from her past to someone building her future. Now, battling cancer with my head bare and my body weakened by chemo, I need this place to remind me who I am beneath the illness. The island's rugged beauty welcomes me as always, and the familiar sight of its kelp forests and rocky shores fills the air with more than possibility—it carries the promise of renewal, of returning to myself.

Our day unfolds with an invigorating yoga session atop the rustic, sunlit rocks, where we stretch and breathe in sync with the rhythm of the waves. The saltwater breeze is therapeutic, its briny tang a sign of nature's raw healing power.

Not quite up for diving with my heavy gear yet, I opt for snorkeling above the other women. The ocean's soothing embrace is a balm for my soul. The Pacific waters are cool and refreshing, easing the discomfort of my treatments. I float effortlessly, surrounded by the brilliant colors of marine life dancing in harmony with the sunlight filtering through the water. With each breath through my snorkel, I absorb the serenity, healing, and connection that the ocean offers.

Here, suspended between the surface and the depths, I find myself practicing what Thich Nhat Hanh calls "mindful floating"—not just physical but emotional lightness. His teachings point out that water can be our teacher, showing us how to yield without losing our essence, how to flow around obstacles instead of fighting them. As I drift with the gentle current, watching fish move with effortless grace, I understand that my cancer treatment is teaching me the same lesson. Some days I must be like water—soft, adaptable, finding a way through rather than demanding a way be made for me.

In just a few weeks, I'll be scuba diving again. I can't wait to reclaim that part of myself, to plunge into the deep, crystal-clear waters that have always been my sanctuary. But first, to celebrate the end of chemo, our family is heading to Ireland—a serene retreat into a mystical world of castles and tranquil landscapes.

Our escape to Ireland feels like the perfect way to mark this milestone. Each day flows with the peaceful rhythm of an ancient river, letting us drift into deep, rejuvenating rest. We indulge in hearty Irish fare, savoring rich stews and warm, freshly baked bread—a comfort that infuses both body and soul.

Exploring age-old castles, wandering through lush green fields, and taking in the sweeping views is like living in the mists of a poetic dream. Every moment—each meal, each nap, every exploration of this enchanting place with my closest loved ones—is a gift. Ireland's quiet beauty becomes the perfect retreat, allowing me to pause, reflect, and fully embrace this new chapter with hope and gratitude.

CHAPTER 18

The Maldives and Fiji: Reconnecting

*Almost everything will work again if you unplug it
for a few minutes, including you.*
– Anne Lamott

If Ireland was a misty, enchanted reverie, I tell myself, *then the Maldives will surely be like a vivid dream coming to life.* The thrill of planning this getaway, a return to crystal-clear waters and vibrant, beloved seascapes, is distinct and electric.

"Pick any place in the world," Hilaire said months ago, "and we'll visit when you're done." We wanted to envision a light at the end of the tunnel, something to look forward to throughout all the treatments and surgeries of this cancer journey. My husband's thoughtful gesture helped turn an excruciating period in our lives into something exciting, a celebration of our family overcoming everything life has thrown at us.

I chose the Maldives, and now it's finally happening.

Life is starting to pick up again, and it feels refreshing. At home in California, I've been diving back into my jewelry business with renewed energy, attending bustling crystal and gem fairs and working on private commissions, all while feeling the call of the ocean once more.

In June, Dr. Burrell finally replaced the expanders in my breasts with permanent implants, and although the surgery was still tough, recovery went faster and more smoothly than with my previous surgeries. I didn't let the fatigue and discomfort beat me. Now it feels like a whole new world. I can breathe easily at last.

After the surgery, I wasn't allowed back in the water for a while. This offered a chance to plan a whole new type of trip with my family: to Yosemite National Park, where the crisp, invigorating air filled our lungs and the soft rustle of leaves underfoot set the pace for our daily wandering. Towering granite cliffs and majestic waterfalls created a stunning panorama as we shared laughter and stories along the trails, our conversations blending with the serenity of the park.

One morning in Yosemite, seated on a large, smooth boulder overlooking a peaceful valley, we took a break from hiking to rest and indulge in the fresh fruit and homemade sandwiches we'd packed. Enzo was full of energy, eagerly exploring every nook and cranny, while Hilaire and I beamed over his enthusiasm and the simple pleasure of being in such a magnificent setting. And I realized something incredible: *I'm not in pain.*

In fact, I was feeling great.

Perhaps I am finally over the hump. My hair is starting to grow back, and things are getting back to "normal." I'm receiving calls for movie productions and private scuba training again. I am ready to close the door on this part of my life and move on, filled with the jubilation of being alive.

En route to the Maldives, we make a captivating two-day stop in Hong Kong, a city brimming with incandescent charm. We have a fancy suit tailored for Hilaire, explore the bustling metro, savor leisurely breakfasts, and discover parks filled with turtles and play areas for Enzo. Every moment feels festive, adding a touch of magic before we even reach our final destination. I rejoice in being alive and all the wonderful things in my life.

The past year has unfolded in a cascade of unexpected milestones, each one a testament to hard work, dedication, and perseverance. I was honored to receive the Platinum Pro 5000 recognition for achieving more than five thousand dives, and to become a PADI Ambassador, a prestigious title awarded to those who have demonstrated exceptional commitment to diving, marine conservation, and the PADI community.

PADI also asked me to collaborate on a community project: an inspirational video about the ocean's healing power. This was a project that speaks to my heart on such a profound level—after all, I am living proof of what they want to capture. So I showed up bruised and bald but full of life, ready to share my story.

The process captured moments of inspiration while demonstrating the deep connection between the sea and our well-being. Walking along the shoreline, my bald head gleaming in the California sun, I spoke about how the ocean had become my sanctuary during the darkest months of treatment. The rhythmic sound of waves had been my meditation, the sand beneath my feet a grounding force when everything else felt uncertain.

"When you're fighting cancer," I told the camera, "your body becomes foreign territory. But in the water, I remember who I am beneath the illness. The ocean doesn't see my scars or my baldness—it simply holds me, supports me, reminds me that I'm still here, still whole, still capable of wonder."

We filmed sequences of me sitting in the sand at the edge of the water, waves gently lapping at my feet as I reminisced about returning to diving after surgery, about how the promise of underwater adventures had sustained me through the hardest days. And I realized something I'd never been able to articulate before: how the ocean's endless rhythm mirrors the persistence needed to heal. The cool Pacific water washing over my toes seemed to carry away the residue of treatment—not just the physical exhaustion, but the emotional weight I'd been carrying.

Sitting there with the vast blue horizon stretched before me, I wasn't just talking about the ocean's healing power. I was embodying it, exposing how the sea had helped restore both my body and my spirit.

I've also been flooded with invitations to speak at events with organizations such as Voices for Our Oceans and to be featured in yoga and scuba magazines. These experiences are deeply moving, and I hope my story in turn moves others, particularly by offering hope to anyone suffering from cancer. My positive outlook on life seems to resonate with people, who sometimes reach out to share their own powerful stories of survival. Knowing that my strength and my mindset help set a course for them to follow is unbelievably uplifting.

I appreciate the validation and experiences, and the opportunity to reflect on my journey and make a difference in people's lives. But right now I'm ready to enjoy a celebration just for me and my family—and get back to the real me.

Upon arriving in the Maldives, our journey continues with a hydroplane flight to our resort. Soaring above the ocean in one of these marvels for the first time is exhilarating, and the resort is a slice of paradise, with an opulent ambiance and personalized touches that make us feel like royalty—an oasis crafted for rest and renewal.

The beauty and tranquility of the Maldives take my breath away. Our days unfold on white sandy beaches, as soft and pristine as powdered sugar, stretching into the horizon. Our accommodations are simple yet elegant, designed to blend seamlessly with nature. Just outside our room, a cozy swing sways gently beneath lush palm trees, inviting us to linger and gaze out over the sea's turquoise hues shimmering in the sunlight. The outdoor shower becomes my ritual of indulgence, with open sky above and the island's tropical humidity all around me.

The privacy here is unexpectedly luxurious, offering a chance to finally relax and let go. Just steps from our room, Enzo and I play for hours in the warm, shallow ocean waters as calm as a pool, a safe haven where he can splash and explore in bright white sand, his laughter mingling with the soft sounds of the waves. And the Kids Club is a game-changer for us, catering perfectly to our needs as a family: Enzo can enjoy a fun-filled, engaging environment while Hilaire and I immerse ourselves in our shared passion for diving.

We cannot wait to dive together again.

Descending into the turquoisewater for the first time, we are eager to be enveloped by the vibrant subaquatic life we've dreamed about for months, but our long-awaited first dive is a letdown. The coral has been devastated by storms and global warming—by ocean waters that reach an astounding 90°F that week. The undersea scene is a cemetery of broken, colorless fragments where a once-thriving reef used to be. We spot a lone turtle and a few scattered fish, but the abundant underwater world we envisioned seems distant and faded.

After another lackluster day, we choose to stop diving and start relishing this experience together as a couple—exploring this miraculous island, indulging in our love for the ocean in other ways, and creating unforgettable memories. We bicycle everywhere we can, discovering hidden coves, secret lagoons, and lush landscapes.

With each slow, sun-soaked day, we savor this rare tranquility. The leisurely pace allows us to pause and fully immerse in the beauty of this paradise—the gentle rhythm of the waves, the golden sun on our faces, the serene luxury that surrounds us. This trip is our reward for the horrible events we've endured, and a deeply personal reminder of how far we've come. We hold close these moments of peace and joy, knowing how precious they are.

The magic of this journey is powerful enough, it seems, to bring incredible, life-affirming news from afar: I'm being inducted into the Women Divers Hall of Fame with the upcoming Class of 2017. This prestigious organization recognizes and commends the remarkable women who have made significant contributions to the diving world and who inspire and support others—women who lead with courage, push the boundaries of diving, and give back to the community.

To be acknowledged among such inspiring women is a profound affirmation of my life's journey. It's a personal milestone, of course, highlighting the impact of my work in stunts and water safety in Hollywood; my role as Miss Scuba; and my professional diving career. It's also a recognition of my deep commitment to making a difference in the lives of young people, through A Chance for Children Foundation—both by volunteering my time to take inner city at-risk youth underwater and in my ongoing efforts to bring gemstones into schools around Mother's Day and Christmas, so underprivileged students can craft meaningful gifts for their loved ones. This accolade is also testament to the shared spirit among women who dedicate their lives to making the world—both underwater and on land—a better place for all.

During our stay in the Maldives, I often imagine how much Mutti would've loved these breathtaking turquoise waters, and the sadness of missing her is tinged with the understanding that life must go on. Things don't always go as expected, but if we continue to seek beauty in each day, that seems to be enough for now.

The thriving coral my husband and I had hoped for is a distant memory, and we had to abandon our original plan. But we've adjusted and embraced this new direction, this new plan and vision for our vacation together. The island's beauty offers its own kind of magic. All we have to do is look for it.

* * *

January arrives with a mix of anticipation and resolve as I prepare for my final surgery: a total hysterectomy. Doctors will remove my ovaries, uterus, and fallopian tubes, marking the end of an intense march against cancer. This drastic measure will preemptively ward off ovarian cancer, a threat I otherwise face with an 80 percent probability.

The urgency of this operation is underscored by its sheer gravity, but my resolve is unwavering. I'm already in menopause, and I have made peace with not giving Enzo a sibling. Although many women speak losing their femininity in such circumstances, my experience is different. I don't perceive it as a loss but rather as a necessary step toward health and survival.

The surgery is laparoscopic, leaving only two one-inch cuts just below my bikini line. Having braced myself for a much more aggressive ordeal, I'm somewhat relieved by the minimally invasive approach. Post-surgery, I don't even require painkillers. The physical recovery is on track, and as soon as I'm medically cleared, I'm eager to leave the hospital and reclaim normalcy.

I'm not a fan of doing nothing. Resting, sleeping, reading, and watching TV is nice for a few days, but I'm done with it. I can't resist going back to yoga, lifting Enzo, and generally refusing to lay low. Both Hilaire and my doctor are frustrated with my inability to stay still, and honestly, I'm frustrated with myself too. But doing nothing just doesn't suit me. I am itching for that next adventure and finally feeling myself again—though not the free-spirited, vagabond self of my past, of course. My travel plans now revolve around balancing our family's needs with my craving for scuba diving.

Our criteria for choosing a destination have shifted to ensure it caters to a young child who loves the water but doesn't swim on his own just yet. I seek places that offer excellent diving while also providing safe and stimulating activities for Enzo, allowing Hilaire and me to dive together without worry. Our choice also has to be land-based, as I am terrified of Enzo falling or jumping into the water if we were staying on a liveaboard. Surprisingly few locations meet all these needs, but Beqa Lagoon Resort in Fiji offers everything we're looking for.

Fiji, a lush paradise just past Hawaii but before reaching New Zealand, is a dream destination for us, and we decide to head there for Easter. The direct overnight flight from Los Angeles to Nadi takes only eleven hours, enough time to sleep soundly after dinner and a movie on the plane. Our trip comes with a twist: We're filming Beqa Lagoon Resort.

On top of our own luggage and everything one needs to travel with an active little boy, Hilaire and I are juggling six Pelican cases, two carry-ons filled with camera gear, and diving equipment—and a stroller. Once again, we've accepted an extraordinary project that will blend our love for adventure with professional filmmaking, and every detail is carefully planned. We're filled with enthusiasm and eager to produce a series of videos that highlight Fiji's natural beauty and vibrant atmosphere as well as the resort's luxurious offerings and family-friendly activities. It's a departure from our usual diving focus, and I'm excited to see Hilaire's creative vision unfold again behind the camera while I step in front of it.

The humid air of Nadi greets us like a warm, energizing embrace, and soon we're making our way to Beqa Lagoon Resort, where the smiling staff welcome us with songs and flowers. After settling into our beachfront bure, we dive into the pool and relax, following it up with a heavenly foot scrub and massage at the spa. The sun is shining. Warm-hearted people surround us. We are barefoot and living free, laughing by the sea.

I am in heaven.

To top it all off, the diving is phenomenal. Fiji's reefs, known as the soft coral capital of the world, surpass my wildest dreams. The vibrant colors and formations feel like an artist's palette come to life. We glide through giant fan coral and sprawling table coral, in every shade of purple, pink, yellow, and green.

What strikes me most powerfully is the contrast with so many other dive destinations I've visited in recent years. Unlike the bleached coral grave-yards I witnessed in Trinidad and Tobago, or the damaged reefs struggling to survive in parts of Thailand's Andaman Sea, Fiji's reefs pulse with life. Where the Maldives' delicate ecosystems face constant threats from rising temperatures and ocean acidification, Fiji's traditional *tabu* system—where local communities protect certain reef areas as sacred, off-limits zones—has created underwater sanctuaries that thrive.

The difference is immediately visible. These aren't the skeletal remains of coral formations I've grown sadly accustomed to documenting, but living, breathing reef systems where soft corals cascade like waterfalls and fish populations flourish. It's proof that when marine protection is taken seriously, and when local communities are empowered to be guardians rather than exploiters, the ocean can still reveal the full spectrum of its magic and abundance.

Exploring the reefs with local divemasters allows us to capture stun-ning footage of the marine life. We particularly enjoy the shark dive at the Cathedral, encountering blacktip, whitetip, gray, and silky sharks, and even a thrilling tiger shark. The dive crew treats us like royalty, setting up and washing our gear daily. And while we dive, the resort staff takes wonderful care of Enzo. Fijians' reputed love for children is heartwarming and fully on display. One afternoon, coming back from another amazing dive, we find Enzo sitting at a table, sandwiched between two Fijian ladies: one feeding him mango ice cream, the other fanning his red, sweaty face. All three are laughing.

Experiencing the world through Enzo's eyes is magical. Traveling is the best lesson Hilaire and I can offer our son; exposing him to diverse cultures and experiences is an invaluable gift. Seeing him so curious, open-hearted, and fearless is a validation that we are doing something right and raising him well. He makes friends everywhere we go and engages with new surroundings and customs—tasting the local dishes, embracing unfamiliar traditions—in countless ways that can only enrich his life. My hope is that our urge for exploration becomes part of who he is, too.

In Fiji, we spend hours swimming with Enzo, and his playfulness in the water is delightful, though it will always be a bit nerve-wracking until he's old enough to fully swim on his own. His love for the water is seemingly as vast as the ocean that stretches around us.

In the afternoons, we hike to waterfalls, kayak in the mangroves, and snorkel along the coral reef that extends directly from the resort's shoreline—what divers call the "house reef" because it's literally at the accommodation's doorstep. One day, as Hilaire is capturing footage of me kayaking over the shimmering atolls, his face suddenly contorts in pain, and his yell pierces through the tranquil surroundings. He has accidentally stepped on a hidden stingray, and the result is instantaneous and excruciating—the kind of pain that makes grown men cry.

Stunned and horrified to witness him in such agony, I quickly dial the Divers Alert Network and explain the dire situation. Following their instructions, we put Hilaire's foot in the hottest water he can tolerate to draw out the poison and ease the pain until he can get to the hospital on the mainland—via an hour's boat ride from our secluded island.

A few days after getting stitched up, Hilaire realizes that the tropical heat has taken its toll: The stingray wound has become infected, complicating his recovery. His condition is monitored closely as the infection is treated, adding an unwelcome layer of difficulty to our peaceful escape. Despite the severity of the situation, we navigate this unexpected challenge together, hopeful for a swift and full recovery.

Needless to say, filming is over for this trip. We are forced to slow down and soak in every moment of our time on this beautiful island. Taking the hint, we kick back in the hammock, read books, and enjoy watching sunsets framed by palm trees. We will come back to complete this project another time.

The Buddha taught that attachment to outcomes causes suffering, and I'm finally beginning to understand what that means. The old me would have been devastated by this setback, already planning how to salvage the project. But watching Enzo play in the sand with crabs and seashells while the ocean whispers its eternal rhythms, I realize this forced pause might be the real gift.

Sometimes what appears to be an obstacle is actually the path.

* * *

All clear.

My four-month check-up following the final cancer surgery deliver results I can hardly believe—and a wave of relief I can hardly describe. My blood tests are all clear.

An enormous weight lifts from my shoulders, leaving room to reflect on the past two years. I wish I could say I faced this battle with unshakable courage and grace, but the truth is, fear was always there. Fortunately, my will to live and my longing to see my child grow up proved stronger than the disease.

I could question why this happened to me: I live healthily, manage stress well, cultivate a supportive community, find wellness in my work. But life handed me this challenge, and I had no choice but to accept it. I lost my hair, underwent double mastectomy, and had a total hysterectomy. My body lurched into instant menopause, ending my chances of having more children. No matter how you look at it, it's a grueling experience.

Cancer is a part of my story now, but it doesn't define me. It's only one part of my life's narrative. I choose to focus on the positive, and I know something amazing is just around the corner. I'm ready to write the next chapter—one where I rise from the ashes, stronger than ever before.

CHAPTER 19

"Pandora": Making the Impossible a Reality

It's not whether you get knocked down.
It's whether you get back up.
– Vince Lombardi

When the phone rings in May 2017, I am taken completely by surprise. "This is John Garvin," the caller says, "the water safety coordinator for *Avatar: The Way of Water*."

My heart skips. Calls like this don't happen anymore, not after everything I've just been through. But it's happening: John wants to meet with me to discuss a role on the project.

I hang up and stare at the phone. Two years ago, I was lying in a hospital bed wondering if I'd see Enzo's fifth birthday. Now someone wants to hire me for the biggest film project in Hollywood.

Meeting with John feels like stepping back into a version of myself I thought was gone forever. The project is massive—bigger than anything I've worked on—and my potential role would involve ensuring the safety of cast and crew during underwater scenes. As we talk, I find myself overcompensating, talking faster than usual, trying to prove I'm still up to the task—still the person I was before, the person who could handle anything.

John values my experience working with women and children, and he wants me on his team as a scuba instructor and safety diver. The best part? Avatar is filming its second, third, and fourth sequels simultaneously in Manhattan Beach, just eight minutes from our house.

I want to say yes immediately, but the voice in my head—the one that's been with me since my cancer diagnosis—whispers: *What if you're not strong enough? What if they find out you're not the person they think they're hiring?*

But sitting across from John, seeing his confidence in me, I realize something: Maybe I don't need to be exactly who I was before. Maybe I just need to be who I am now.

"Yes," I tell him, and for the first time in two years, I feel like I'm moving toward something instead of away from it. "Absolutely yes."

* * *

Walking onto the *Avatar* set for the first time, I'm not prepared for the scale of what James Cameron has built. The tank, where we will create a fictional underwater world on the habitable moon Pandora, dominates the soundstage—one hundred twenty feet by sixty feet around, and thirty feet deep. I've worked in plenty of pools, but this feels different, more like standing at the edge of a small lake that someone boxed up and dropped inside a building.

The glass walls rise two stories high, and there's something both impressive and slightly unsettling about all that water contained behind glass. A steep ladder descends into the depths, and I find myself calculating how long it would take to get someone out in an emergency. Old habits die hard.

Special effects technicians demonstrate the wave makers—two massive ship propellers that can churn the water from calm to turbulent with the push of a button. Cameron calls it his "Swiss army system," because he can do just about anything to imitate real-world conditions. The current they generate looks manageable, maybe ten knots, but I can see how the camera angles and lighting will make it appear much more violent on screen.

The glass walls are a filmmaker's dream, allowing for camera views from both inside and outside. Four or five camera operators, led by Pete Zuccarini—whom I worked with on *Piranha 3D*, and who is also known for his work on *Life of Pi, Into the Blue*, and the *Pirates of the Caribbean* saga—dive underwater to capture every angle of the action. A multitude of mounted cameras on the walls ensure nothing is missed. It's a high-tech setup, perfect for intricate underwater scenes.

Glimpsing the prep area with its retractable platforms, I'm already thinking through the logistics: How many people can we safely have in the water at once? Where are the blind spots? What happens if someone panics in thirty feet of water with all this equipment around? The underwater camera rigs, lighting systems, and mechanical platforms create a maze of potential entanglements. In a panic, people don't think clearly—they might swim into camera cables or get caught under the retractable mechanisms while trying to reach the surface. As I watch the water settle into mirror-calm perfection, I have to admit that this is going to be unlike anything I've worked on before.

And when the first major technical challenge arises, it changes everything.

"We can't have a lot of air bubbles," Cameron explains. He's using sensitive motion-capture technology that can't work properly with the bubbles we exhale while scuba diving. Every bubble creates reflective interference that disrupts the system's ability to track the tiny marker dots on the actors' bodies. For the water to remain crystal clear—essential for accurate motion capture—we have to abandon scuba gear entirely.

This means training the entire crew in freediving.

Accustomed to bulky scuba gear, all of us—water safety team, grips, lighting technicians, special effects team—must adapt quickly. Kirk Krack—known for his water work on *Black Panther: Wakanda Forever, The Cove*, and *Suicide Squad*—from Performance Freediving International, who is already training the actors, comes in to transform us from scuba divers into freedivers, and the adjustment is more exacting than anyone anticipated. After more than twenty-five years of scuba, I'm not sure freediving will be my thing.

To my surprise, I fall in love with it.

Scuba diving has always made me feel at home in the water, like it's where I truly belong. It's like shedding the tether that held you to shore and finally swimming free—unencumbered, unrestricted, purely connected to the water. I thought I was weightless before, but this is a completely new sense of freedom, raw and liberating.

No tanks.

No gear.

Just me and the water.

I feel becoming part of the water.

The mornings start quietly. I am usually first in the water with our water safety team—vacuuming the bottom, testing platforms, securing equipment. Next, the stunt team, special effects crew, and grips arrive, preparing everything before the actors show up. It becomes ritual, the daily routine that keeps this massive production running.

John Garvin, known for his work as diving coordinator on *Sanctum*, *Last Breath*, and *Deepsea Challenge*, is the quiet genius behind it all. He runs the show with a calm authority that has earned him the respect of everyone on set. And Kirk, the freediving supervisor, moves through the water with lifelong practice, precise and efficient. His internal compass guides him— and the rest of us—through every scene.

We train to stay underwater for two to four minutes at a time, which makes long filming days far more efficient even without scuba tanks. Freediving lets us move with ease and agility, so the ten-to-fourteen-hour shoots are not just manageable but genuinely enjoyable. It also allows for a quicker, more effective response in case of emergency, ensuring safety while maintaining the fluidity of the shoot.

The training itself becomes an intensive boot camp. We begin every day with stretching and yoga to loosen our muscles and get centered, followed by a deliberate breathing routine that helps slow the heart rate and prepares the body for the dive. After the basic freedive training, we focus on freedive-specific dive rescue scenarios.

Safety is paramount, and we dedicate an impressive amount of time to preparation for any emergency. We even practice spinal injury air lifts using a basket, which is more intense readiness than I've seen on any other movie set. My immediate boss, Matt O'Connor, the marine coordinator, is a true professional—known for *Perfect Storm*, *Pearl Harbor* and *Deja Vu*—and I'm learning something new every day from him and the other seasoned pros all around me.

Work hasn't been this physically exhausting for me in years. From sunrise to sunset, the core water safety team—me, Kirk, Alex Krimm, Katie Klosterman, Danny Bailey, and Freeze Jeffrey—is submerged in the tank, practicing freediver rescues. Unlearning techniques we've relied on for decades stirs up a lot of frustration, but Kirk is adamant that we all execute the rescues using freediving methods. As the hours drag on, the 90°F water turns into a suffocating embrace. By the end of each day, I can barely peel off my wetsuit.

The real challenge comes with the latest production requirements. To perfect the lighting for bringing Pandora's oceans to life, almost a million tiny, white plastic balls are added to cover the pool surface, eliminating reflections and achieving consistent lighting. This makes water safety even more difficult, of course, obscuring the safety team's view as we monitor the actors and crew. The balls also present a choking hazard: They're the perfect size to inhale while gulping that precious air when you ascend after a long dive.

This happens on our first day of filming, when one of the stunt performers breaks the surface after an underwater chase scene. Luckily, Kirk is right there to respond when the stunt guy's eyes go wide and his hands fly to his neck—a universal sign for choking.

The stunt team, mainly from Cirque du Soleil, is incredible, performing underwater choreography while holding their breath for up to seven minutes. I watch for shallow water blackout, a condition that can happen without warning, especially to divers pushing their limits. It typically occurs during ascent, when oxygen levels drop dangerously low, causing a diver to lose consciousness just below the surface. Staying vigilant is important because often no clear signs lead up to this critical event. When a stuntwoman faints one day after an impressive performance, our rescue drills pay off as we fly into lifesaving action.

The physical demands of this project are very real, yet it's super rewarding to see the immense level of attentiveness and professional behavior among everybody on our team. Garrett Warren, our stunt coordinator—known for *Logan, Alita: Battle Angel*, and *Road House*—orchestrates the operation with precision, guiding accomplished team members Steve Brown, Chris Denison, Mike Avery, Andy Jones, Benoit Beaufils, Juliana Potter, Molly Miller, Lea Catania, Emilie Siemer, Liz Parkinson, and many other skilled stunt performers. Each one brings expertise in their craft, executing complex maneuvers with professional precision.

Meanwhile, the props add another layer of complexity. Today we're testing the whale, a massive, detailed piece that looks convincing enough for film but creates blind spots and entanglement risks that I'm constantly calculating. During rehearsals, when I mount this sleek creature to stand in for Lo'ak—the young Na'vi who forms a connection with this whale in the story—the wonder of the scene fills me from head to toe. Still, my mind remains split between the magic and the mechanics: *Where are the exit routes if something goes wrong? How quickly can we reach someone if they get trapped underneath?*

Production ramps up over the first few months on set, with a focus on testing props and developing the technical systems that Cameron envisions. It's mostly grips, stunts, and special effects—a relatively relaxed atmosphere, where various departments collaborate to solve problems that have never been solved or even presented before. We're working to bring Cameron's underwater vision to reality, from the vivacious marine life to the sprawling aquatic environments.

Then the principal cast arrives, and the air shifts.

* * *

Sigourney Weaver, at age sixty-eight, is no natural in water. She freely admits this yet pushes herself harder than anyone else, consistently performing underwater takes two and a half minutes long. Her resilience and quiet grace inspire everyone around her. She quickly becomes my favorite person on set, a beacon of strength and kindness amidst the chaos.

What strikes me most, however, isn't her ability or her kindness—it's her methodical approach to a skill that doesn't come naturally. She asks questions, follows protocols, never pushes beyond her limits. From a safety perspective, she's exactly the kind of performer you want: professional, self-aware, respectful of the environment.

Kate Winslet presents the opposite side of the coin. She takes to freediving immediately, moving through water like she's been doing it for years. For instructors like Kirk, the concern with natural talent is overconfidence, which can lead to pushing too far, too fast. But Kate listens to direction and respects the limits we set. Her smile underwater isn't manufactured movie magic; it's genuine enjoyment of the medium.

While I want to marvel at the performances unfolding before me, my job isn't to be starstruck. It's to watch for the subtle signs of someone approaching their limit—a slight shift in posture, a change in rhythm, anything that signals it's time to surface. Whether it's an A-list actor or a stunt performer, oxygen deprivation looks the same. The celebrity aspect becomes irrelevant when you're responsible for keeping people alive.

On massive productions like this, crew can easily become invisible or blend into each other. So, the first time James Cameron uses my name, I do a double take. Calling me by name speaks to his awareness of the entire operation—every single detail, not just the marquee elements.

Sets this size can make you feel like just another piece in the machine, but with Cameron, I feel like part of a carefully orchestrated operation. He operates with precision I've rarely seen, telling you exactly where to look, what specific action to perform, where to place your hand. Most directors might say, "Let's try that again, but better." Cameron gives the exact adjustment needed. It's clear and efficient, though demanding. His reputation for intensity is well earned.

His passion is just as legendary, and perhaps that is what fuels his ability to push people beyond what they think they're capable of. He expects excellence, but he provides the tools, vision, and direction to achieve it. When you finally nail that one particular movement he envisioned and he nods in approval, you know you've contributed to something significant.

As they work, both Kate and Sigourney are covered in sensors, their faces inked with tiny dots—for tracking their every move and slightest emotional impressions. They wear neoprene motion-capture suits bristling with sensors and cameras, equipment that transforms simple swimming into a technical ballet. The technology adds another layer of fascination—and confusion. Watching the actors adapt their performances to accommodate the gear while maintaining character authenticity is impressive. Gone are the days of just playing a character or role. These actors are problem-solvers finding ways to serve the storytelling—magicians who make the sometimes burdensome technology disappear.

In one scene, Sigourney floats motionlessly near the tank's center, her neoprene suit transforming her into some hybrid sea creature as she "converses" with digital fish that will be added later. The tiny cameras mounted on her headgear capture every micro-expression while she holds perfectly still, twenty feet underwater.

Fifteen feet away, Kate perches on an elaborate "coral" structure that reaches nearly to the surface—a twisted sculpture of foam and tubes, designed to mimic Pandora's underwater fruit trees. The artificial coral sways with the tank's subtle current, and dozens of prop "fruits" hang from its branches like oversized apples. Kate's job is to demonstrate the harvesting technique to the child actors clustered around her, their small bodies barely visible behind their own bristling sensor equipment.

The lighting rig above creates shafts of "sunlight" that penetrate thirty feet of crystal-clear water in calculated angles, casting moving patterns across the coral and actors alike. Everything looks ethereal—the kind of shot that will take your breath away on screen.

But from my position on the underwater platform, I'm counting seconds, not admiring visuals. My job? Make sure nobody pushes themselves too far.

This balance of art and responsibility keeps me grounded. I know my role is critical to ensuring the filming continues, safely and seamlessly. Take after take, twenty-plus people hold their breath while Cameron adjusts microscopic details: "Kate, shift your left hand two inches toward the fruit above your elbow. Sigourney, tilt your head slightly down—I need to see more of your eyes." Each adjustment means another four-minute breath hold, another test of everyone's limits.

The magical scene that will captivate audiences is, in reality, a grueling test of endurance. By the fifth take, a camera operator's movements have become less fluid. By the seventh, one of the child actors surfaces early, gasping, and I'm already moving toward him. Fatigue is the enemy of safety underwater, and my job is to spot it before it becomes dangerous. The coral structure itself becomes a hazard as tired performers brush against its sharp edges, forcing me to signal the underwater grips to reposition it between takes. On my watch, no one gets hurt in pursuit of perfection.

My role extends far beyond the safety of the principal actors. I scan the water constantly, my eyes darting to all the people sharing the space: the camera operators submerged with their specialized rigs, the grips and lighting technicians hovering just out of frame, the stunt performers executing daring maneuvers with split-second timing, the child actors who require an especially watchful eye as they eagerly push themselves to embody the aquatic grace of the fictional Metkayina Clan—the reef-dwelling Na'vi who take in Jake Sully's family when they seek refuge by the ocean. Each component adds layers of drama and realism to the filmed scenes in a precise and intricate underwater dance.

I remain vigilant as the weight of responsibility presses on me. A tangle of hoses from the breathing apparatus, a rogue wave from a jet-propelled device, or a slight misstep from any of the performers could turn this orchestrated symphony into deadly chaos. My heart pounds each time an actor dives deep or a camera operator ventures too close to a sharp prop. I cannot afford a lapse in focus; every moment demands my vigilance.

Amidst this contained pandemonium is undeniable beauty. The entire team's relentless pursuit of excellence—the actors giving their all, the crew tirelessly fine-tuning every shot, the technicians crafting a world that will transport moviegoers to Pandora—is compelling. As the scene comes to life, the power of collaboration is made tangible, with each person playing their part to make the impossible a reality.

Together we're creating magic.

* * *

Days blur together on the set of *Avatar* as we push through increasingly complex sequences. Some of our most adrenaline-pumping sequences are the "dogfights"—complex chase scenes that transform the tank into an aquatic battlefield, pushing both technology and human endurance to the breaking point.

The choreography calls for high-speed pursuits through a kelp forest, with one or more creatures fleeing while others give chase, weaving between swaying pillars of vegetation, executing sharp turns that send spirals of bubbles through the water. The "creatures" are stunt performers riding jeto-vators—sleek, underwater propulsion devices that look like a cross between a mechanical dolphin and a fighter jet.

Each device is about eight feet long, painted gunmetal gray, and emits a constant, low hum punctuated by sharp whooshes as the jetovator changes direction. The riders lie prone on top, gripping handlebars while their legs trail behind in the current created by the jet propulsion. The jetovators can accelerate from zero to twenty knots in seconds. Their high-pressure water jets creating thrust powerful enough to lift a rider completely out of the water if they hit the surface at the right angle.

Our lead "pilots" are expert freedivers—mostly Mike and Chris—who move through water with supernatural efficiency. They're followed by four other stunt performers, each maneuvering through the artificial kelp at speeds that make my pulse race. Pandora's underwater jungles—towering, alien, and beautiful—are an obstacle course of entanglement hazards. The kelp is constructed of flexible green tubing that sways from floor-mounted anchors, creating a dense, three-dimensional maze that extends from the "sea floor" to just below the surface. It's not hard to imagine the "kelp" wrapping around limbs or equipment and trapping someone underwater.

At these speeds, a collision with the tank's glass walls could be just as catastrophic—not only by injuring the rider, but also by cracking the entire containment system and causing even more injury and destruction. Plus, with six high-speed vehicles operating in a confined space, the risk of mid-water collisions is significant. The dangers here are immediate and constant.

On the fourth take, one freediver executes a move that makes my stomach drop. Pursued by two other riders, he suddenly dives straight down, threading between two vertical kelp stalks with maybe eighteen inches of clearance on either side of him. His pursuers follow, and for a moment all three disappear into the depths of the tank.

I hold my breath.

When they surface for air, all three are grinning with adrenaline, water streaming from their hair.

The footage on Cameron's monitor shows exactly what he wanted—a heart-stopping chase through an alien underwater forest that will look seamless once the digital creatures are added in post-production. But from where I stand, all I can think about is how many ways that sequence could have gone catastrophically wrong.

One Monday morning, the energy on set picks up when Sigourney Weaver arrives, her silver hair already pinned back in preparation for the headgear. Next comes Zoe Saldaña, moving with that dancer's grace she never loses, even when weighed down by motion-capture equipment. And then Sam Worthington brings his quiet intensity. But it's the arrival of the child actors that transforms the atmosphere.

Six kids between the ages of eight and fourteen cluster near the tank's edge, their excitement palpable despite the early hour. Their motion-capture suits are smaller versions of the adult gear—silver neoprene second skins dotted with reflective markers, topped with head rigs that look oversized on their young faces covered in black dots. The children's natural liveliness bounces off the soundstage walls, a sharp contrast to the controlled professionalism of the adult cast.

Today's scene is designed to be emotionally wrenching: a rescue sequence where one of the children (played by Jamie Flatters) becomes separated from the family group during a violent storm and is wounded by the enemy during a fight. The tank's wave makers are set to maximum intensity, and the water roils with artificial fury. White foam crests roll across the surface, tugging an underwater current that pulls with surprising strength—strong enough that even the tank's most experienced swimmers struggle to maintain position.

The mechanical waves crash against a constructed shoreline at one end of the tank, sending spray fifteen feet into the air. The lighting rig strobes intermittently, simulating lightning, while massive fans positioned around the tank create "wind" that whips water droplets across anyone standing nearby. The sound is overwhelming—crashing water, mechanical propellers, fans roaring. I'm looking at a massive storm at sea.

The water churns with the hum of activity. At its center, Jamie—playing the character of Neteyam, Jake Sully's eldest son—must appear to fight the current while several adult actors search for him. Watching him get tossed by artificial waves makes my heart rate spike. When his limp body washes up on shore and is discovered by his parents, Zoe releases an ear-piercing primal scream. The pain in her voice is real, and we all feel the devastation of losing their child.

Both the actors and the crew work with military precision around this manufactured storm. Camera operators in waterproof housings capture close-ups while staying clear of the crashing waves. Sound technicians monitor levels through headphones to distinguish the actors' voices above the mechanical thunder. Every few minutes, Cameron calls, "Cut!" and the tank systems power down, leaving an eerie, sudden silence broken only by the actors' heavy breathing and the gentle lapping of settling water.

By noon, we've completed only three takes of a sequence that will last maybe ninety seconds on screen, but each attempt has pushed everyone to their physical and emotional limits.

The set buzzes every day with controlled chaos like this—crew members scurrying between cameras, sound equipment, and various props, and the safety team training our eyes on the underwater action to ensure everything runs smoothly. The pressure is constant as everyone pushes to meet tight deadlines. As production progresses, a strong bond forms among our water team, forged through these intense shared experiences. Our core group of ten or so spends hours floating on the surface, chatting about past dives, close calls, mutual friends, and travel destinations while waiting for the next directive from Cameron or for his approval of our latest shots. By now, we know everything about each other. The suspense of whether Cameron will approve the take or ask for another one becomes part of the demanding but inspirational rhythm.

On top of the mental exhaustion from a marathon shoot, the physical strain is an onslaught from every side. I've invested in specialized earplugs, antibiotics, and ear drops to combat the relentless strain on my ears from being underwater. The harsh air conditioning hitting our heads as we emerge from the warm water adds another layer of discomfort. Even so, amidst the constant fatigue and the daily grind, there's an undeniable thrill in every moment beneath the water's surface.

Most days end with a text message at around ten p.m. from John or Matt: *Come back tomorrow. We need you in the water.* If the text never comes, I dive into crafting my jewelry the next day and try to spend quality time with my husband while Enzo is at preschool. Occasionally, I carve out some me-time for yoga or a pedicure, indulging in a bit of self-care. But I'm constantly in limbo, checking my phone in case I am called in to the *Avatar* set on an hour's notice. Our life becomes a constant state of standing by, of *hurry up and wait.*

By workday 120, I'm exhausted in ways I didn't know were possible. My freediving record now stands at four minutes and thirty-seven seconds—a personal achievement that feels both meaningless and monumental. Some days, I wonder how much more my body can handle.

But then something extraordinary happens—Kate Winslet glides through the water like she was born to it, the kids master their underwater choreography, raw footage transforms into something otherworldly—and I remember why I said yes to this impossible job.

* * *

Once again, a stranger looks out from my bathroom mirror. A red, angry rash circles my hairline—chemical burns from months of chlorine exposure that no amount of specialized shampoo could prevent. Bruises map my arms and shoulders—purple smudges where underwater equipment knocked against me in the commotion of filming. My ears, despite the expensive custom plugs and daily antibiotics, still throb with the echo of my latest infection. It's the third one this month.

Working on *Avatar* has been exciting. We've pushed every limit and given our best every day. What I didn't anticipate is how the job would consume everything beyond the tank. A few months of water scenes has stretched into nearly two years. No one seems to know how long filming will go on, and I stop asking. The uncertainty becomes its own exhausting challenge, and the unpredictability wreaks havoc at home. Yet each day, I'm grateful to read the words: *Come back tomorrow.*

My body has done what it was trained to do for more than twenty-five years. Every successful dive, every emergency I've prevented, every day I've kept up with performers half my age feels like a victory over everything that tried to stop me. I think about the person I was when I got that cancer diagnosis—how small and afraid I felt, how convinced I was that my life was effectively over.

That woman couldn't have imagined any of this: holding her breath for over four minutes, keeping A-list actors safe, being trusted with a $350 million film production. She couldn't have imagined that her body—scarred, rebuilt, fundamentally changed—would still be capable of this kind of work.

I'm back in the water, the place where I've always felt most myself. I'm proving that I'm still here. Still capable. Still valuable.

But the proof comes with a price. Some nights I collapse into bed so exhausted, I can barely kiss Enzo goodnight. Some mornings I wake up and wonder if today will be the day my body says no, the day I'll have to admit I've pushed too far. The line between proving myself and destroying myself feels thinner and thinner each day.

When people ask me about working on *Avatar*, they expect stories about celebrities and movie magic. What they don't expect is the grueling reality of shooting a movie of this caliber. Still, working at this level of production, with performers this committed and technology this advanced, reminds me of the reasons I chose this profession—not the famous names or behind-the-scenes looks, but the complex problems we're solving, and the people pushing themselves to solve them and to create something that entertains and inspires millions.

As we eventually wind down after two years of experimenting and shooting, the main unit moves on to New Zealand. Only a skeleton crew remains to dismantle the massive tank in Manhattan Beach. Standing on the platform for the last time, watching the water drain from the tank that's been my second home for so long, I think about the journey that brought me here. Two years ago, I thought cancer had ended my career. I worried that I might never feel truly useful again—that my body, irrevocably altered, wouldn't be capable of the work I'd spent a lifetime mastering.

This project proved me wrong in ways I couldn't have imagined. I didn't just survive it. I excelled at it.

I didn't just keep up with performers half my age. I led safety protocols that kept everyone alive.

I didn't just adapt to new technology. I used my expertise to train others.

I didn't just return to my old self. I discovered capabilities I never knew I had.

The prestige of having *Avatar* on my resume matters, certainly. The relationships I've built with this talented team will serve me well. But the real victory is more personal: I've proven to myself that survival isn't just about making it through the hard times. It's about discovering who you become on the other side.

I've found my place in this industry again. Not as the person I was before cancer, but as someone stronger, more confident, more capable than I ever imagined possible.

The water, as always, showed me the way forward.

CHAPTER 20

Australia:
From Burnout to Bliss

Gratitude ... turns what we have into enough.
– Melody Beattie

Hilaire's eyes flutter open, immediately finding mine across the room. "Good morning," he murmurs, his voice rough with sleep. "How long have you been up?"

"About an hour," I say, settling back into the chair. My mind is slowly, finally drifting into vacation mode, though my body still hasn't gotten the memo that the *Avatar* marathon is over. "I'm just thinking."

"About?"

I gesture toward the window, toward Sydney Harbor, where the morning sun paints everything golden. "About how maybe it's time to stop running so hard toward what's next and start appreciating what's right here."

Travel is what makes me happy, and as soon as production finally wrapped, our family set out on a long-awaited, three-week expedition through Australia. Hilaire has orchestrated every detail impeccably, starting with a direct, long-haul flight from Los Angeles to Sydney.

The first wave of gratitude hit me yesterday, before we even left the plane. Watching Enzo stretch his small arms above his head after fourteen hours of travel, seeing his eyes light up as he spotted Sydney Harbor through the aircraft window—I was in awe of his resilience, for the way children can adapt to adventure.

At seven years old, Enzo is a pro traveler who possesses a quiet confidence that catches adults off guard, with things like methodically organizing his carry-on backpack all by himself: travel journal with colored pencils, a small pouch of Australian currency, snacks, water bottle, and his favorite books. When we checked into the InterContinental Hotel, right beside the Sydney Opera House, the view from our room was revealed to be nothing short of spectacular. But it wasn't the massive, iconic white shells catching the harbor light that made me pause—it was the sound of Enzo's delighted gasp when he saw a hotel bed big enough for all three of us.

"We can have a family sleepover every night!" he announced.

That caused the second wave of gratitude: my son's ability to find joy in the simplest things.

Waking early this morning, I curled up on plush pillows in the hotel window seat, cradling my cup of coffee, watching Hilaire sleep peacefully beside Enzo, who was sprawled across the king-size bed in that boneless way only children can manage. The room was blessedly quiet—no production schedules, no tank equipment humming, no urgent calls about safety protocols.

For the first time in months, I could hear my own thoughts.

I felt grateful—again!—for the luxury of drinking coffee while it's still hot. For the absence of a phone buzzing with last-minute schedule changes. For the profound quiet that comes when your nervous system finally receives permission to rest.

I felt grateful for Hilaire's methodical planning—how he researched every detail of this trip while I was submerged in chlorinated chaos, how he understood that what I needed wasn't another adrenaline rush but the gentle rhythm of a real, honest-to-goodness vacation.

The exhaustion is not exclusively from *Avatar*. It's deeper than that. It's the bone-deep weariness that comes from forty-odd years of operating in "fighter mode"—always braced for the next challenge, the next crisis, the next person who might let me down.

I learned early to operate in this mode, when I was two years old and crying myself sick in a bathtub, when my mother had to return to work and leave me with strangers. By fourteen, when my father died and I became the keeper of our family's fragile stability, it was second nature: *Don't depend on anyone. Don't expect anyone to catch you when you fall. Keep your guard up, keep moving, keep fighting.*

It served me well through diving in cold, surging California waters where most women wouldn't dare venture.

It got me through Hollywood's cold-hearted stunt world, where showing vulnerability could end your career.

It carried me through building businesses, traveling to remote corners of the world, facing down cancer.

But sitting here, watching my husband—my best friend—sleep in the golden morning light, I realized something has been shifting. Slowly, quietly, like water wearing away stone.

When Hilaire stirred slightly, I reached over without thinking to brush a strand of hair from his forehead. He didn't wake, but a small smile crossed his face, as if he sensed my touch even in sleep—this man who saw past my armor from the very beginning, who waited patiently through years of friendship while I learned to trust, who never tried to change the fierce independence that both protected and isolated me.

Marrying Hilaire wasn't just about love—it was about finally having a teammate. Someone who doesn't need me to be smaller or quieter or more conventional. Someone who celebrates my strength while showing me that being strong doesn't mean being alone.

And now, our kid will never know a childhood where love comes with conditions, where affection must be earned through achievement or good behavior. He takes our presence for granted in the most beautiful way—

assumes we'll be there when he falls asleep and when he wakes up, trusts completely that we'll catch him if he stumbles. It is not how I felt as a child.

All those years, I thought depending on people was weakness, when it's actually the ultimate strength. It takes courage to let someone see your fears, your doubts, your middle-of-the-night anxieties about whether you're enough.

Outside our window, Sydney Harbor bustles with early morning ferry traffic, people beginning their daily routines. But here in this quiet cocoon of family, I feel something I haven't experienced since I can remember: the luxury of being completely, utterly safe.

That's why, when Hilaire's eyes flutter open, I tell him exactly what I was thinking about: "Maybe it's time to stop running so hard toward what's next and start appreciating what's right here."

He props himself up on one elbow, studying my face with the gentle attention that first made me fall in love with him. "The great Szilvia Gogh, considering slowing down? Should I be worried?"

I laugh softly, careful not to wake Enzo. "Not slowing down. Just ... changing direction. Toward something... something that includes leisurely morning coffee and watching our son sleep and not feeling like I have to conquer the world before breakfast."

I'm struck by a realization that feels both incredibly philosophical and embarrassingly simple: For the first time in my adult life, I don't want to be anywhere else or achieve anything more. Where I am right now, and what I have, is enough.

This feeling is so foreign it takes a moment to identify it. Since I was fourteen years old and my world collapsed with my father's death, I've been in constant motion—always climbing toward the next goal, the next certification, the next adventure.

Youngest female PADI Course Director in the world.

First Hungarian woman to earn that title.

Hollywood stunt performer.

Women Divers Hall of Fame.

Avatar crew member.

Each achievement was supposed to fill the void. Instead, each success only revealed how much more there was to want.

I remember standing at my course director graduation, officially at the pinnacle of my profession, and feeling nothing but cold dread. *If this isn't enough to fill the void inside me*, I had wondered, *what will be?*

The answer, it turns out, wasn't another accomplishment at all. It was discovering that the void I'd been trying to fill was actually an illusion— that gratitude could transform what I already had into more than enough.

The Buddha taught that we can acknowledge our wounds without being defined by them, that suffering can become the very foundation of wisdom and compassion. The fighter in me will always be there—she's part of my DNA, forged in childhood trauma and tempered by years of proving myself in male-dominated industries. But maybe she doesn't have to be the only voice anymore. Maybe there's room for the part of me who wants to build sandcastles with Enzo, who craves lazy afternoons reading books, who lunches with friends and dreams of surfing lessons.

I've been learning about a Buddhist concept called *metta*—loving-kindness meditation that begins with offering compassion to yourself before extending it to others. When I think of that fourteen-year-old girl sitting by her dying father's bedside, I want to tell her: *You don't have to carry this alone. You don't have to become invincible to survive.*

As if sensing our conversation, Enzo rolls over and opens one sleepy eye. "Are we going to see kangaroos today?" he asks, his voice thick with dreams.

"Whatever you want, buddy," I say, and for the first time in years, I mean it completely. No hidden agenda, no ulterior motives. Just the simple pleasure of making our child happy.

The revelation settles over me like warm sunlight: I don't have to fight for everything anymore. Some things—the best things in life—are given freely.

"Thirty years," I realize out loud. "Since Dad died, I've been in constant motion, as though if I stopped moving, stopped achieving, stopped proving myself, I might … disappear."

But here I am, sitting still, and I'm more present than I've been in decades.

* * *

As the heat intensifies, we catch an overnight train to Melbourne, where we are greeted by sweltering temperatures of 114°F. We cool off at St. Kilda Beach, relaxing on the golden sands and swimming in the cool waters. Our days are filled with long, leisurely walks and hours of dining at local spots, taking in the ever-changing parade of people strolling along the river.

What strikes me most during this Australia trip is how slowing down has allowed us to become true companions rather than just family members managing schedules. Amid the turbulence of *Avatar*, family time was squeezed into gaps between work calls. Enzo would start telling me about something he'd learned at school, only to be interrupted by my phone buzzing with set updates. I'd find myself nodding absently while mentally reviewing shoot schedules for the next day's complex underwater scenes.

One of our most memorable excursions is a drive to the Twelve Apostles, the magnificent limestone stacks that were my favorite spot in Australia eighteen years ago, and are still as majestic as when I first laid eyes on them. Standing before them now, I'm overwhelmed by nostalgia for the privilege of returning. How many people get to revisit the faraway places that marked significant chapters in their life?

The Twelve Apostles evoke a sense of timeless beauty and impermanence, except only eight remain standing due to erosion. I'm grateful for this reminder that everything changes, even ancient rock formations. The *Avatar* shoot that felt endless will become a memory. The exhaustion will fade. But this moment—watching Enzo sprint along the clifftop while Hilaire captures his joy through the camera lens—is eternal.

We stop in Port Campbell, where we explore a local beach surrounded by more towering rock formations—a perfect place to delight in the serenity of the ocean. There is nobody around, as far as we can see. This isolation, which might have felt lonely in another context, now feels like an extraordinary gift.

Enzo and I splash around, laughing as we walk barefoot on the beach … running in and out of the water … picking up rocks, shells, and other treasures. I can't stop smiling at Enzo's delight—the way he shrieks when a wave catches him off guard, how he examines each shell as if it might contain the secrets of the universe.

"Mama, look!" Enzo calls, holding up a piece of sea glass worn smooth by waves. "It's like a green diamond!"

In my old life, I would have immediately started planning: Where could we find more sea glass? Which beaches were known for the best specimens? Should we research the geology of glass formation to enhance his learning experience?

Instead, I simply admire his treasure and watch him carefully place it in the small collection he's building. Sometimes appreciation is enough. Sometimes the experience doesn't need to be optimized or turned into something bigger.

For the first time in months, I enter water purely for pleasure. No scuba gear, no camera, no responsibility for anyone's life but my own. The feeling of happiness is so intense, it brings tears to my eyes—tears that mix with salt water as I float on my back, watching clouds drift across the impossibly blue Australian sky.

During lunchtime at a seaside café, other diners are constantly checking phones, photographing their meals, live-updating their experiences. They're working so hard to document, summarize, and share their vacation that they're missing the actual experience of being on vacation.

I deliberately leave my phone muted in my bag and focus on the taste of fresh fish, the sound of Enzo chattering about marine ecosystems, the feeling of Hilaire's hand resting casually on my shoulder. This moment doesn't need to be documented or shared or optimized. It just needs to be lived.

This is the extreme shift I couldn't have predicted: the recognition that having enough isn't about accumulating the right experiences or achievements. It's about being fully present for the ones you're already having.

On our last evening in Sydney, standing on our hotel balcony overlooking the harbor, Hilaire asks the question I've been avoiding: "What do you want to do next?"

In the past, this question would have unleashed a torrent of possibilities: new diving locations to explore, certifications to pursue, businesses to build. The old me would have already researched our next adventure before this one was even over. But now, watching the lights twinkle across the water while Enzo points out constellations he's learned, I realize I don't want to do anything next. I want to do this—this being present, this appreciating what we have, this radical act of contentment.

"I want to go home," I say, and for the first time, the word *home* doesn't feel like giving up. It feels like arriving.

As our three-week road trip draws to a close, I realize that gratitude has become the theme song of this trip. Not the forced appreciation of someone trying to convince herself she's blessed, but the deep, cellular appreciation that comes from having something precious nearly taken away and then returned.

I'm thankful for the *Avatar* experience because it led me here—to this profound understanding that having enough isn't about accumulating more extraordinary experiences or achievements. It's about fully inhabiting the ones you have. It's about mornings with coffee and family, afternoons with friends who've known you for decades, evenings watching your child collect treasures from foreign beaches.

Most of all, I'm blessed for the realization that I don't have to fight for everything anymore. Some gifts—the love of your family, the loyalty of true friends, the healing power of salt water and sunshine—are freely given. The trick is simply learning to receive them.

* * *

Just back from our grand Australian journey, I'm hit by fierce chills and a fever that knock me harder than anything in recent memory. Even so, I make it to my six-month post-cancer check-up, where the doctor reassures me: Everything is still on track. It's been three years since my first cancer surgery, and while I'm committed to another two and a half years of taking my cancer medication, I dream of the day I can start a full detox to purge the built-up toxins. I figure I'm presently at about 80 percent of my former health and strength. I'm determined to rebuild my energy level to 100 percent.

Spring break brings a breath of renewal as we head to Utah. The landscape there is otherworldly and breathtaking, with orange mountains shaped as if sculpted by hand. Inspired by this Mars-like environment, I snap photos for my website, of my jewelry against Moab's vibrant tableaux. My approach to marketing is deeply personal—using friends, family, and real travel moments instead of studio models. I want others to absorb fragments of my own life and free-spirited essence when they purchase my creations.

Thankfully, my jewelry continues to resonate with people, and orders flow in steadily, allowing me to make a good living. I've resolved to pursue only ventures where I maintain total control of my business, focus on driving traffic directly to my website and communicating through newsletters and SMS marketing. I purposely steer away big middle-men or hyping consumerism, and focus instead on less competitive opportunities, such as Lucky Friday the 13th, National Yoga Day, or World Turtle Day.

This shift toward mindful business practices reflects my overall transformation. Though I haven't gone full digital nomad, I manage to be away from Gogh Jewelry Design for a month at a time. If someone can't wait a few weeks for my bracelets, I prefer to offer a refund rather than stress myself out. I want to savor the fruits of my labor by traveling with family and friends. I work to live—like most Europeans—rather than live to work as most Americans do.

The new perspective on life naturally leads me toward service. As May comes around, I join A Chance for Children Foundation for a heartfelt Mother's Day event, making necklaces with underprivileged kids. I pick Enzo up from school early—he likes to volunteer with me—and we head to an elementary school in Los Angeles's underserved area, our partner for the outreach program this time. Watching Enzo engage with children is heartwarming. He even asks to take the lead, confidently taking over the microphone from my hands to direct the next group of one hundred participants. His enthusiasm is contagious, and it's clear the kids admire him.

Helping others opens my eyes to the need for facing and healing my own childhood traumas—those that I buried so deep, I didn't even know about them. Through a friend, I discover the Sweat Lodge in Bakersfield, led by Sarah Bennett, a grandmotherly woman initiated into Lakota Indian rituals. The experience proves profoundly transformative.

Inside the igloo shaped sacred space, as hot lava stones are brought in for four progressively intense rounds, we engage in deep conversations about our desires and struggles. We use no mind-altering substances—this is a pure ceremony focused solely on sweating and experiencing visions that feel like connections with a higher realm. After these rituals, my spirit is fully recharged, brimming with renewed energy and strength.

This spiritual exploration continues when I head back to Hungary for the Samsara Festival, a vibrant celebration of music, art, and spirituality, with my childhood diving friends Nóra, Reni, and Vica. We arrive in a torrential downpour, but as the storm eases, a breathtaking sight unfolds: a herd of wild horses galloping through the mist, their manes whipping in the wind. It's a surreal experience that feels like a sign.

Trusting that sign brings us to the Deep Forest concert, which takes place in an actual forest sparkling with endless strings of lights. The electrifying music pulses through my body, and I close my eyes, letting the rhythm wash over me. I feel release, renewal, vitality, and a deep connection to something greater.

Since my journey through cancer, I've noticed a profound shift in how I see the world and what's really important to me. I'm finally ready to confront and heal the wounds of my childhood—something I hadn't allowed myself to face before. After spending the first forty years of my life in constant "go mode," always chasing the next trailblazing exploration, I'm learning to slow down and do the inner work.

Back in California, I continue to explore the power of sisterhood at a Warrior Women's Weekend—a transformative retreat in the rugged mountains near San Diego. Eighteen "strong women" gather on a secluded ranch, and we sense immediately that this weekend will be special.

My friend Szilvi leads challenging yoga sessions; another friend, also named Szilvi, introduces us to archery. Cindy guides horseback rides that bring euphoria and power, and I lead jewelry-making workshops where women intuitively choose gemstones for their healing journey. Zita's cacao ceremony opens our hearts unexpectedly, while Melissa's intense breathwork sessions push us to confront buried emotions.

By weekend's end, I realize how far I've come since my tomboy days. Here I am, embracing womanhood and the incredible energies in this circle of female friends. Together, we brave a profound rite of passage and emerge as sisters, empowered by the strength we find in ourselves and each other.

Next, I visit my cousin Andi in Florida for a restorative weekend at her salt cave business. We indulge in salt yoga, foot detoxes, and lymphatic massages, each session revitalizing both body and spirit. After my surgeries, these treatments offer much-needed relief, reminding me of the importance of self-care.

Then the pandemic strikes, and suddenly I'm not the only one taking a much-needed pause.

* * *

COVID-19 changes everything. All around the world, people's lives slow down. As sad and frightening as this time is for many, I relish the opportunity to reconnect with loved ones over leisurely video chats from our backyard. Schools and businesses are closed, and we have no choice but to embrace this slower pace, filling our days with hiking, cooking together, and meaningful family time.

Homeschooling with Enzo becomes our new routine, blending work and family life seamlessly. We create vision boards and crystal grids, and spend countless hours outdoors. Despite the media pressure, I embrace this time with Enzo and work to remain positive while surrounded by global uncertainty.

Indeed, this unexpected pause unfolds as a sacred journey of growth and resilience, deeply intertwined with the rhythms of nature and our family's love. I discover a newfound delight in the simplicity of home life, and gardening becomes a new hobby. Each moment spent in nature's embrace—whether tending to my plants, walking barefoot on the beach, or wandering through the woods—feels like a spiritual awakening, connecting me to life's cycles around me.

A few months into the shutdown, we venture back to Yosemite for quiet trails and river swimming—the kind of serenity only nature provides. Then we continue on, driving to Mount Shasta and Oregon, camping and exploring beautiful landscapes. On the road, I manage my jewelry business while Enzo completes his homework, maintaining a healthy work-life balance. Remarkably, my business thrives during this period. People seem to crave the positive messages I share through my creations.

Back home, as things gradually reopen, we visit my beloved Santa Catalina—this time for an extended stay as I teach Enzo to swim with fins and we bond over our shared love for the ocean. No one would ask for a deadly pandemic, but since it's here, I find something to be grateful for: Our family has become an even stronger unit, and we appreciate every moment together.

My colleagues desperately hope the arrival of the COVID vaccine will usher in the return of movie jobs at full speed. Just as the film industry starts to regain momentum, however, the looming SAG-AFTRA strike brings everything to a grinding halt once again. The excitement and optimism that followed the reopening of TV and movie sets quickly fades as negotiations stall, leaving the entertainment industry in an unprecedented state of bewilderment.

In the midst of all this upheaval, I come to a sobering realization: I'm burned out from teaching scuba diving. For years, it's been my drive, my livelihood, and my connection to the ocean—but somewhere along the way, the bliss I once felt began to fade. The spark that drew me underwater now feels dulled by the routine of instructing others.

I long to return to my roots, to rediscover that pure, unfiltered elation of diving for myself—without the pressure of teaching. Without the weight of responsibility on my shoulders. Without holding a camera or posing for one. Without overseeing others' safety or doing stunts. Without pointing out pretty fish for clients. I miss that feeling of being completely immersed in the ocean, with nothing but the quiet hum of the deep and my own breath to guide me.

Deciding to forgo my career as a dive instructor and focus instead on my jewelry design business frees up my time for more thoughtful, intentional travel. I make the conscious choice to step away from regular dive instruction, accepting only the occasional movie project and working exclusively with scuba clients who specifically seek me out—people who resonate with my approach and values. For the first time in my career, I realize I don't have to say yes to everything. This selective approach transforms work from obligation into choice.

While many families always travel together as a unit, Hilaire and I share a different perspective, opting to travel apart sometimes. We feel that taking this time for ourselves is not only beneficial but necessary. So, he embarks on annual mountain biking trips to places like Scotland, Italy, and Croatia, connecting with friends and challenging himself physically in new landscapes.

Meanwhile, I begin my own tradition: reuniting with my childhood scuba diving girlfriends from Hungary in exotic locales around the world, like Morocco, Spain and Portugal, where we explore stunning destinations, forge new memories, and enjoy deepening friendships. How satisfying it is to cultivate the simple, genuine connections that matter most in our lives!

I start making more time for friends living close by, too. During one of Hilaire's bike trips, Betti—whom I met thirty years ago at goldsmith school—arrives from Oregon with her little girl, Violett. The moment they step through our door, Enzo and Violett light up with sheer joy; their instant connection is heartwarming. Betti and I fall into our familiar rhythm, setting up a booth at a bustling crafts festival. As we chat and catch up, laughter and nostalgia fill the air, and we cherish our time together. When they leave, Enzo's tears show how deeply he forms such bonds, too, with friends who are actually family.

One day, an email from Csilla appears with a photo of her children, Hanga and Peti, wrapped in a tender embrace. Their hug speaks volumes about their bond—a pure, unspoken love that tugs at my heart. Csilla's message is reflective, expressing how she wishes we had experienced this level of closeness during our own childhood. The deep connection her children share reminds us of what we missed, but also highlights the progress we've made in building a relationship that reflects the closeness and equality we've always wanted.

This discussion sparks a new tradition: Csilla and I decide to travel together once each year—just the two of us—to a beautiful, distant place we both long to discover. Spending time together with our kids and husbands around is always a whirlwind of coordinating schedules and managing responsibilities. Meeting in the places of our dreams, a long way from home, will serve as our sacred time to connect without the usual distractions.

We decide first on Iceland, where we explore breathtaking landscapes—glaciers, volcanic craters, geothermal baths—and rekindle our sibling bond. What a relief to discover that we've reached a beautiful point in our relationship where we can actually enjoy each other's company, free from family tensions and competition.

The following year, we embark on a ten-day trip across Malaysia, avoiding touristy spots and instead visiting temples and places like Batu Caves. Next we head to Borneo, focusing on the islands of Mabul and Sipadan. Despite the pollution concerns we confront at some locations, our love for the underwater world makes this trip unforgettable. During one memorable dive, Csilla frees trapped fish from an abandoned net while I document her effort, eager to promote awareness about ocean protection.

The year after that, we decide on island-hopping through Thailand's southern island chains, with no concrete plan. We discover Koh Adang's jungle paradise with gorgeous waterfalls and swim with dugongs at Koh Mook. We find Koh Libong to be a rare haven where environmental sustainability is deeply ingrained in the community. After backpacking through nine islands in thirteen days, laughing and growing closer with every step, finally parting ways brings tears to our eyes.

Traveling continues to be the best investment in myself, and now in strengthening my bonds with loved ones. I may have decided to "slow down," but to me that just means a different way of wandering, infused with intentional presence and gratitude.

* * *

As much as I love the untethered moments in my life, there are plenty of blissful moments of mindfulness and joyful wellness right here at home. Hilaire and I feel grateful to be in a wonderful place both physically and mentally, as we exercise daily, eat well, and enjoy many activities together. We are supremely fortunate to have created a life that allows us to step away from the traditional nine-to-five grind and make the most of every moment.

With no blood family nearby, and given the sometimes complicated costs and logistics around babysitting, my husband and I invent "date days" while Enzo is at school. This is usually about cherishing simple experiences: scuba diving in our local waters, playing backgammon in the garden, in-line skating along the beach. For special events like birthdays, Hilaire likes to plan extraordinary moments such as an exciting Porsche driving experience.

But this year I ask for something different: surfing lessons for the whole family. It turns out to be one of my best decisions ever.

Enzo falls in love with surfing, showing impressive skill. And me? I find it exhilarating. Each wave I catch fills me with pure ecstasy and the feeling of freedom I've always relished.

One sunny day at the beach, I strike up a conversation with a woman my age whose child is effortlessly riding the waves. She tells me about a group of local moms who meet once a week after dropping their kids off at school to learn surfing. Intrigued and hungry to connect, I decide to join them.

I've been puzzled about who to enlist as a surf buddy. My old diving buddies tend to have grown children or no kids at all, so we've gotten out of sync for now. My local Hungarian friends aren't really water people, and Hilaire isn't into surfing either. I was preparing to just be on my own if I wanted to continue with surfing. So, it's refreshing to find women in their forties who are eager to explore new things and push limits.

Meeting MJ and Becci feels like a breath of fresh air. I join them in training with Surf Moms owner: Robbie and Ryan, a seasoned surfer who brings motivation and energy to our sessions. What I love most about our group of surf moms is our collective clumsiness, tempered by our love for the water. We cheer each other on, celebrate successes, and offer encouragement when someone struggles. The joy of building new connections and sharing meaningful experiences kicks the thrill of surfing up another notch.

On perfect days, when the waves are just right, it feels like we're flying.

Surfing in the morning fills me with radiance that carries through the day. As with diving, the salt water washes away my worries, recharges my spirit, but surfing fits seamlessly into my schedule: I drop Enzo off at school, surf at a nearby beach, and am home by lunchtime, refreshed and ready for the rest of the day. This new routine balances my wanderlust with my daily life.

Things seem so clear to me now. I've found that elusive equilibrium in life, where every piece of the puzzle fits. I am happy and content. The constant chase that churned inside me for three decades—that relentless need for "more" that drove me from certification to certification, from country to country, from achievement to achievement—has finally quieted.

I know exactly where I am: standing on the bridge between who I was and who I'm becoming. Now I see that the constant chase for more—more stimulus, more complexity, more experiences—was actually keeping me from experiencing the life I already had. That insight came when and how it had to: The *Avatar* tank taught me about pushing my limits and achieving a perfect performance. The quiet hotel room in Sydney, and all the moments that followed, have taught me about the courage to stop pushing and simply be.

The old me would have seen this as settling, as losing my edge. The new me understands it as finally winning the only game that really matters: the one where the prize is appreciation for what's already yours.

What's more important than the enjoyment of seeing my beloved friends and family thrive, and knowing we are living fully and authentically? This energized, all-encompassing contentment comes from a focus on "having enough"—not wanting something different or more, but basking in gratitude for what we have.

This is the secret to satisfaction, the ultimate purpose, the essence of all my dreams: a realization that fills me with gratitude and peace, knowing I've created a life rich with love, triumph, and contentment.

Having Enough

Let go of what no longer serves you.
– Buddha

The Pacific swells roll beneath my board in perfect four-foot sets, each wave announcing itself with a distant hiss before building into glassy perfection. I paddle out through the lineup, salt spray kissing my face, as the familiar burn in my shoulders arrives like a greeting. The water is crystal clear this morning—so clear I can see kelp dancing twenty feet below, swaying in underwater currents that mirror the gentle breeze above.

I sit up on my board—legs dangling in the cool water as the sun warms my back through my wetsuit—and scan the horizon. The water cradles the board with the gentleness of an old friend.

Becci floats nearby, her easy smile reflecting the same contentment I feel, while MJ paddles over with unhurried grace. No film crews setting schedules. No dive tables to calculate. No safety protocols to review. Just the three of us, the ocean, and the endless rhythm of waves that have been rolling toward this shore for countless millennia.

Movement catches my eye about fifty yards out—a pod of dolphins arcing through the water in perfect synchronization. One, two, three sleek bodies launch into the air, their silver forms glistening as they catch the morning light before slicing back into the blue.

"Look at that," MJ whispers, her voice full of the same wonder I feel. The dolphins surface again, closer now, blowing misty breaths that sparkle in the sunshine, and we all share knowing smiles. No cameras rolling. No need to document this magic—just the pure gift of sharing the ocean with these graceful creatures and the women who've become my chosen family in the water.

A set approaches—three perfect waves marching toward shore in formation. We don't scramble or compete for position. Becci nods toward the first wave, MJ takes the second, and I choose the third, each of us moving with the measured strokes of mothers who've learned that the best waves aren't always the biggest ones. There's no script, no director, no pressure to perform. There's just the pure joy of being present in this moment with friends who understand that surfing, like life, is better when shared.

As I drop into the wave face, the world goes quiet except for the rush of water beneath my board. The wave wraps around me like liquid silk, and for these few seconds, I understand what the Buddhist masters mean when they speak of being fully alive in the present moment. No past achievements to validate me. No future goals to chase. Just this: the salt air filling my lungs, the sun painting diamonds on the water's surface, the dolphins playing in the distance, my surf mom friends riding their own waves nearby, and the profound peace of knowing that right here, right now, I have everything I need.

When the wave finally deposits me near the shore, I paddle back out with no urgency, rejoining Becci and MJ in the lineup. This is what "enough" feels like.

I have everything I need.

Every member of my family is healthy and thriving—a blessing I never take for granted after our battles with cancer, loss, and the fragility that life has taught us to recognize. We're navigating life on calm waters now, without the shadow of immediate crisis, and I understand what a rare and precious gift this is.

We have enough, and that's everything.

Having enough means that I don't envy the influencer with millions of followers, the actress with the Oscar, or the entrepreneur with the IPO. I don't wish for a bigger house, a more prestigious career, or exotic adventures I haven't yet experienced. What I have feels complete. My years of chasing the next best thing are behind me, replaced by something I never expected: the understanding that happiness comes from savoring the present moment, not constantly reaching for the next one.

True happiness is not acquisition or accomplishment, but alignment—knowing that the life I'm living reflects who I actually am, not who I thought I should become. Today, my deepest satisfaction comes from watching Enzo discover his own passions, from the comfort of Hilaire's hand in mine during our evening walk, from my morning coffee before the world wakes up. We've made the deliberate choice to prioritize presence over productivity, quality over quantity. Working from home with flexible schedules means we can spend entire afternoons reading together on the beach, take impromptu bike rides with our son, or spend a whole morning making smoothies from our garden while discussing the science of fermentation.

And the future? It excites me more than ever, but now I look forward to it with quiet, profound delight—not the frantic urgency that once drove me from one escapade to the next, but a calm anticipation that welcomes whatever path wants to emerge. Wanderlust still pulses in my veins, but it has evolved from desperate escape to curious exploration to mindful presence. True contentment lies not in reaching the destination, but in the journey itself.

The future holds endless possibilities, and we never know exactly what's coming. The key is to make peace with that uncertainty, to trust that life will unfold in ways we can't predict. That's where the magic lies. Whether it's Enzo's next developmental leap, a new creative project, or an unexpected opportunity to share what I've learned, I'm ready—not with the armor of my younger self, but with a heart that is finally open.

The thrill of exploration and discovery remains a part of me. There are still so many places I wish to see, experiences I long to have, and ways I yearn to keep growing. But I no longer rush toward any goal. I seek beauty in stillness, reflection, and the quiet, in-between moments. I am fully present in whatever experience is arising, savoring every moment, and embracing the lessons that want to teach themselves. The ocean, my constant teacher and guide, has shown me patience—how life ebbs and flows, the way tides always return, the power that exists in both stillness and storm.

Once, adventure meant moving fast, checking destinations off my list, proving something to myself and the world. Now I understand that true growth lies in the depth of experience, not the speed of accumulation. Some of my most profound journeys happen in our backyard, in quiet conversations with my husband and my son, in the slow healing of my relationship with trust and vulnerability.

What hasn't changed is my deep, deep love for living a curious life. Journeys aren't just about diving into the unknown or traveling to faraway places—they're about welcoming life's unpredictability with open arms, about seeing each twist and turn as an opportunity for growth, even when it's scary or uncertain. Life, like the ocean, is vast and full of currents we can't always control. But if we learn to flow with it, we find ourselves exactly where we need to be.

Journeys are for everyone. Expeditions aren't just trips to far-off places; they're the choices we make every day. They're about embracing life in all its forms, stepping outside our comfort zone, and discovering new experiences and a deeper understanding of who we are. Adventure comes from living with curiosity, taking risks, and believing in the possibility of something greater than what we can see. Finding the courage to listen to that inner voice urging you forward, even when the path is unclear, is the greatest adventure of all.

Life, like the sea, is both powerful and gentle, unpredictable yet purposeful. As I move forward, I'm filled with gratitude for the quests I've had and the ones still waiting on the horizon. Never-ending pursuits have been my compass in life, guiding me through successes and challenges alike. That's the true gift of any sojourn—it will push you to grow in ways you never imagined, leaving you changed for the better every time. My wandering soul helped me navigate my cancer journey, build a family life that feels authentic, and stay grounded in the present while still dreaming about what's ahead.

I feel a responsibility to keep living adventurously, not just for myself, but for my loved ones and anyone else who might be inspired by my story. Exploration can be found in the smallest moments—the decision to take a different path, try something new, or follow a long-neglected hobby. In the end, life is one big odyssey—an ever-evolving journey that surprises us at every turn. And I, for one, am ready to dive in again.

So here's my advice: Embrace your own journey, and recognize that *you* are capable of extraordinary things. You don't need to have all the answers or know exactly where you're headed. The right adventures for you may be the ones you don't plan. The key is to keep moving forward, exploring, and trusting that each step will lead you where you're meant to be.

It's never too late to start diving into your dreams.

About the Author

Szilvia Gogh is a stuntwoman, entrepreneur, and world-renowned scuba diver who has been inducted into the Women Divers Hall of Fame—a true Renaissance woman. She has explored more than fifty-six countries and contributed to twenty-seven Hollywood films, working with A-list actors including Zoe Saldaña, Kate Winslet, and Sigourney Weaver, and serving as stunt double for Drew Barrymore.

Szilvia made history as the youngest female PADI Course Director ever, later becoming a celebrated PADI Ambassador who has inspired divers worldwide. In Hollywood, she built a successful career as a stunt performer while founding Gogh Jewelry Design, a brand inspired by her love for the sea and her unwavering perseverance.

A breast cancer survivor, motivational speaker, and advocate for holistic women's healthcare, Szilvia shares her extraordinary adventures through her media company Miss-Scuba.com. She lives with her husband—her best friend—in California, where they are raising their child to be a confident, open-minded, open-hearted world traveler.

Dedicated to giving back and paying it forward, Szilvia has volunteered for over twenty-five years with A Chance for Children Foundation. Her first book, *Diving into Dreams*, captures her journey of courage, creativity, and compassion.

To learn more about her story, visit www.SzilviaGogh.com.